LABRADOR RETRIEVERS

TODAY

CAROLE COODE

HOWELL
BOOK HOUSE

New York

Maxwell Macmillan Canada
Toronto

Maxwell Macmillan International
New York Oxford Singapore Sydney

Howell Book House
Macmillan Publishing Company
866 Third Avenue
New York, NY 10022

Maxwell Macmillan Canada, Inc.
1200 Eglinton Avenue East
Suite 200
Don Mills, Ontario M3C 3N1

Macmillan Publishing Company is part of the Maxwell Communication Group of Companies.

Library of Congress Cataloging-in-Publication Data

Coode, Carole.
    Labrador retrievers today / by Carole Coode.
            p.   cm.
    ISBN 0-87605-207-3
    1. Labrador retriever.   I. Title.
SF429.L3C665 1993
636.7'52–dc20   93-17878
                                                                    CIP

Macmillan books are available at special discounts for bulk purchases for sales promotions, premiums, fund-raising, or educational use. For details, contact:

Special Sales Director
Macmillan Publishing Company
866 Third Avenue
New York, NY 10022

10 9 8 7 6 5 4 3 2 1
Printed and bound in Singapore

CONTENTS

This book is dedicated to Lawnwoods Hot Pants of Warringah:
A great brood bitch, pictured at twelve years of age.

Picture by Anne Roslin Williams.

ACKNOWLEDGEMENTS

Many people have given me their time and encouragement but most thanks must go to my husband, David, for his help and encouragement. If he had not taken so much of the daily work-load off my shoulders, I would not have been able to write this book.

Thanks must also go to my son, Aaron, who pulled his weight and helped out with the dogs every time he was home from University; to Malin-Maria Landwall for the line drawings in the book; Theo Berstrom, photographer of the Pedigree Chum photographs; Jim Hutchinson, Art Director for the Pedigree Chum photographs; to photographers Anne Roslin-Williams, David Dalton, Marc Henrie, Sally Anne Thompson, David Bull, and Jan West and Hilly Hoare (English Field Working section); to Joy Venturi for her chapters on the Field Trial Kennels and Training.

Overseas, my thanks must got to Katarina Inglehoff for her help in compiling the Swedish chapter; Hugh Gent for help in compiling the history of the breed in Australia; Pat Dunstan for her help in gathering information on Australian kennels; Mary Wiest for her help in gathering the information for the American chapter, and Mike and Pat Lanctot (Ebonylane) for the excellent coverage of Canada.

My veterinary surgeon, Colin Clark, has kindly checked the chapter on Health Care; and finally thanks to Gary Johnnson, whose book *Post War Labrador Bench Champions* has been such a source of information.

This past year has been at times terrifying, until I really got started, but then so rewarding and so enjoyable, and I feel I have gained a great deal from the experience.

Jacket photograph courtesy of Pedigree Petfoods, makers of Pedigree Chum.

Chapter One

ORIGINS OF THE LABRADOR

THE FISHERMAN'S DOG

The origins of the Labrador Retriever are not clearly defined, but we know that the breed came from the East coast of Canada – from the Newfoundland and St John's Island area – and was commonly called the Newfoundland or smaller St John's Dog. In the early eighteenth century, fisherman from the Atlantic shores of Europe had, for many years, been going to the Cod Banks off Newfoundland to fish, and they utilised the local dog who showed such ability to be an all-round worker. This dog could haul wood during the winter, going over terrain where horses would have been of little use. The wood was stacked ready to be used for the summer job of smoking part of the fish catch. The rest was preserved by salting, as there was no refrigeration in those days, and was then shipped to Europe. During the summer months the local dogs proved their use by helping the fishermen to drag the fishing net ropes ashore, as well as retrieving fish that had fallen overboard. The dog's short weatherproof coat (with its thick undercoat) was ideal for handling jobs on land and in the water in these cold conditions.

No doubt, dogs taken by the fishermen from their own countries were occasionally crossed with the local dog, and the Labrador Retriever was born. In Portugal today, the Labrador has a yellow cousin, the Cane di Castro Laboreiro Waterdog, who bears a striking resemblance to the Labrador. It is only a surmise on my part, but I believe that a bastardization of this name has given us the name Labrador, bearing in mind that the Canadian dogs were from the Newfoundland and St John's area, an area that is south of Labrador.

I think some of the Labrador's distinctive characteristics were established early on, particularly in relation to appetite. The dogs were probably fed by the fishermen during the winter when they were hauling wood down from the interior to the shore, and then turned loose to fend for themselves in the summer. The dogs would have had to feed on fish offal and fish heads, and some fish hunting, in order to survive. Hence, the Labrador seems quite happy to eat almost anything – and survive. I call them 'walking dustbins', and most owners would agree that the most well-fed Labrador will still scrounge for food.

THE ALL-ROUND RETRIEVER

As is well documented, fisherman brought the Canadian dogs back to England, and landed in the fishing harbours of Dorset. The news of their retrieving ability had spread, and wealthy landowners decided to see if they would make suitable gundogs. The Labrador came, saw and conquered. Within a very short space of time this new breed had made its mark as a good all-round retriever, working as well in water as on the land, and being steady and biddable in temperament.

The Labrador established itself as good all-round retrieiver, working as well in water as on land.

Jan West Photography

These early importers did a marvellous job for us, laying strong foundations, keeping the line pure, keeping good kennel records, and setting a standard that has altered little to this day, and we remain grateful to Colonel Peter Hawker, the Dukes of Buccleuch, the Earls Home and Malmesbury, and the Hon. A. Holland-Hibbert (later to be Lord Knutsford, of Munden kennel fame).This solid foundation of the breed in Britain became increasingly important following two pieces of legislation. In 1885 a law was passed for the destruction of practically all Labradors in order to promote the breeding of sheep in the Newfoundland area; not too long after that quarantine laws were introduced into England. The combined effect of the two laws virtually brought about the end of the trade in Labrador dogs between the two countries. So, although the Labrador originated in Canada, the breed was moulded, refined and promoted by British landowners in the nineteenth century, who recognised its wonderful retrieving and game-finding ability.

DRAWING UP A BREED STANDARD

The Labrador Retriever Club was set up in England in 1916 to promote the pure-bred Labrador, and the UK has always been regarded as the Labrador's country of origin. Prior to this the Kennel Club allowed Retriever crosses, and the offspring were registered into the breed they most resembled. For example, a litter of Flatcoat/Labradors would have some entered as Flatcoats and some as Labradors. Those early committee members were among many influential in the breed: Mrs Quintin Dick (later Lorna Countess Howe), Arthur Holland-Hibbert (Lord Knutsford), Lord

*Mary Roslin Williams with four Mansergh
Champions: (left to right) Ch. Mansergh
Groucho, Ch. Mansergh Antonia, Ch. Mansergh
Moleskin and Ch. Mansergh Damson.*

Anne Roslin Williams.   *Gwen Broadley: 60 years in the breed.*

Chesterfield, Lord Lonsdale, Lord Vivian, Lord Harlech, Mr Burdett-Coutts, Mr R. Heaton and Mr A. Nicholl. A Breed Standard was drawn up by the Committee, which was accepted by the Kennel Club, and this remained unaltered until 1950.

The FCI, which covers the European countries, follows the British Breed Standard, as they always adopt the Standard drawn up by a breed's country of origin. The United States has its own Breed Standard, and this has a few minor differences from the British version (See Chapter Four: The Breed Standard). There are now thirteen Labrador Clubs covering the British Isles, plus a Labrador Breed Council, which meets once or twice a year. This is made up of two representatives from each club, and the aim is to discuss any problems that we might have as a breed, to find solutions if possible, to promote our breed, and to speak as one voice to the Kennel Club.

INFLUENTIAL KENNELS
It is hard to choose which kennels had the greatest impact in the past, and they have been well documented elsewhere. However, a number of kennels have been highly influential, such as the KNAITH kennels of Mrs Arthur Wormold, who made up the breed's last Dual Champion (in field and ring) with Dual Ch. Knaith Banjo; the STAINDROPS, owned by Mr and Mrs Edgar White and their daughter, Joan Hays; and the BANCHORY kennel, owned by Lorna Countess Howe, whose Dual Ch. Banchory Bolo was Best in Show at Crufts in 1932 and 1933. Audrey Radclyffe's good-looking ZELSTONES were always worked and shown; there were the famous BLAIRCOURTS of Mr Grant and Marjorie Cairns, Mr and Mrs Saunders (LIDDLYS), Mrs

The Mansergh Labradors are famous for their beautiful heads. Mansergh Spring Songress (left) and her mother, Mansergh Blackthorn Winter.

Anne Roslin Williams.

Saffells (ROOKWOOD), Keith Hart (LANDYKES), Ann Wynyard (BRAEDUKES), Mim Kinsella (BRENTCHASE), Louise Wilson-Jones (DIANT), Mr and Mrs Fred Wrigley (KINLEY), Lt Col. and Mrs Hills (GARSHANGEN), Mr and Mrs Horace Taylor (WHATSTANDWELL) and Peggy Rae (CORNLANDS – still going strong today). Horace Gilliat and his daughter, Daphne Walters had the famous HOLTON Labradors, and Ch. Holton Baron was the breed CC record holder for many years with twenty-five CCs, as well as Field Trial awards. Until her untimely and brutal death in 1988, Joan Macan's TIMSPRING kennel produced a strong line of sound dogs that worked well and were good show specimens. Joan was one of the foremost people to promote hip X-rays in Labradors, and she personally paid for hip results to be published, so they were available in an easily readable book. To their great credit, the Labrador Retriever Club took over this work for the breed following her death.

BALLYDUFF
This kennel, owned by Bridget Docking and her first husband, Dr Acheson, was highly thought of round the world for their marvellous line of dual purpose dogs that were shown in the summer months and were worked during the winter. The Ballyduff dogs were influential in the foundation of many kennels both in the UK and overseas, including the famous Lockerbie kennel in the USA. Some of the better-known dogs were Ballyduff Whatstandwell Robin, Whatstandwell Ballyduff Rowene (BOB at Crufts twice), Ballyduff Seaman, Ballyduff Marina, Curnafane Seamansal, Ballyduff Marketeer, Ballyduff Marshall, Ballyduff Squire, Ballyduff Spruce, Ballyduff Spark, Ballyduff Candy and Ballyduff Lark. Dr Acheson, and Bridget's daughter, Sheelin Cuthbert, now own the Ballyduff prefix in the UK. A couple of year's after Bridget's death, Sheelin started to show her line of good blacks, which goes back on to her mother's strong line.

MANSERGH
Mary Roslin Williams, nicknamed affectionately 'Black Mary', is well-known for her wonderful line of black Mansergh Champions. She is no longer judging at Field Trials or Championship Shows, but still competing in the ring with two very good typical bitches, with the beautiful heads that she is so famous for, and strong, but actively-built bodies. They both go back to her

foundation bitch, Carry On Mansergh. Two of her early Champions, who were among her particular favourites, were the father and daughter, Ch. Midnight of Mansergh and Ch. Bumblekite of Mansergh. A further nine Champions have been made up in the UK: Damson, Groucho, Moleskin, Antonia, Ooh-la-la, Ships Belle, Mayday and Nokeener Black Spark. Mansergh Sailor Beware was made up by Didi Hepworth, though owned by her son. One of the highlights for this highly successful kennel was when Mayday went best in Show over thirty-three Champions at the Labrador Club's 'Ruby' Championship Show in 1984.

There have been numerous Champions made up abroad including Field Trial Champions. The Mansergh Labradors were campaigned at trials for nearly twenty years, gaining many Field Trial awards. Carry won the first trial they ever attended, and eighteen years later Mansergh Black Grape won their last trial.

SANDYLANDS
Through all this time, Gwen Broadley's Sandylands kennel has been at the forefront – and everyone in the breed today owes so much to her. More than seventy Labrador Champions have been made up since the kennel was founded in the early thirties. The first Champion came in 1934 – in fact, it took Ch. Jerry of Sandylands five years to gain his title. The latest Champion (to date) is Sh. Ch. Sandylands Bliss made up in 1992, celebrating over sixty years in the breed.

Sandylands has made the strongest single impact on the breed as it is today. Every country in the world that has Labradors will have dogs that go back to these lines. Mrs Broadley's Labradors have laid solid foundations for so many show kennels both in the UK and overseas. Sandylands Tarquin and Sandylands Markwell have been highly influential in America, and Sandylands Tan has done so much for Australia. These dogs have produced some of the top sires of all times. They include Ch. Sandylands Tweed of Blaircourt, bred by Mr and Mrs Grant, who dominated the sixties becoming a legend in his lifetime, Ch. Sandylands Tandy, and then Ch. Sandylands Mark, who sired no less than twenty-nine UK Champions. He died in 1979 at just under fourteen years of age, and his influence on the breed is still felt today. Indeed, all those who have come into contact with the Sandylands dogs have been enriched, benefiting from Mrs Broadley's immense knowledge and dedication to the Labrador.

Mrs Broadley (known as 'Aunty Gwen') no longer shows her own dogs in the ring, but she attends shows whenever possible. Erica Smith has been with Mrs Broadley for many years, and handles the Sandylands dogs with great success.

We now come to the breed as it is today, with three of these important early kennels still taking a very active part, namely Cornlands, Mansergh and Sandylands. In the last twenty years many new kennels have come to the fore, and these are highlighted in Chapter Six, along with Didi Hepworth's world-famous Poolstead kennels, which started in 1959, and remain such a strong force today.

Chapter Two

CHOOSING A PUPPY

There are several reasons why you might want to purchase a Labrador puppy. It could be that you are simply looking for a nice puppy as a companion; you may have been bitten by the show-going bug, and so you are looking for a puppy of quality that has the potential to succeed in the show ring, or it could be that you have started breeding your own Labradors, and now realise that you need to up-grade your stock by selecting a top-class puppy. In all these instances there are a number of guidelines which are helpful when trying to choose a good puppy from a litter.

CHOOSING A BREEDER
Prospective buyers that are interested in showing and breeding should not confine themselves to going to the local shows in their area when trying to locate a breeder. They should try to go to Championship Shows which are patronised by Labrador people from all over the country – and they can then assess the type of Labrador they like.

If you are thinking of buying a good bitch puppy who will form the basis of your kennel line, it is essential to buy from someone who has already established themselves as a breeder of note, producing good quality stock time after time. This will be important if you want your new acquisition to do the same for you. A marvellous 'one-off' from a litter of mediocre puppies, with no strong breeding line in the pedigree, will not necessarily reproduce herself. In fact, the odds are that she will reproduce offspring of the same type and quality as the rest of the litter she came from.

If you are serious about getting good stock, be prepared to be patient. Put your name on the list of the breeder whose stock you admire, making sure that the breeder knows that the bitch you are looking for is intended for showing, and that you eventually plan to use her for breeding. The breeder will then ensure that you get a good-quality puppy, because the pup will carry the breeder's prefix and this will reflect on the kennel's reputation.

It might take many months – but it is worth a wait to get the right puppy. Years can be lost, breeding up to a higher standard, if you settle for an available puppy that is of mediocre quality. I find these days that pet puppies from stock no-one has heard of go for the same price as top-quality animals – so price is no guide. You should, perhaps, not expect to get the pick of the litter. I only breed a litter when I want something for myself, so I would always have first choice.

However, I am always very hard on myself, and if I find the best in the litter does not have that little extra something, I will sell the whole litter and try again, keeping nothing for myself. This is the point where, I think, many 'novice' breeders come unstuck. It is sometimes hard to see that although it is a 'nice' litter, there is nothing outstanding in it that will lift the breeder up another notch. The tendency is to keep the 'pick of the litter', not realising that you are getting no further ahead in the goal to breed a truly great Labrador.

ASSESSING A LITTER

I am often asked to go and look at litter, and help to choose the pick – and I enjoy this very much. Each time you go over dogs you, hopefully, learn a little more. I am very seldom asked "Would you keep it yourself for a potential show dog?" The answer on some occasions would be a definite "No". Then again, when I have been asked to visit a litter, sometimes one pup really catches my eye, even before I have handled it. Once I have gone over the puppy and the quality has been confirmed, I have been told: "That one is just a pet, and is already sold!" This has happened on four or five occasions to date – the breeder just fails to see the real gem – perhaps because it is the wrong colour or the wrong sex! My advice is never look at any litter with a closed mind: I have bred litters hoping for a yellow dog, and I have ended up with a black bitch because it was the best and was a cracker.

You are now going to see the litter. Every kennel line is slightly different. I have seen gorgeous puppies at six weeks of age belonging to some breeders, when I think my own are definitely less than cute at the same stage; but by nine weeks mine are looking great, so, personally, I do not make the final choice until this age at the very earliest. At six weeks you can certainly assess the lay of shoulder, topline, tail-set, turn of stifle, sufficiency of bone, type of feet and coat. Heads can still change a lot, but you can tell if you have good ear placement, and assess the length and width of muzzle, and the eye shape.

I do not think I am particularly clever at picking out puppies. I can never pick them at birth, as some claim they can. I make my choice methodically, and it usually works on my own stock. I like to watch the pups playing around as a group, but I am more interested in standing them up, and going over them, and writing my assessment down as a critique, highlighting the good points and the failings. I do this to the whole litter, then I bring back the ones I have marked as good prospects and go over them again. I do this at five, seven, and nine weeks of age, when, hopefully, I make my final choice.

When I stand up a pup, and view from the side, I like to see a nice, solid shape, slightly longer body-wise than the height at the shoulder. I want to see a good topline and deep bodyline, with well-sprung ribs, and only two fingers width between the end of the ribs and the start of the rear quarters, i.e. in the loin area. I want to see the tail-set going straight off the back, and level with it. I do not mind if the tail is held a little gay at this stage (if the tail-set is still correct) because worms seem to play a large part at this stage, and the tail usually comes down over the next six to eight weeks or so. I want to see some prow at the front, a good lay of shoulder and upper arm, well-boned legs, tight feet and well-turned stifles.

A useful test is to lie your index finger along the puppy's back, with your fingertip just lying between the shoulder blades, and then gently press the pup's head down with your other hand. You should find that the shoulder blades just nip your finger. If this doesn't happen, you will usually find that the shoulder is not soundly constructed, and you will later discover that the dog is loose at the elbow when coming towards you.

I want the eyes set reasonably well apart, and, as to shape, not round or bulbous eyes; we prefer diamond-shaped eyes on a Labrador. The pup should have a bump on top of the head to grow into, so the ears are not stuck on top of the head when the head has finished growing. I like the muzzle to be as wide as it is deep, so I have a nice square muzzle, not snipey, when the dog is grown up. I also look for a reasonable length of muzzle; a short muzzle like a Rottweiler's, looks horrific on a

A nice, typical looking Labrador puppy, aged nine weeks.

Labrador head. Teeth should be checked to confirm the bite is scissor – top incisors just lapping the bottom. Labradors usually have very good bites, but it is still something that should always be checked in a puppy. While the dog is growing up, do not panic if, at some stage, the top jaw seems to be growing more quickly than the bottom. The balance is usually redressed by the time the head is fully grown, at nine to ten months.

Coats can be difficult to assess. I can remember some years ago being asked to look at a pup because the owners thought the coat was all wrong. This was a black puppy, and the coat was a rather mousey colour, and it was very dense. I said I would buy the pup right away, but, sensibly, the owners declined my offer. They kept the pup and won a Reserve CC at Crufts only eighteen months later! The rather mousey colour, or reddish tinge on a black, is often the sign of a good coat with thick undercoat in later life. Smooth, shiny black pups seen in a litter aged six to nine weeks, will not have double coats in later life. The same applies to yellows or chocolates. The rather woolly puppy coats, with only a few longer guard hairs coming through, are preferable to smoother coats at that age.

When you are trying to make your initial mark on the show scene, even for some years to come, it is a good idea to stay with bitches. You need a really outstanding dog to stand at stud successfully. Most people tend to use a Champion dog, hoping to improve their stock, so even good males tend not to be used very often. Economics must come into it a little, and if there are a couple of particularly good, top-winning, well-known dogs in your area, your dog will not be used at stud too often, and he will sit there eating his head off, and perhaps deprive you of a space for a good, young bitch. I found this hard at first when I started out in the show world on my return to England, as both my husband, David, and I rather favour the males. Given the choice of having only one dog, I would always keep a male; I feel they have more personality and give much more affection.

SELECTING SHOW STOCK

When David and I arrived back in England eighteen years ago, we had already spent eight years in Labradors – four in Australia and four in Malaysia – and we had drawn up our ideas on the type of Labrador we wanted to breed. We enjoyed our first two Labradors, they remained very special to us, but, so far, we have never been kennel blind, and we did realise all their faults and failings as well as their good points. We went to a few Championship shows when we came home, and we decided we would like a Lawnwoods bitch. We bought a young eighteen-month-old youngster to use as our foundation bitch – this was Brentville Marcella of Lawnwood. She had lovely classical lines, very similar in type to her great granddaughter, Ch. Warringahs Fair Dinkum, and her great great granddaughter, Ch. Warringahs Waltzing Matilda. They were good up-to-size bitches, with the nice length of back that I like, good chunky rear ends, nice second thighs, with beautiful feminine heads.

If you are lucky enough to get a grown-on bitch from a good breeder, much of the hard work is already done for you. If they have the space, many breeders will run on two bitches and decide at some time between six to twelve months which to keep. If you can bide your time and wait for one, you will be off to a good start. You will, of course, be expected to pay a fair and reasonable price: after all the dog has been fed, housed, inoculated, X-rayed, eye-tested and perhaps even shown, so do not expect to be handed the youngster on a plate.

Some breeders go in for breeding terms when selling a grown-on puppy or young stock; I personally do not like the idea, having seen the pitfalls that can occur. That said, I have tried it twice, both times selling on a six-month-old pup to a family home on the understanding that the bitch would have one litter at approximately two years of age. I was to choose the stud dog, and have one pick-of-the-litter puppy. On both occasions I was very successful – my two pick-of-litter pups were Ch. Warringahs Fair Dinkum and Sh. Ch. Warringahs Fair Clemency. The mothers became the sole property of the owners from the moment I had my pups.

However, I have heard horror stories concerning breeding terms, with the breeder asking for three or more pups, not necessarily from the same litter. There can also be confusion over when the breeder releases the 'owner' from from the contract. My advice would be to steer clear of breeding terms, or, otherwise, make sure that you are happy with the terms, i.e. try to ensure the pups are all from one litter, or if it is a small litter that the contract ends with the first litter. The contract should state clearly the points that have been decided upon, detailing when the bitch is your property solely, and it should be signed by both parties.

There might be a very good reason why the breeder cannot run on the youngster that you are being offered – perhaps a better one is coming on – but you should have got a good bitch with brood potential. I would suggest that any youngster bought from six months of age should be X-rayed, just to see what the hips look like, although we know that they cannot be put through the KC/BVA Hip Dysplasia Scheme at this age. If the youngster is a year-plus, KC/BVA Hip and Eye Certificates are a must before you make your purchase.

Assuming you have now got a good-quality, grown-on, young bitch, please do not go and undo all her good breeding by using the wrong dog on her. I would take the breeders' advice on which dog to mate her to, as they will know which dogs are most suitable, and which to avoid.

Chapter Three

THE MATURING PUPPY

PLAY AND REST

Careful management is vital at all stages from pre-mating through to when the pup is ready to leave home, and it is equally important in raising your puppy through to adulthood. I think that where so many people go wrong is in not allowing the small pup to rest for sufficient periods of time. This is especially true if the pup is newly introduced into the household. Everyone wants to play with and hold the new baby, but, while the pup certainly needs attention and should be introduced to all manner of new experiences, long periods of sleep are essential. This is in order that the food that is consumed goes into steady growth, and not just on energy which is used up in play. The puppy will go on playing for as long as you will – the Labrador has a big heart – but this is not good for a growing dog.

THE PLAY PEN

If you already have adult dogs in the house, you will obviously want the pup to learn to live in harmony with them – and vice versa. Remember, a pup can be very annoying, continually playing and hanging on to an older dog's ears. Equally, an older dog can also wear out a pup. I have found that a small pen, 4ft by 4ft, set up for the pup is an ideal solution. Mine is actually a compost container, consisting of four welded mesh panels, 2ft by 4ft, held together by strong rubber clips. This can be bought at any good garden centre; it make an ideal puppy pen, and what is more, it is useful in the garden afterwards.

   This pen can be used until the pup is four months old, for rest periods and for sleeping in at night. You can put a cardboard box bed in there, lined with a warm blanket (I can never see the point in buying expensive beds while the puppy is growing so quickly, and the boxes can be replaced whenever it becomes necessary, at no extra cost). Make sure you put newspaper on the floor of the run for the inevitable mistake. The pen becomes a special, private place, where the puppy can sleep undisturbed after play periods, as well as letting the older dogs have some peace and quiet. The pup will learn also to be quiet and content without company for part of the time, and this is a very important lesson, for a dog cannot be with you twenty-four hours a day.

   I let my small pups play for a short time after every meal with the adults, while I am there to keep an eye on proceedings. I do not want a puppy getting injured in the rough and tumble of the more exuberant young adults. By the time my pups are five to six months old they are fully integrated into the pack, and I feel they are big enough to hold their own in strength and in character. We have to remember that the Labrador is a fairly fast-growing breed, and that means that the bones are not fully hardened, and too much rough and tumble can injure them. I do not

A fast-growing breed needs controlled exercise, and should avoid too much rough-and-tumble. These pups are confined to the small run, but by five to six months they will be fully integrated into the pack.

believe in mollycoddling my pups; I just take sensible precautions such as keeping them a little lighter in weight, until they are fully grown (which is, surprisingly, about seven months old in my line), ensuring they do not get knocked about by the bigger, heavier adults and are not over-exercised. One of the diseases that is a bane to Labradors is osteochondrosis dissecans (OCD), which can cause lameness and pain in the shoulder, elbow or hock. In the Labrador it is mostly the elbow which is affected (see Chapter 16, Health Care), and it is careful management during the crucial growth times that may help to alleviate this painful condition.

EXERCISE
Once the pups have had their inoculations they need to start going out and meeting the world. I start this off, along with lead training, by just going and sitting outside the front gate and watching the cars go past. I then progress to a little road walking, to a maximum of a quarter of a mile, to get the pup used to the passing traffic. On the country lanes where I live, it is most important that the dogs are not shy of traffic – we have no pavements to separate us from the cars. As a car approaches, I get the pup to sit, by giving the command and pressing gently on the rear end. I then stroke the puppy reassuringly as the car goes past, giving plenty of praise.

At three to six months, we go out for a short walk every day – a quarter of a mile stretching to half a mile a day by the time the pup is six months old. From six to nine months, the walks get longer, increasing to about one mile a day, and from nine months to one year, well, by then we have made the *big dog* time, and we go for two to three miles each day. I take every opportunity I can, at this time, to approach my house from different directions, so if a dog ever became lost, hopefully the surroundings would be familiar and the lost dog would find the way home. When I was in Australia twenty-five years ago, I found a Labrador puppy that was lost; it took me three days to find the owners, and they were only in the next road! It was a lesson that I have never forgotten.

Once *big dog* status is reached, the youngster goes road walking once a week (two miles round the block). This helps to keep the feet, nails, and pasterns in good working order. I have to make a point of this for my dogs, because all our other exercise is taken on soft ground in the woods behind our home. I am not advocating that this exercise routine is kept to without deviation; if you want a good long walk in the country at the weekend with your family and the puppy, that is fine, but you should not do it every day.

TRAINING

As I hope my dogs will be show-dogs, I take them straight off to show classes as soon as the inoculations are complete. This gets them used to inside venues, to noise, to other breeds of dogs, and lots of new people – all great learning experiences. I try also to take my pups into the local market town to get them used to walking on pavements and seeing dozens of cars and people, although the number of shops or banks that will allow dogs inside is diminishing rapidly. The short drives to training classes, and to the town also help the pups to get used to the car.

Having started many years ago in Obedience, I really do not subscribe to the theory that you cannot do Obedience training with a show dog. All of my dogs have a certain amount of basic Obedience drummed into them. I cannot stand dogs that pull on the lead, and if I tell a dog to sit and stay, I expect the correct response to the command. I like to know that when I open my car door, the dogs will stay there until I ask them to come out, and at shows, I can put my dogs up on to the benches, knowing they will sit and stay while I go from one to the next putting on the collars and benching chains. If you see a strange woman walking along with six dogs from the car park, mostly Labradors, but with a Sussex and a German Shorthaired Pointer thrown in for good luck, that's me – and hopefully the dogs are not pulling!

When you are training your puppy for show it is important that the difference between 'Sit' and 'Stand' is clearly established. When your pup is standing, give plenty of praise and repeat the command 'Stand', drawing out the word. Then, when the pup learns 'Sit', make the command short and sharp, and the dog will soon differentiate between them. I still instruct at Obedience classes once a year at my local club (I am the club's president), and on these occasions I like to teach the beginners. I always start off the first lesson by teaching 'Sit' and 'Stand', because, as they come to a halt, the dogs will do either one or the other. To my mind, it is so easy at this stage to put a command to their action.

As your puppy becomes more responsive to house training, allocate an area of your garden, and always take the pup to this spot for toilet purposes. Make sure that you clean up the area at least once a day or twice a day. It is old stools that incubate the toxacara canis worm that can do so much harm to children.

WORMING

Remember, that as the pup grows to adulthood, it is essential to worm on a regular basis. Youngsters seem to be more prone to re-infestation of roundworms than adults. After my initial worming regime up to nine weeks, I worm again at three months, six months, nine months, and at twelve months. From this time onwards, a twice yearly regime should be adequate, and this should be maintained for the rest of the dog's life. However, as I am most likely to have young stock at home, I personally stick to the three months regime for the entire kennel. I worm on January 1st, April 1st, July 1st and October 1st, and in this way I do not forget. It is a very good idea to keep to a three-monthly programme if you have young children; it lessens the risk of infection to them.

DIET

As the pup matures, four meals a day decreases to three meals at three months (cutting out supper), to two meals at six months (there goes breakfast), and finally to one meal at a year old. This should be fed at whatever time of day is most convenient to you. I feed at noon after everyone has been walked in the morning – they then all settle down to a good snooze in the afternoon with full stomachs. I find that at twelve weeks my pups are eating roughly the same quantity as they will consume for the rest of their lives. A daily diet would be:

> **Breakfast:** Three Weetabix plus milk.
> **Lunch:** 7oz meat and 3oz biscuit.
> **Tea:** 7oz meat and 3oz biscuit.
> **Supper**: One-third of a can of rice pudding
> (A total of 14oz meat to 12oz cereal over the day.)

When I drop the supper at twelve weeks, I increase the Weetabix up to four, as well as putting up the biscuit to 4oz at each meal; the meat remains the same. By six months, when the breakfast goes, it becomes 6-8oz of biscuit at each meal, depending on the pup. Eventually, at one year, the dog is on one meal only, having combined the two meals into one.

I am not one for additives. I use only fish-oil tablets for the coat, and a multi-vitamin palatable tablet. If you are using the complete foods, remember that these already contain all the additional nutrients that you should require, and no more should be added. More harm than good is done by over-doing the vitamins and calcium. I used to be a believer in giving a small daily addition of calcium (in the form of bone meal) until the pup had reached maturity, but for the past couple of years I have not given this to my Labrador puppies. The reason for this is that recent reports have suggested that added calcium has not helped cases of OCD in the Labrador. One of the earlier treatments of OCD was to push calcium into the puppies, but this has since been found to be a detrimental factor. I can see no lessening of quality in my pups since I dropped the calcium addition, so, until proved wrong, I will stick to my rather spartan routine.

MALES AND FEMALES

As I said previously, I am a believer in Obedience classes. I ask all my puppy owners to take their dogs along to class when they are six months old, and I think it is a good idea for the young males, in particular, to do some lessons, especially when they are becoming sexually mature. It does them good to do as they are told, surrounded by other dogs, when all they really want to be is macho men. I think of our young Labrador males as being a bit like teenagers, with lots of muscle, but they do not know quite what to do with it. It is your job to make sure that your dog is guided in the right direction. Labrador bitches vary considerably on when they come into season for the first time. I have heard of some coming in as early as seven months, although the earliest I have had is nine months. In most cases, I would expect a bitch to come in season at some time between eleven and thirteen months. One of my bitches did not have her first season until she was sixteen months old, and I have heard of bitches that have been later than that. When they do eventually come in, I find Labrador bitches are pretty regular, and come in season every six months.

Now that you have a grown-up pup, the bitch has had her season and the boys have learnt to lift their legs (again nine to twelve months is normal), what do you hope to do with them in their lifetime? Obviously, if you are going to show or breed, you will want your dog or bitch to be entire, but if you do not intend to show or breed, I am in favour of spaying or castrating at this point.

This a very emotive subject. The arguments that neutering leads to obesity hold little water. This is just bad management, as you should simply adjust the diet to suit the amount of energy the dog is using up. I worked for the Guide Dogs for the Blind, and so I was in contact with hundreds of spayed or castrated animals – just look around at the guide dogs you see out on the streets, and none of them are fat! If you decide to neuter, you must let your dog or bitch grow to sexual and physical maturity before surgery. I have seen notices in some vets' surgeries (not mine, I hasten to add) that encourage the spaying of bitches at four to five months, and some canine organisations recommend nine to twelve weeks, but I would be totally against this. I believe in letting an animal grow to its full potential before either spaying or castrating.

I am also not of the opinion that every bitch needs a litter. I have often been presented with this argument by someone who is enquiring about using a stud dog. It is either a "friend" or "the vet", who has said it would be a good thing for the bitch to have litter "before being spayed", or, in the case of a bitch who is having problems in frequent seasons or phantom pregnancies, a litter will "sort her out". In fact, it is far more important to debate whether it is wise to be putting yet more puppies on to the pet market. You also have the other request, more infrequently I must admit, when you are asked to find a bitch as a mate for their beloved pet dog. I gently try to explain that even very good show dogs or working dogs do not always get used at stud, because people usually try to go to the very top when it comes to choosing a mate for their bitch. I also stress that it is not a good idea for a pet dog be allowed one, single experience of stud work – this is almost certain to lead to behavioural problems in the future.

Last, but not least, make sure you enjoy your puppy. Use a good dose of commonsense (and if you have chosen a Labrador you must have lots of that already) and all will go smoothly. Your Labrador will reward you with love and loyalty for many years to come.

Chapter Four

THE BREED STANDARD

In most countries of the world the British Kennel Club Breed Standard is in use; Britain is considered to be the Labrador's country of origin. The FCI (Federation Cynologique Internationale), with all its aligned countries, also uses the British Standard. In America the Breed Standard differs slightly, and so I have included this Standard, and will comment on the differences between the two.

BRITISH BREED STANDARD (1986)

GENERAL APPEARANCE Strongly built, short-coupled, very active; broad in skull; broad and deep through chest and ribs; broad and strong over loins and hindquarters.
CHARACTERISTICS Good-tempered, very agile. Excellent nose, soft mouth; keen love of water. Adaptable, devoted companion.
TEMPERAMENT Intelligent, keen and biddable, with a strong will to please. Kindly nature, with no trace of aggression, or undue shyness.
HEAD AND SKULL Skull broad with defined stop; clean-cut without fleshy cheeks. Jaws of medium length, powerful, not snipey. Nose wide, nostrils well developed.
EYES Medium size, expressing intelligence and good temper, brown or hazel.
EARS Not large or heavy, hanging close to head and set rather far back.
MOUTH Jaws and teeth strong, with perfect, regular and complete scissor bite, i.e. the upper teeth closely overlapping the lower teeth and set square to the jaws.
NECK Clean, strong, powerful, set into well-placed shoulders.
FOREQUARTERS Shoulders long and sloping. Forelegs well-boned and straight from elbow to ground when viewed from either front or side.
BODY Chest of good width and depth, with well sprung barrel ribs. Level topline. Loins wide, short-coupled and strong.
HINDQUARTERS Well-developed not sloping to tail; well turned stifle. Hocks let down, cow hocks highly undesirable.
FEET Round, compact; well-arched toes and well developed pads.
TAIL Distinctive feature, very thick towards base, gradually tapering towards tip, medium length, free from feathering, but clothed thickly all round with short, thick, dense coat, thus giving 'rounded' appearance described as 'otter' tail. May be carried gaily, but should not curl over back.
GAIT/MOVEMENT Free, covering adequate ground; straight and true front and rear.

COAT Distinctive feature, short dense without wave or feathering, giving fairly hard feel to the touch; weather resistant undercoat.

COLOUR Wholly black, yellow, or liver/chocolate. Yellows range from light cream to red fox. Small white spot on chest permissible.

SIZE Ideal height at withers:

Dogs 56-57cm (22in-22½in)

Bitches 54-56cm (21½in-22in).

FAULTS Any departure from the foregoing points should be considered a fault and the seriousness with which the fault should be regarded should be in exact proportion to its degree.

NOTE Male animals should have two apparently normal testicles fully descended into the scrotum.

Reproduced by kind permission of the English Kennel Club.

AMERICAN BREED STANDARD (1957)

GENERAL APPEARANCE The general appearance of the Labrador should be that of a strongly built, short-coupled, very active dog. He should be fairly wide over the loins, and strong and muscular in the hindquarters. The coat should be close, short, dense and free from feather.

HEAD The skull should be wide, giving brain room, there should be a slight stop, i.e. the brow should be slightly pronounced, so that the skull is not absolutely in a straight line with the nose. The head should be clean-cut and free from fleshy cheeks. The jaws should be long and powerful and free from snipiness; the nose should be wide and the nostrils well developed. Teeth should be strong and regular, with a level mouth. The ears should hang moderately close to the head, rather far back, should be set somewhat low and not be large and heavy. The eyes should be of a medium size, expressing great intelligence and good temper, can be brown, yellow or black, but brown or black is preferred.

NECK AND CHEST The neck should be medium length, powerful and not throaty. The shoulders should be long and sloping. The chest must be of good width and depth, the ribs well sprung and the loins wide and strong, stifles well turned, and the hindquarters well developed and of great power.

LEGS AND FEET The legs must be straight from the shoulder to ground, and the feet compact with toes well arched, and pads well developed; the hocks should be well bent, and the dog must neither be cow hocked nor be too wide behind; in fact, he must stand and move true all round on legs and feet. Legs should be of medium length, showing good bone and muscle, but not so short as to be out of balance with rest of body. In fact, a dog well balanced in all points is preferable to one with outstanding good qualities and defects.

TAIL The tail is a distinctive feature of the breed; it should be very thick towards the base; gradually tapering towards the tip, of medium length, should be free from any feathering, and should be clothed thickly all round with the Labrador's short, thick, dense coat, thus giving that peculiar 'rounded' appearance which has been described as the 'otter' tail. The tail may be carried gaily but should not curl over the back.

COAT The coat is another very distinctive feature; it should be short, very dense and without wave, and should give a fairly hard feeling to the hand.

COLOR The colors are black, yellow, or chocolate and are evaluated as follows:

a) **Blacks:** All black, with a small white spot on chest permissible. Eyes to be of medium size, expressing intelligence and good temper, preferable brown or hazel, although black or yellow is permissible.

b) **Yellows:** Yellows may vary in color from fox-red to light cream with variations in the shading of the coat on ears, the underparts of the dog, or beneath the tail. A small white spot on chest is permissible. Eye coloring and expression should be the same as that of the blacks, with black or dark-brown eye-rims. The nose should also be black or dark brown, although 'fading' to pink in winter weather is not serious. A 'Dudley' nose (pink without pigmentation) should be penalized.

c) **Chocolates:** Shades ranging from light sedge to chocolate. A small white spot on chest permissible. Eyes to be light brown to clear yellow. Nose and eye-rim pigmentation dark brown or liver colored. 'Fading' to pink in winter weather is not serious. 'Dudley' nose should be penalized.

MOVEMENT Movement should be free and effortless. The forelegs should be strong, straight and true, and correctly placed. Watching a dog move towards one, there should be no signs of elbows being out in front, but neatly held to the body and with legs not too close together, but moving straight forward without pacing or weaving. Upon viewing the dog from the rear, one should get the impression that the hind legs, which should be well muscled and not cow hocked, move as nearly parallel as possible, with hocks doing their full share of work and flexing well, thus giving the appearance of power and strength.

APPROXIMATE WEIGHTS OF DOGS AND BITCHES IN WORKING CONDITIONS
Dogs 60-75 pounds. Bitches 55-70 pounds.
HEIGHT AT SHOULDERS Dogs 221/2in-241/2in
Bitches 211/2in to 231/2in
Reproduced by kind permission of the American Kennel Club. (Due to be revised in 1993).

INTERPRETATION AND ANALYSIS

PHYSICAL APPEARANCE
GENERAL CONFORMATION

In general conformation, the Labrador should be a sturdy, strongly built, of good substance, but not a fat dog. A Labrador has got to be strong enough to carry a really heavy hare or bird, to be able to jump over obstacles with it, to swim against strong currents, and still have enough reserves to do all this again and again during the day. Those that tend towards breeding Labradors too far either side of this desirable norm, will have dogs that do not have the staying power, because they have no reserves of strength, or are so heavy or badly-constructed that they tire too easily. We must always remember that the Breed Standard was drawn up by people who used the Labrador as a working dog. We have chosen to own this breed, and when breeding, we must never lose sight of the breed's working potential, even if we know that our dogs may never have the opportunity of fulfilling their role as retriever in the field.

HEAD AND SKULL

The skull should be broad but not coarse, with enough brain room, and it must have a definite stop. Cheeks should be flat; fleshy cheeks give a very foreign look to the head. The muzzle should be of

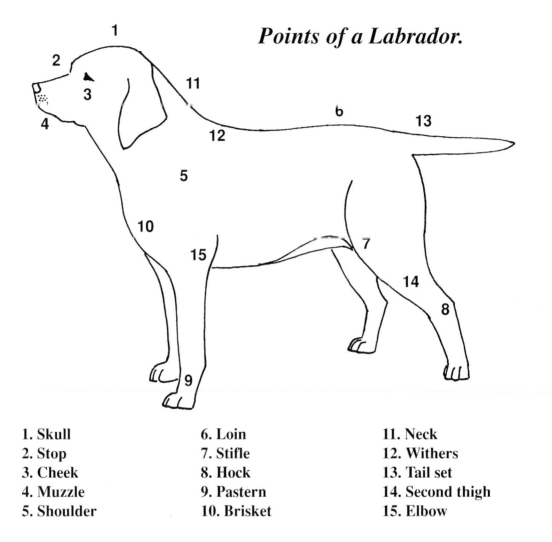

Points of a Labrador.

1. Skull	6. Loin	11. Neck
2. Stop	7. Stifle	12. Withers
3. Cheek	8. Hock	13. Tail set
4. Muzzle	9. Pastern	14. Second thigh
5. Shoulder	10. Brisket	15. Elbow

a moderate length (bearing in mind its game-retrieving capability), and have a square appearance. A thin, narrow muzzle is referred to as snipey. The nose should be wide and the nostrils well-developed for good scenting ability.

EARS The ears are set quite far back, and should be reasonably low. Ears that are set right on top of the head, give a hard untypical look; they should hang close to the skull, and be of a neat size.

EYES The eyes should be set fairly wide apart, and they should not be round or bulbous, as these are too vulnerable to damage for a working dog. We look for a diamond-shaped eye that is not too deeply-set. The colour can range from hazel to brown, although the colour of 'burnt sugar' is preferred. Black eyes are allowed in America, but they are frowned upon in England. However, what is most important of all is the expression. The eyes should give an immediate impression of kindliness and good temper. A hard expression is penalised.

MOUTH The British and American Standards differ in the wording on the bite. The English Standard asks for a "regular and complete *scissor* bite", and the American Standard states "*level* mouth". I always ask the Societies that I judge for in America to clarify this, and I am told to look for a scissor bite. Perhaps when the American Standard is updated in 1993, this point will be looked into.

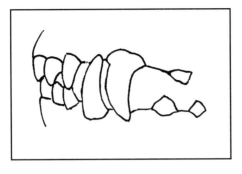

Correct scissor bite.

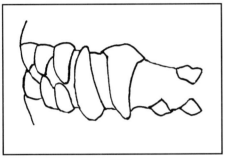

Level bite.

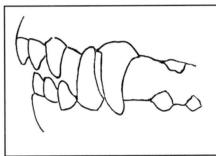

Overshot mouth.

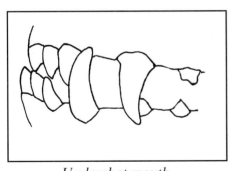

Undershot mouth.

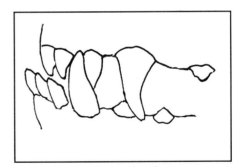

Badly undershot.

NECK AND FOREQUARTERS

The forequarters are of vital importance; the way they are formed significantly affects the manner in which the dog can work.

NECK We are looking for a clean neck, meaning not throaty with dewlaps, set into a long, sloping well-laid shoulder.

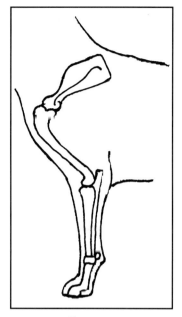

Correct.

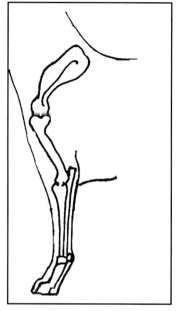

Incorrect: Too straight and upright.

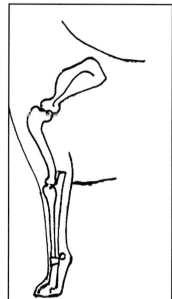

Incorrect: Good lay, but short, straight upper arm.

SHOULDERS The upper arm should not be too short and should have a good lay back – the angle formed between the two being about 90 degrees. The correct angulation gives the dog the balance that is required to carry game in the least tiring manner, with most of the weight being carried through the shoulders, and not in the mouth and neck.

CHEST The chest should have a hand's width between the front legs, and the depth of chest should reach the level of the elbow when viewed from the side.

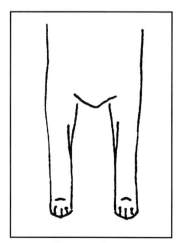

Correct front.

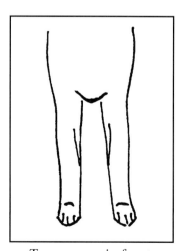

Too narrow in front.

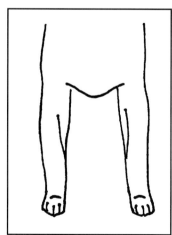

Too wide in front.

FORELEGS The forelegs should look straight when viewed either from the side or from the front. They should be of medium length and have good bone and muscle. The pasterns should be strong, and have a little give in them, but they should not be too sloping.

FEET The feet should be round and compact, with well-arched toes, and good pads. The long, thin hare foot is incorrect, and would be inadequate for the work the Labrador has to perform. Likewise, the very tight cat-foot with the bone going right down to the foot, like a Terrier, with no give in the pasterns at all, would be incapable of sustaining prolonged exercise.

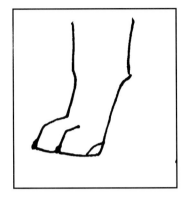

Correct foot; pastern with just a little slope.

Incorrect: Longer hare foot; pastern too soft and sloping.

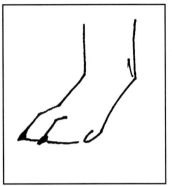

BODY

The Labrador should have well-sprung barrel ribs and well-ribbed back. The loin should be short, wide and strong – not tucked up in the body. The topline should be straight, not dipping or sloping off to the tail-set.

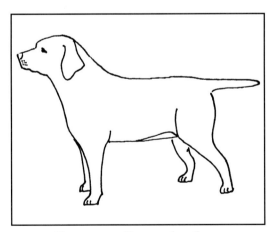

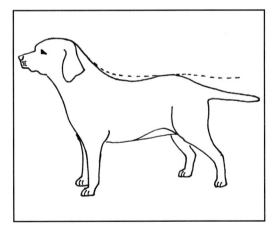

Correct topline and tail-set.   *Incorrect: Soft topline, low tail-set.*

HINDQUARTERS

These should be well-muscled, with a good turn of stifle. The Labrador should have a well-made second thigh, and well let down hocks. When viewed from behind, the hocks should be straight.

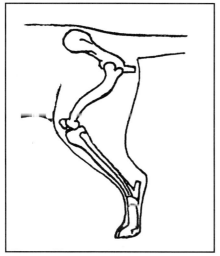

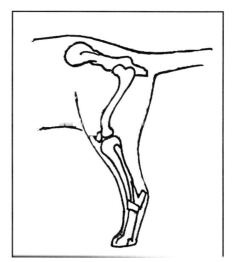

Correct: well-bent stifles, and well let down hocks.

Incorrect: Rather straight in stifle and hock.

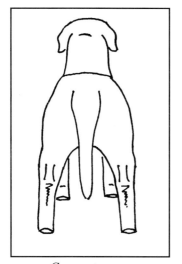

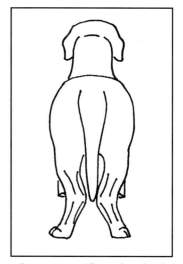

Correct rear.

Incorrect: Cow-hocked.

Hocks that turn in, known as 'cow hocks', are considered a serious fault. Incorrect hind angulation will not supply the power to thrust the body forward. Powerful hind limbs should look as if they are pushing the ground away behind them.

COAT AND TAIL

These are two of the most distinctive features of a Labrador, and they are related. It is the correct clothing of the tail that gives it the thick otter-like appearance. There should be no feathering on the tail; it is thick at its base and narrows to the tip. There is no detailed mention of tail-length in

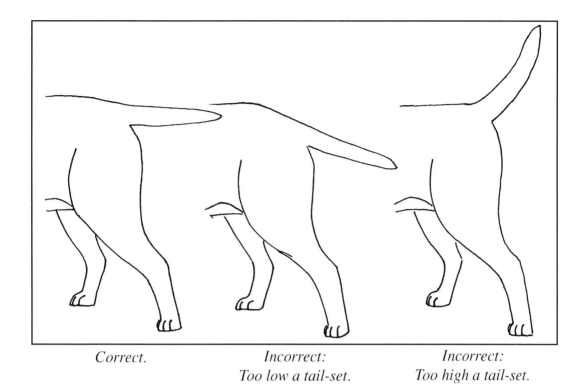

Correct.   *Incorrect:*   *Incorrect:*
                           Too low a tail-set.   *Too high a tail-set.*

either the British or the American Breed Standard – 'medium length' is stipulated. However, a tail that is too long, or too short, does not give a balanced look. A tail that reaches to the hocks is more pleasing. The tail should be carried horizontally, but it is often carried higher. This is referred to as a 'gay' tail, and it is permitted in the Standard, but the tail must never be carried curling over the back – this is considered a bad fault.

The coat should be short and dense and feel hard to the hand. When the coat is turned back, it should reveal a soft, thick weather-resisting undercoat, quite covering the skin. This is often of a lighter shade than the top coat – many a good black has a quite mousey-coloured undercoat. I also have a black who has the top two-thirds of its outercoat length black, and the third nearest the body is white.

A soft coat would be of no use to a Labrador, as it soaks up the water, and so this fault must be penalised. In the American Standard there is no mention of the all-important undercoat, although, in my experience, all American breeders do breed for a good undercoat, and the true 'otter' tail is one of their strong points.

COLOUR
The coat colour in the Labrador comes in three colours, black, chocolate (liver) and yellow.
BLACKS: All black – a small white spot on the chest is permissible. Many Labradors are born with white pads just behind the ankle, especially on the front feet. These are nicknamed 'bolo-pads' after Dual Ch. Banchory Bolo, and most serious breeders quite like them, and would certainly not penalise them when judging. Eye colouring should enhance the coat, with brown or hazel being preferred.

YELLOWS: This term can cover any colour from light-cream to fox-red, with variations in shading on the ears and coat. What is objectionable to many of us is the darker mask that some yellows have over the muzzle. It tends to give a hard, untypical look to the head. Again, a small white spot is permissible on the chest. Eye colouring should be the same as the blacks, with black or dark brown pigmentation on eye rims and nose. The nose fading to a pink in winter weather is not serious.

 CHOCOLATES: Shades do vary from light milk-chocolate to a dark chocolate; to my mind, the darker shades with good, brown eye colour are the more attractive. Again, the eye colouring should enhance the coat colour.

MOVEMENT

Movement on a Labrador is most important. It should be free and effortless – if constructed correctly, a dog will move correctly. A Labrador should move truly, coming and going. When coming towards you, you should not see a dog that is out at elbow, or toeing in, and only the front legs should be visible. When going away from you, only the rear legs should be visible, with the hocks flexing well, and doing their job of propelling the dog forward. The movement, fore and aft, should be neither too wide or too narrow.

HEIGHT

Again, the British and the American Standards differ slightly, with the American Standard going for a slightly larger dog. The English wording allows leeway, and an experienced judge will put up a good dog if it is below, or above the 'desired' height, as long as the animal has overall balance.

   To sum up, I quote from Mary Roslin Williams: "A typical Labrador looks like a Labrador and nothing else. If he reminds you of any other breed then he is not typical." A wise, and true, saying.

CHARACTER

I have discussed the looks of the Labrador, and lightly touched on the breed's greatest attribute, its temperament, when referring to expression. To my mind, the Labrador is unbeatable in temperament. This dog has a great, noble soul, and is always kind and steadfast with people, especially young children. My first Labrador was not used to having young children about, but when a friend visited with her toddler daughter, he took over the role of nursemaid. When they were out in the garden, he watched over her, putting himself between the little girl and a short, sharp drop, and steering her away from it. Of course, all Labradors have another side to them, and this same dog used that same bank to launch himself at my washing-line, grabbing any article of washing he could reach, and then demolishing it with great relish!

   The good temperament, unflappability, and intelligence of the Labrador makes the breed suitable for many different jobs, such as Guide Dogs for the Blind, Police Dogs and Therapy Dogs, and we have to thank the breeders of yesteryear, and those of today, for insisting that this marvellous temperament remains the same. Any dog showing signs of bad temperament in the show ring, or on the benches, is dealt with ruthlessly. In the ring such a dog would be asked to leave immediately, no matter how good the animal might be in terms of physical appearance. I keep other breeds of Gundogs, namely German Shorthaired Pointers and Sussex Spaniels, and the Labrador is by far the quietest, both at home and in the show ring.

COLOUR INHERITANCE
There are three colours in Labradors.

BLACK AND YELLOW

Black and Yellow colour inheritance is reasonably simple to explain and follows the simple Mendelian principle of Dominant (black) and Recessive (yellow). Dominant Black Labradors when mated together will only produce dominant black puppies. Dominant Black mated to an impure black (i.e. carrying the colour yellow) will produce all black puppies, but half will carry the (recessive) yellow gene.

Two impure blacks mated together will produce approximately two yellow puppies in a litter of eight. Of the remaining six puppies, two will be dominant blacks and four will be impure blacks carrying the yellow gene. An impure black mated to a yellow will produce four impure blacks and four yellow pups. A dominant black mated to a yellow will produce a litter of blacks, but all will carry the recessive yellow gene. Yellow mated to yellow will not produce any blacks at all. *A dog that carries the gene for black will always be black.*

The above proportions are based on an average of one hundred puppies. Obviously the bigger your litter, the nearer you will be to the expected ratio; small litters can be inconclusive.

SIRE / DAM	PUPPIES		
	DOMINANT BLACK	BLACK CARRYING YELLOW	YELLOW
BB x BB	●●●● ●●●●		
BY x BB	●● ●●	◑◑ ◑◑	
BY x BY	● ●	◑◑ ◑◑	○ ○
Y x BY		◑◑ ◑◑	○○ ○○
BB x Y		◑◑◑◑ ◑◑◑◑	
Y x Y			○○○○ ○○○○

CHOCOLATE/LIVER

The colour inheritance pattern that produces the chocolate colour is more complicated than the Black/Yellow inheritance patterns. Up to now we have been using the accurate but simple genetics of B = Dominant black and y = recessive yellow. To understand the relationship of Chocolate/Liver it is necessary to understand the slightly more advanced genetic principles, as follows:

B = black.

b = brown (in Labradors we say chocolate or liver).

E = the ability to express pigment or coat colour.

e = the inability to express dark pigment or coat colour i.e. can only express light colour such as yellow.

Dominant genes are always written as a capital letter, and recessive genes (or genes which can have their effect masked by the corresponding capital letter of the alphabet) are always written as a small letter. For example, B is dominant over b, therefore the dog carrying Bb is black, but the dog carrying bb is chocolate. However, the little e (represented by a small letter) is not necessarily recessive to other letters of the alphabet, only to a capital E. Therefore, when ee is present in the Labrador it masks the effect of B's or b's, and the dog (being unable to express black or chocolate) is yellow in appearance.

In other words, the E or e sequence has the ability to affect the B or b sequence. The effect is called epistasis. Therefore, for a dog to be black or chocolate, it must also carry at least one E gene. If the dog only carries e genes then it cannot express black or chocolate (even if it is carrying B or b), and will be yellow. Dogs inherit one colour gene, of each pair of genes, from each parent, one of the pair being present in the sperm and the other in the egg. When the egg and sperm fuse the result is two genes representing each given characteristic in the progeny (puppies).

The possible genetic make-ups of the Labrador are as follows:

BBEE = BLACK Double dominant black (BB) and double dominant expression (EE) means black appearance and can only pass on Black appearance.

BBEe = BLACK Will be black in appearance (BBE), but the small e means that the dog can pass on the non-expression gene. If it mates with another dog carrying the non-expression (little e) gene, yellow pups can be born.

BbEE = BLACK Black gene masking the effect of the chocolate (small b) gene, and double dominant expression (EE) means the dog will be black, but has the ability to pass on the chocolate (small b) gene. If it mates with another dog which carries the chocolate gene (small b), chocolate pups will be born.

BbEe = BLACK Black gene masking the effect of the chocolate gene (small b), and expression gene (E) masking the effect of little e (non-expression of dark colour) gene. However, if this dog is mated to another dog carrying a little e, yellow pups can be produced, and if mated to a dog carrying little b, chocolate pups can be produced.

bbEE = CHOCOLATE The two chocolate genes (bb) and the two expression genes (EE) means the dog can express dark (in this case chocolate) colour, and is chocolate. This dog can only produce chocolate, unless is mated to a dog which carries a B gene, when black can be produced.

bbEe = CHOCOLATE The two chocolate genes (bb), plus one expression gene (E), means the dog can express chocolate and will be chocolate. However, the dog also carries a small e (non-expression gene), which means that if mated to another dog carrying the small e, yellow could be produced. Likewise, if this dog was mated to a black dog, the black dog's capital B would override the small b, and black could be produced. And, of course, if mated to another dog carrying a small b, chocolate could be produced. In other words, all three colours could be produced with the right mating. However, mating to a yellow dog or one carrying yellow is not advised, as the skin pigment may be very pale or pink.

bbee = **YELLOW** (with pink skin pigment). This dog (ee) cannot express dark pigment; this combined with the double chocolate genes (bb), results in a yellow dog with very pale skin pigment. This is not desirable.

Bbee = **YELLOW** (with normal skin pigment). The two small e genes mean the dog is unable to express the capital B gene which it carries, or the small chocolate gene which it carries, and will therefore be yellow. However, because it carries a B gene, this somehow manages to influence a darker skin pigment, which results in a normal yellow dog. If mated to a dog carrying an expression gene (E), black or chocolate could be produced. However, if mated to a dog carrying a small b (chocolate) gene, the possibility of producing a bbee type yellow exists. Remember, normal yellows can hide small b (chocolate) genes.

BBee = **YELLOW** (with normal skin pigment). The two small e genes (non-expression of dark colour) mean that the effect of the BB genes is masked, and a yellow dog is produced. Skin pigment will be normal because of the influence of BB.

It is not possible for two yellows mated together to throw any colour other than yellow – even though they may hide B or b influences. This point is illustrated below:

BBee			mated to		**BBee**		
(YELLOW)			X		(YELLOW)		
	B	**B**	possible genetic			**B**	**B**
e	Be	Be	combination of	e	Be	Be
			sperms or eggs				
e	Be	Be			e	Be	Be

Fusing of resulting eggs and sperms:

	Be	**Be**	**Be**	**Be**
Be	BBee	BBee	BBee	BBee
Be	BBee	BBee	BBee	BBee
Be	BBee	BBee	BBee	BBee
Be	BBee	BBee	BBee	BBee

All the possible sixteen combinations are the same; all are unable to express the BB combination because of the influence of the ee (non-expression of dark coat colour genes).

We now look at two yellows with different genetic make-ups:

Bbee			mated to		**bbee**		
(YELLOW)			X		(YELLOW)		
(normal skin colour)					(pale pigment)		
	B	**b**	sperms and eggs			**b**	**b**
e	Be	be			e	be	be
e	Be	be			e	be	be
PARENT **A**					PARENT **B**		

Fusing of sperm and egg combinations:

P		Be	be	Be	be	PARENT A
A	be	Bbee	bbee	Bbee	bbee	
R	be	Bbee	bbee	Bbee	bbee	
E	be	Bbee	bbee	Bbee	bbee	
N	be	Bbee	bbee	Bbee	bbee	
T						
B						

Half the pups have normal pigment, half have pale pigment.

The results of a black-carrying chocolate and yellow (BbEe) mated to a yellow carrying chocolate (Bbee):

BbEe		mated to	**Bbee**	
	B b	sperms and eggs	**B b**	
E	BE bE		**e**	Be be
e	Be be		**e**	Be be
PARENT **A**			PARENT **B**	

Fusing of sperm and egg combinations:

P		BE	bE	Be	be	PARENT A
A	**Be**	BBEe	BbEe	BBee	Bbee	
R		(black)	(black)	(yellow)	(yellow)	
E	**Be**	BBEe	BbEe	BBee	Bbee	
N		(black)	(black)	(yellow)	(yellow)	
T	**be**	BbEe	bbEe	Bbee	bbee	
		(black)	(choc)	(yellow)	(yellow pale skin)	
B	**be**	BbEe	bbEe	Bbee	bbee	
		(black)	(choc)	(yellow)	(yellow pale skin)	

Six black puppies, two chocolate puppies, six normal yellows, and two pale skin pigment yellows.

It must be remembered that these are all ratios which will run true over several repeat matings. Nature decides at each mating which egg and sperm meet (we rarely get sixteen puppies in a single litter, thank heavens!), but the ratio of 3/8th Black, 1/8th chocolate and 3/8th normal yellow and 1/8th pale skin yellow would follow through. Therefore, in a litter of eight you would expect approximately three blacks, three normal yellows, one chocolate and one pale pigment yellow.

My grateful thanks to Joy Venturi for her help with the chocolate inheritance pattern.

Chapter Five

THE SHOW RING

STARTING IN THE SHOW WORLD

In my early years in Labradors, I was told that it takes at least five years to learn what you like in your breed and do it justice in showing it well, and to clarify your thoughts on how to interpret the Breed Standard. Perhaps I didn't entirely believe this at the time, but looking back, I would say that five years is a conservative estimate. I think the majority of people see their first Labrador through rose-coloured spectacles. It takes a few years to realise, if you ever do, that your prized dog has faults and failings, and that you are never going to get to the top of a line-up at a show. This should never detract from the fact that this first dog (or two, in our case) is very, very special, but as far as shape goes ... well, you could do better!

So, a couple of years into showing, you get yourself a better-bred animal with show prospects. Your dog may look as good, in your eyes, as the stock owned by the 'big breeders', but you are still failing to beat them at shows. It can take years for some people to learn how to feed, exercise and present a dog to the optimum level – and some people never learn. Speaking as a judge, when I have six or more good dogs in a class, I may well have to nit-pick for placings. Therefore, dogs with a better depth of coat, those that are better conditioned, those with tighter pasterns, and those not carrying the extra weight will have the advantage. The judge may also be influenced by the dog that is being handled more skilfully (new handlers often get nervous and tend to fuss the dog too much). All these factors are taken into account, and this is where the experienced breeder comes to the fore.

The 'big breeders' are not untouchable – we all love to talk about our dogs, and the snippets that we have found useful in breeding and showing, we are only too happy to pass the information on. So never be shy about asking questions: what could be a major hurdle to you could be solved quite simply by some one with more experience.

Although I now have a reputation as a 'character' in the breed, for years I was very quiet (believe me, it was true), sitting and listening to my elders and betters. I learnt a great deal this way. I remember very vividly one day, some years after I had arrived back in this country, when Mrs Woolley (Follytower), Mr Kelly (Bradking) and Mrs Macan (Timspring) rounded me up and said "Really, Carole, it is about time you called us by our Christian names." I replied that I would be delighted to do so, but I had been waiting to be asked. I was brought up in the old school where you did not call people by their Christian names until requested to do so – and certainly not those who were older and further up the ladder. To a certain point I enjoy the informality of today, but a bit of me still hankers for the more formal manners of the past.

A good judge of an animal (not just in the ring) is not manufactured. It is something you either have, or you do not have. You can learn a great deal, but that final, essential part is something that you are born with, and only a few are lucky enough to have it. My vet is always surprised that good breeders can spot slight abnormalities so quickly on their dogs. But every time you look at your own stock you are assessing without knowing it, and some small point that doesn't ring true will ring alarm bells. It may be a lack of lustre in the eye or the coat, or the dog may not be moving so freely. If you fail to spot these details, you may well find that a judge, with a more perceptive eye, will penalise you in the ring.

You never stop learning. I still go to handling classes, and I find that I am still picking up good points from other handlers and teachers. It is those that know it all, after being in the breed a few years, that will never get on, for they have effectively closed their minds. They will be either the five-year, or the ten-year wonders. Five years is the average length of time for people to come into a breed, and to go out of it disillusioned. Some make it to ten years, and then they fall by the wayside. The rest of us plough on – only a few ever reach the top spots – but many are happy in niches lower down the ranks. We all have one thing in common – a continuing love of our breed, the Labrador.

TYPES OF SHOWS
BRITAIN
The show scene of today has changed dramatically from the past, and expense has had a great deal to do with this. As well as exhibiting my dogs, I am involved in organising shows, and so I am only too aware that costs have to be covered. To this end Sanction and Limited shows are now few and far between. The venues can cost so much that it becomes uneconomical to stage a show, due to the restriction in class numbers that these shows incur by their very nature. Consequently, in the UK, we are now left for the most part with Open shows and Championship shows.

OPEN SHOWS: The Labrador, being a popular breed, nearly always has breed classes scheduled at Open shows, where thirty to fifty dogs are usually divided into four separate classes; there would normally be fifty to seventy entries at a Gundog Group (Sporting Group in America) Open show, when six to eight classes might be on offer; and an entry of 150 plus would be expected at a Breed Club Open Show, where eighteen to twenty classes may be allocated. Puppy classes take us up to 12 months, Junior classes up to 18 months, either Novice, Graduate or Post Graduate classes will take care of the maturing Labrador, and Open for the mature dog. A full definition of the class classification will be in each and every schedule printed, so you can choose the right class to put your dog into.

An Open Show is now the only training ground for would-be up-and-coming judges to actually get their hands on dogs, although the Labrador Breed Clubs around the country also try to do their part and put on judges training days. However, you will not know how much experience a judge has had until you know more about the show scene. Judges do vary a great deal, so do not be put off by one judge; you need to go under a number in order to get a good, overall opinion. That first judge may be a raw novice and as nervous as you. Equally, the judge's opinion may be correct – only competing in many shows will give you the overall answer.

CHAMPIONSHIP SHOWS: The Championship Show is quite a big step up. In the UK, we expect an entry of between 250 and 400 Labradors, depending on whether it is an All Breeds Championship show or a Breed Club show. However, this is a step that you should aim for, if it is your purpose to breed and show good Labradors. It is here that you will see a much broader spectrum of good dogs. The dog that beats you every week at the local Open Show, even taking Best of Breed, may not get too much of a look in at the Championship Show. This you must observe, so that you see the correct type of Labrador winning – not just the one that wins locally. Challenge Certificates ('tickets') are only on offer at Championship shows.

UNITED STATES OF AMERICA

The USA has, on average, ten times more shows than the UK, but the numbers entered in individual classes are usually far smaller.

MATCHES: These are organised by Specialty breed clubs and all-breed clubs, and are often used as a training ground for puppies. Champions are not eligible.

ALL-BREED SHOW: Points are awarded towards a dog's Championship title, and the classes, which are the same for each sex, at both All-Breed and Specialty shows are:

Puppy (6-9 months, and 9-12 months), Novice 12-18 months (at Specialty shows), Bred by Exhibitor, American Bred, Open.

SPECIALTY SHOWS: These are held annually by the single breed club concerned, and they usually attract much larger entries, ranging from 100 to 400. The annual Labrador Club National Specialty can sometimes go as high as 800 to 1100 dogs, depending on the area where it is held. Each year it is moved from one American time zone to another. Even at these shows, the maximum points awarded for each Winners Dog or Winners Bitch is five, for a really tremendous win. This is why Specialty Shows are so highly regarded among breeders – to gain all your Championship points from Specialty wins is a major achievement.

FORTHCOMING SHOWS

Shows are advertised in the canine press, and entries must be made some weeks in advance – up to six weeks for a Championship show. This is not just a whim on the part of the Society holding the show. I have worked as a club secretary, and I know that this is the minimum time needed to get the schedules printed. The schedules or flyers, as they are known in the USA, contain full details of classification.

BECOMING A CHAMPION

BRITAIN

Britain is widely recognised as being one of the hardest places to make up a Champion. Each dog must win a total of three Challenge Certificates under three different judges to gain the title, and the third CC must be won after a dog's first birthday. At Championship Shows, where entries are huge (ten to twelve classes for each sex), Champions and non-Champions compete against each other for the CCs. There are currently forty-three sets of tickets on offer every year at Championship Shows; usually about a dozen new Champions are made up in the breed yearly, usually split fairly evenly between the sexes.

UNITED STATES OF AMERICA

To become an American Champion, a dog must gain fifteen points. Of these, two blocks have to be 'Majors' awarded by different judges. A Major is a show where three or more points are awarded to Winners Dog or Winners Bitch. Five is the maximum number of points awarded for each sex at any show, no matter how large the entry.

   The USA is divided into five areas. Each year the point system is evaluated for shows, depending on the number of dogs of the breed exhibited in that designated area in the previous year. It often happens that dogs and bitches of one breed have different points on offer at a show, perhaps two for the dogs and three for bitches. If, in this instance, the dog should go Best of Breed, he would take the higher points i.e. three, and the bitch would still retain her three points.

Let us take a three point Major for example. If you lived in the Boston area, twenty-five dogs (of one sex) may be all that is needed to be exhibited for Winners Dog to gain three points. If you lived in Florida, it might well be only ten dogs, and if you were in California, it could be many more dogs. So the number of dogs you need to beat, in order to gain the Championship title, can vary considerably. Dogs gaining their titles in the USA do not have to compete against other Champions. Once Winners Dog and Winners Bitch have been chosen from the competitive classes, and have their points, they then go into the final class with the Champions to decide on who should go Best of Breed.

In America, the Conformation rankings or 'top dog' each year, are evaluated in different ways. In one system, one point is credited for each Labrador defeated by virtue of Best of Breed wins. In another system, one point is credited for each dog defeated (of any breed) by virtue of Best of Breed, Group, and/or Best in Show wins. Some dogs are campaigned vigorously for these rankings, and it is interesting to note that Specialty winners seldom come near the top of the rankings.

PREPARING YOUR DOG

When you are planning which shows to enter, make sure you are not wasting your money by entering a dog or bitch, that will have shed its coat in a big way by show day. A good double coat in a Labrador is so important, that it can be a complete waste of your entry fee if your animal is coatless on the day. If you are showing a bitch, make a note in your diary of when she is due in season. It is highly likely that two months prior to her season, she will be in a pretty hairless state. It is only when she is in season and the following few months that she will be in full coat – looking at her most attractive for the males. The dogs do not usually cast coat quite so heavily – unfortunately I have one that does – so make notes from year to year and you will build up a pattern of your dog's coat-loss times.

When your Labrador is going out of coat, do not make the mistake that so many do, of putting extra weight on your dog in an attempt to compensate for the dropping of an undercoat, which can make a dog look some five pounds underweight. The problem arises when the coat comes back, and the extra weight stays on, and all of a sudden you have a real roly-poly on your hands. If your dog is coatless, go to the show by all means, but leave your dog at home. You will probably learn more by just sitting, watching and listening, without the worry of a dog to look after.

A dog must be well presented, ready for the judge's examination. It is not a necessity to bath your dog before every show. I occasionally have to bath my yellows because of the grey sandy soil that gets into their undercoats and discolours it. This is done at least three days prior to the show, to enable the oils to be replaced, and the correct hard feel to the coat to return. If you enter a freshly-washed dog with a soft coat, under a judge, it will be presumed that the coat is of incorrect texture – it would not do its job of protecting the dog in bad weather – and so you would be placed down the line accordingly.

However, you do want a clean, well-groomed coat, free from dust and dirt – and that requires hard work and a good brush. It is most discouraging to be judging, and then to find that you need to rub the dirt and grease off your hands after going over a dog. This has happened to me quite a few times; you usually know before your hands even get to the dog – your nose has told you what to expect. You would not go out with dirty, greasy hair; and neither should your dog. Preparing a Labrador for a show is relatively simple. The only trimming that is required is to take the twist of hair off the tip of the dog's tail. This should not present a blunt-scissored, rounded look, that is seen so often in the ring; it is only the twist that should be removed. The dog should be given a good brush, and for blacks, a final polish with a soft chamois or velvet glove will bring a shine to the coat. Do ensure that the dog's nails are kept short. Long nails tend to splay the foot, and you will certainly be placed below a dog of equal merit that has good, tight feet. Fasten on your show lead, and you are ready to go.

Show leads are strange things. Many of us get a favourite one and we use it exclusively, while some handlers prefer to ring the changes. However, what is more important when showing a Labrador is that the lead is reasonably thin and supple, and one that complements the coat colour. Many handlers use a thin leather thong, well-oiled so that it is supple – a plain slip, which is long enough to lay back on the shoulders (giving an illusion of good lay-back of shoulder). I personally use long thin rope leads, which are the same colour as my dogs. I do not like to break up the line of the neck, which happens when a thick brightly-coloured lead is used. Try out different leads on your dogs; ask a friend to hold the dog, and you will see how the bright, thicker lead gives the illusion of making your dog's neck appear much shorter and thicker, which is not the picture you are trying to create for the judge. A handler needs to use a lead that will enhance a dog's good points, not detract from them.

HANDLING IN THE RING

So now you are ready to go into the ring, in the correct class for the age or maturity of the dog, or according to the dog's wins. Make sure you display the dog's ring number clearly on your person – not tucked into a pocket, or turned over so that the number is not evident. If you are looking at a dog from the ringside, it is important to see the ring number so that you can check on parentage and breeding in the catalogue.

When you come into the ring, have a good look around, and place yourself in an advantageous position. Some dogs tire easily, so it is better to be seen first. Other handlers like to go last, in order to leave an impression with the judge. I usually try to position my dog near another of similar size, as I tend to show well up-to-size animals. I would never position myself between two dogs that are a little on the short size, as my dog would look over the top.

It is also important to study the ground. Outside rings are very seldom as smooth as a bowling green. If the ring slopes off at all, make sure that your dog's rear-end is facing downhill, otherwise your dog will present a distorted picture and will appear as though the rear-end is too high. The same applies when you go into the centre of the ring for the judge to go over your animal. Always assess the lie and slope of the land, and place your dog accordingly. Remember, if you have a dog with an eye that could be darker, do not show the dog looking into the glare of the sun: it will only make the eyes appear even lighter.

When you are at an inside venue, the lighting can be an advantage or a disadvantage. Showing blacks inside can certainly be a little tricky. Try to position yourself under a light, if possible, because a black dog can disappear into the surrounding gloom. So although you do not need to assess the lie of the land (essential at an outside venue), this time your eyes are on the areas with the most light. One onlooker once said: "You were lucky, Carole, that sunlight (from a window) just fell on your dog and he really shone." I had already looked around, seen the patch of sunlight and placed my black dog in it. It was not luck, just good sense. We won the class, by the way.

Try to handle as little as possible. If you are always fretting and moving your dog, your nerves

Ch. Warringah's Waltzing Matilda, showing reach and crest of neck, being shown by the author at Crufts.

will go down the lead to the dog Even if your dog is in not the nervous type, too much fussing and over-handling could result in the dog switching-off and appearing lack-lustre and bored. So, in most cases, *minimum handling is best.* Although we tend to bait Labradors, please do not let your dog have any food while the judge is trying to assess the head. However, once the head has been looked at, a little bait may help to bring the dog right back on to its toes, making the neck and head stretch out, giving an impression of good length of neck, and tightening the topline.

The art of showing is to enhance the good points, and, hopefully, hide any failings. When a dog is standing, you can, by skilful baiting, hide (to a certain extent) slack pasterns, a ten-to-two front, and a slack topline. In other breeds, where the convention is to stack the dog, the handler can 'hold' the dog in the correct position. When baiting, you are are doing the same by bringing a dog on to the toes with bait. Everyone has their favourite bait. I use pig's kidneys, boiled, chopped into four, washed again, and frozen on a tray. I then put the bait into a plastic box in the freezer, free flow, and take out what I need on show day. The dogs love it, and because of its texture it leaves your hands clean when you go to shake hands with fellow exhibitors, or the judge, depending on how successful you have been in your class.

When you are in the ring, make sure that you have enough room to show your dog: be careful not to be boxed into a corner, and try not to keep edging either backwards or forwards with your dog. In my early handling days I once had to set my dog up fifteen times in one class, because the handler behind me was so intent on her own dog that she, unknowingly, kept moving backwards into my dog. By the end of the class I had moved some ten feet from my original position. I now know a great deal better, and if my dog gets backed into, I quickly swap positions. No one backs into me more than once – as I am not going to move!

It is equally important not to crowd your own dog. Many handlers get so close to the dog that the only way the dog can see the handler is to look straight up. The neck drops back into the shoulders, and the dog does not reach for the bait with an out-stretched neck, which gives the judge a much better outline to look at. When your dog is standing, do not worry too much about all four legs being 'just so'. All you need is three correctly positioned legs – the two front legs and the hind leg facing the judge. A dog will always stand more comfortably over its centre of balance, so do not worry if one back leg is slightly in, or out, on the judge's off-side. If you try and get that

Ch. Warringah's Harlech, winner of the Gundog Group, and third Best in Show at the Scottish Kennel Club, 1987. Note the loose lead, and that the handler is standing well back.

Dave Freeman.

fourth leg perfectly positioned, you will most likely make all the others go out of line. My motto when handling is always *least is best*.

MOVING YOUR DOG

When you are on the move in the ring, do as the judge asks. This may seem like a simple rule, but it is seldom observed. If the judge asks you to move in a triangle, make sure you follow the lines of a triangle – and do not set off in a circle. Make sure that your dog can be seen properly, and is lined up with the judge's line of vision. Do not expect the judge to go hopping round the ring in order to see your dog's movement. On the outward and return runs, make sure that the dog is lined up with the judge, and that you, the handler, are not obscuring the picture. The judge is trying to assess, back, side and front movement, and a neat, precise triangle will give the maximum amount of time to see all three angles. A funny little 'rounded' triangle cuts off at least one-third of the outward journey for hind movement assessment, about two-thirds of the topline assessment as the dog curves around the top of the ring, and a further third of the front movement assessment on the return journey. I prefer to move all my dogs on a loose leash. I know their movement is good, and I am confident that they will show that to the judge better on a loose leash than having one tucked up under the chin. It also shows that you have confidence in your animal. I must admit, as a judge, I always have a slight suspicion of those dogs that are 'strung up' on the move. I think to myself "What are they trying to hide?"

The handler has a very short space of time to show off the dog's movement, so make sure your practising has been done before you get to the show. Every time you jerk the lead when a dog is on the move, it will take at least three paces before the dog is balanced and moving well again. Some of our rings are so small that one jerk can take up half the length. It is a point to remember. What can you do if you have a dog that 'crabs' when moving? If you watch a crab moving across a beach, you will know exactly what 'crabbing' means. If a dog has this sideways tendency, you must practise by moving your dog alongside a fence or a hedge. If the dog is restricted to a width of twelve to eighteen inches, there is not sufficient space to crab, and the dog will get used to moving correctly. If your dog still persists in crabbing in the ring, all is not lost. As you head back towards the judge, make the dog run on your right side, instead of the left. The shock of the change-round is usually enough to make the dog come towards the judge in a straight line – so your money is not wasted!

If you have a pacer, a dogs whose legs on one side move in unison, life is not so easy. But you can break this habit. I have had a couple of natural pacers in my kennels, and I always show them with a little trepidation. It is not until you are on the move that you know if the dog is going right or not. I always start a pacer off with a short jerk on the lead, putting the dog off-balance, and set off at a fast walk. This usually does the trick. However, if the dog starts pacing (I can feel it up the lead), I stop, and start again. Once the dog is moving correctly, I allow nothing to stop me, for fear of giving the dog a chance to start pacing again. If the judge has elected that we go straight up and down the ring, then I would break the unwritten rule of never allowing the handler to come between the judge and dog. At the end of the ring I would make the dog go round the outside of me to keep the momentum going, while I almost come to a standstill and twirl round on the spot. This means that the dog's movement keeps flowing, and as long as the dog is moving correctly, this is the main objective.

THE IN-SEASON BITCH

It occasionally happens that your bitch is in super condition; there is a show scheduled with a judge that likes her type – and the bitch comes into season. What do you do? Much has been said on the subject, and I am merely adding my own thoughts. At a Championship Show, where classes are split between the sexes, and the dogs are benched, I do not think it does any harm to enter a bitch that is in season. Some people say it is not fair on the dogs, although I have found that this situation makes my males more on their toes, and looking and showing all the better for it. I would not take my in-season bitch to a show where the classes are mixed sex – that really would be unfair on the males.

I recall showing a thirteen-month-old dog, called Fair and Square, at an Open Show. He sniffed a bitch sitting beside the ring, and she told him in no uncertain terms to "get lost". I apologised for my dog bothering the bitch, and the owner replied "She's five days in season." My eyebrows went up, but I didn't say anything. One week later we saw the same bitch at another Open Show, now twelve days in season. I told the owner to stay away from my dog, informing her that my dog was an experienced stud, and that we would have a 'freebie' mating in the middle of the ring, if she came too close. Needless to say, she kept her distance. The lovely thing was that some two years later, Fair and Square, now a Champion, had just mated a yellow bitch and was still tied, when I realised it was the same person, and the same bitch. I did refrain from reminding her that I had offered a 'freebie' two years earlier in the ring, and now here she was, paying for it!

When showing, it is important to remember, above all else, that it is a hobby, and it should be fun. Sometimes we are going to win, mostly we are not, and if you take it so seriously that you are unable to accept losing gracefully, then perhaps you should reconsider if you want to continue with showing. One day Gwen Broadley (Sandylands) came up to me and said: Mrs Coode, can I have a word with you?" My first thoughts were, oh dear, what have I done? However, she said that she wanted to congratulate me for always being there with a smile and a handshake for those who had just beaten me, even though at times it must have been very hard and must have hurt a lot to smile. She said it was refreshing, and she wished more people were like that. This compliment paid to me by such a marvellous sport, rates as one of my highspots in dogs.

The person who has just won should always be able to enjoy their win and their day. Make it a good occasion for them – give them your warmest congratulations, and mean it. Tomorrow it could be your turn, and you would want that sort of treatment for yourself, wouldn't you?

JUDGING

Some people, regardless of their wealth of experience and the time have been in a breed, will not judge. Others are only too impatient to take on the mantle of judge, often with very little knowledge. I was once approached by someone who said they had been in the breed for two years and knew all there was to know, so where did they apply for judging appointments? I believe that person is still waiting for an appointment! Fortunately, we are more likely to get the medium line, and a first judging appointment would usually go to someone who has been around a minimum of five years, with a reasonable degree of success in the show ring.

It is usually with some fear and trepidation that you take on that first appointment, but as long as you have studied the Breed Standard long and hard, and formulated ideas in your mind on what a good Labrador consists of (we all interpret the Breed Standard slightly differently), you have no need to worry. You must go into the ring and sort out your classes to the best of your ability, and be honest. That is all that anyone can ask of you.

THE ROLE OF THE JUDGE

When you are in the centre of the ring, you must isolate yourself from the exhibitors, no matter how well you may know some of them. A handler should be referred to as 'Sir' or 'Madam' – first names terms are definitely "not on" in my book. I believe that you need to distance yourself, to a certain extent, in order to give yourself the space to judge the dogs honestly. It is hard enough to be called on to judge dogs you know well and dogs belonging to friends and well-known breeders, without the added pressure of first-name terms. I am not saying that you should ignore people you know when you see them on the show site. A nice cheery "Hello" is fine, but it is not a good idea to go into a huddle and catch up on the latest gossip, before you judge.

Dress is also important. A judge should look the part on the day; this is not an occasion for jeans and trainers. Ladies should wear something that allows freedom of movement, without hindering or giving the ringside glimpses of what they would rather not see. Men always look good in suits or sports jackets. Neat and tidy is the order of the day.

People will always appreciate you if you are an honest judge. I remember having a falling out with one judge, and I was entered under them a couple of weeks later at a Championship Show. I was told I would be wasting my time and money; but I knew that the person concerned would judge only my dogs, and not me, and I had a good and fair assessment on the day. A few years on, and we are friends once more.

The worst judges of all are the vocal, ringside judges, who state with authority that they have it on good information that "So and So" and "So and So" will get the tickets (if it is a Championship Show) or the Best of Breed (if it is an Open Show). Obviously, anyone can make a fair guess as to who will get the CCs or BOB if some excellent dogs of the type the judge is known to like are entered. It is the fact that these people do so in loud voices, to as many present as possible, that is so objectionable. It casts a slur on the judge's integrity. The expense of showing your dog means that you are not going to enter under a judge that does not like your type of dog. You enter under judges when you think you have a chance.

JUDGING PROCEDURES
When you are judging, it is important to remember that every exhibitor has paid an entry fee, and therefore you must ensure that each and every exhibit is treated with the same care and consideration. When the class first comes into the ring, and you have seen the dogs standing, and possibly moving, you will earmark those dogs that really appeal to you. When you go over the dogs individually, this will either confirm that initial assessment or not. The only time I ever look at the handler is when I have found something I do not like when going over the dog which is not evident when in the standing still position. I then note either their number or something the handler is wearing; I still do not look 'up the lead', as the expression goes. The exhibitor is not meant to engage the judge in conversation; but a smile and kind word from you might well make them feel more at ease (some people do get so nervous), and they will enjoy their day more.

Initially, each exhibitor should be asked to move their dog following the same pattern. If you have a big class of twenty plus, cut the class to the more promising dogs after going over them individually, and cut again if necessary. After my first pruning, I like to see the dogs move once more, straight out and back, to refresh my memory on their movement. If I have made a mistake and kept a bad mover in, I can always drop the dog out at this stage. It is important that you leave yourself with room to manoeuvre; so never leave yourself with just five dogs, or even six (the exhibitor who is number six, will be faced with an embarrassing solo exit from the ring), so cut to seven as a minimum.

Ring procedure is important. The judge should look happy and confident, make clear decisions, and consider the well-being of the exhibitors and their dogs – do not leave the entire class standing out in the blazing sun, while you dither in the centre of the ring. Obviously, not everyone is going to agree with your judging; that never happens. But an exhibitor should feel as though they have got their money's worth – their dog has been looked at by someone who knew what they were doing – and perhaps they will come back another day to try their luck.

I sometimes watch a judge going over a dog, and I know amazement must show on my face, because the thoughts going through my head are: "Whatever are the judge's hands telling his/her brain?" – I really feel that there is no connection there at times. You see a pair of hands sweeping over the dog in long flowing movements, time after time on the same dog, or else, at other times, a little flick down the back is all you get. I suppose, knowing my own limitations, I do like to feel the dog I am going over. That means I walk round to the front end first, check the shape and balance of the head, the ear placement, and look to see if the forelegs are straight and true. I walk round to the back to check for cow hocks. From the side, I assess topline, feet, and pasterns. And that is before I lay a hand on the dog.

Once I start handling, I am looking for eye shape, length and breadth of muzzle, correct bite, the lay of shoulder and upper arm, length of neck, spring of rib, depth of chest, how well ribbed the back is, the length and strength of loin, width of stifle and second thigh, quality of bone, shape of foot, tail-set, coat type and depth. You must know how a dog is constructed, and how the parts work together to enable the dog to do the job it has been bred for. This must always be in the forefront of your thoughts. If you lose this objective, you will end up by placing a dog that is incapable of picking up a heavy cock pheasant or a goose Once you have worked your way through your classes, and made your placings, I then like to send the winners round the ring once more, so that I can applaud them – hopefully having chosen the best under me that day.

Chapter Six

THE LABRADOR IN BRITAIN

LEADING KENNELS

Due to space I have limited my study to the British kennels that are in the forefront of the breed today. It is also important to bear in mind that it is universally acknowledged that the UK is the most difficult place in the world to make up a Champion. There are approximately forty-three sets of Challenge Certificates (CCs) on offer in a year, and a dog must gain three CCs under three different judges to become a Champion. The dogs are competing against the cream of the country, for Champions are entered every time. This is highlighted by the fact that only twenty-one Champions were made up in the UK in the past two years – and this covers both dogs and bitches.

Comparing the situation with the United States and Australia, it is equivalent to gaining all your points at Breed Speciality shows, and in the case of America, without the established Champions challenging for the points. So the modest single figure number of Champions per kennel do, in fact, compare more than favourably with the more numerous Champions made up in other countries.

ARDMARGHA: MR & MRS H. CLAYTON

Harold Clayton writes: "Labradors started for me in 1943 when I acquired my first black Labrador, sired by Ir. Ch. Black Prince of Marlu out of Ir. Ch. Lady of Ballyholme, whom I called Finn of Ardmargha, once I had obtained my kennel name, Ardmargha in 1944 (the Irish name Armagh). From this bitch line, through a bitch by Dual Ch. Bramshaw Bob (Lady Howes), I had three more Finns, all black. Temperaments became doubtful and I started again with a black bitch, Hollybarn Ebony, bred from Ch. Sandylands Tweed and a Ch. Holton Baron bitch. This line produced Monarch – a very well-known yellow who won at shows (Reserve CC) and at Trials, trained and handled by John Forbes.

"At this time Gwen Broadley had two lovely black bitches in a litter by Sh. Ch. Kinley Skipper out of Ch. Sandylands Truth, and she let me have them both. One was Komely, who was too small, but she had a really sweet feminine head, and from her Margaret and I have bred our present line. We have usually used Sandylands stud dogs, especially Tweed, Tandy, Mark and Aust. Ch. Jaysgreen Jasper, who was mated twice to Komely before he left for Australia, and we whelped three Champions from the two litters.

"I have always been a keen shot, and all my dogs until recently have had to work and run in trials; I thank 'Pinky' Collard for his help and encouragement in this, and also for allowing his trainer to train and handle all my dogs.

"After 1966 we started to show seriously, and whereas I had never previously had a yellow, we

Sh. Ch. Ardmargha Mad Hatter: Group winner and Reserve Best in Show winner.

Anne Roslin Williams.

now seemed to get nearly all yellows. Margaret was by now fully involved in both breeding and showing. We have had sixteen Champions (five black and eleven yellow) at home and abroad. Seven of these are British Champions or Show Champions. The best known are Kilree, Faith, Kimbo and Mad Hatter, but one should not forget Faith's sister Hope, who was to be the dam of four Champions, though never shown herself.

"Kilree was very much like my present bitch, Heidi, to look at, and was a good worker. Faith 'owned' the ring, and was made up before she was two. She was a Group winner, as was Kimbo, who also was very good in trials; he made up as a Junior. Mad Hatter was another who won Groups and was Reserve Best In Show (All Breeds) at WELKS. He only mated twenty-four bitches (we were very particular about pedigree 'mix') but the number of his winning children and grandchildren is proof of his potency as a sire. They can nearly always be identified as 'Honk' children.

"The Ardmargha characteristics, in my opinion, are deep muzzles, very kind, pleading expressions, and really good coats which 'stand up' significantly when fingered the wrong way. The blacks nearly always have a lovely 'mousy' undercoat.

"We have reduced the numbers to six, and these are all bitches. With this number we can have a permanent 'house dog' and the others take turns. We still breed when we want a puppy. Since the KC/BVA HD and Eye schemes were introduced our dogs are regularly examined – so far with good results."

BALRION : JOHN, GLENDA & LOUISE CROOK

The Balrion kennel was founded in 1970, the foundation stock being Hindlehurst Cuban Prince and Tayfield Tapestry. When these two were mated together they produced Balrion Royale Princess, who when mated to Sh. Ch. Clarence of Rossbank, produced four title-holders in the one litter. They were: Sh. Chs. Balrion King Frost, B. Wicked Lady, B. Black Ice, and B. Royal Mischief of Rodarbal.

King Frost was a most superb showman and has been the kennel's top winner to date, with

Sh. Ch. Balrion Black and Tan: The latest addition to Balrion's excellent list of Champions.

twenty-eight CCs, five Groups, three Reserve Groups and one Best In Show All Breeds Championship show – a fantastic record. He held the CC record for the breed, taking over from Ch. Holton Baron, and, in turn, handed it on to Ch. Fabracken Comedy Star.

King Frost proved to be a good sire and soon his son, Sh. Ch. Balrion King's Ransom, joined the ranks of Champions at Balrion. Sh. Ch. Balmurune Psalm of Balrion, bred by the Murdens, was made up, as was Sh. Ch. Balrion Miss Behave of Loxdale, owned by the Mr Charlesworth, and bred by the Crooks. The latest addition to a list of excellent Champions is the dog, Sh. Ch. Balrion Black and Tan (a solid black, I can assure you) sired by Rodarbal Royale Tan of Balrion, out of Brentcalm Miss Fawks.

Glenda and John have sent many dogs abroad with a great deal of success, and to date have a total of thirteen Champions spread over Australia, New Zealand, South Africa, America, Norway, Sweden and Germany. Their daughter, Louise, has always shown a great interest in the dogs, being a Junior Handling finalist in her time, and has gone on to own, train and show her own dogs, sharing the family affix, and has now joined her parents in the judging arena.

BLONDELLA: HAZEL & KEN BURTON
Hazel and Ken's kennel was started in 1970, their foundation bitch being Kupros Marcia of Blondella. It has always been their aim to breed to the Standard as they interpreted it, and their first Champion and stud dog, Ch. Keysun Teko of Blondella, was an excellent example of this. He was a dog of super type, with a very sound temperament – the first requirement for any Labrador. They were so pleased to acquire him from Mrs Spencer, after only four years of showing. His first CC came at just twelve months old, with the second following within three weeks. He went on to win eleven CCs, two Groups, and several Reserve CCs, and at three years old, in 1977, he was top winning Labrador of the year.

He sired several Champions, one of them being Ch. Keysun Krispin of Blondella, who in turn went on to sire many more Blondella Champions, both here and abroad. His two Champion offspring at Blondella out of Sh. Ch. Blondella Ballerina were the brother and sister Sh. Chs. Blondella Balance and Balalai'ka, both being Best in Show winners. Two superb wins for Balance

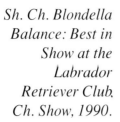

Sh. Ch. Blondella Balance: Best in Show at the Labrador Retriever Club, Ch. Show, 1990.

were when he went Best in Show at the Labrador Retriever Club Championship show in 1990, with a record entry of 418 dogs, and the previous year he also won the Group at WELKS.

Although only a small kennel of seven to eight Labradors, breeding approximately one litter a year, Hazel and Ken have had considerable success, with four more dogs gaining either CCs or Reserve CCs. They have eight overseas Champions, the most famous being Blondella Bonny Lad, owned by Jef and Mariette Verrees Vanhoof in Belgium. This dog has been campaigned with great success and is a Champion in no less than eleven different countries, as well as being a Field Trial Champion in his own right.

BRADKING: ARTHUR & PEGGY KELLEY

Arthur writes: "It was by choice that this kennel's first Labrador was chocolate. This dog was purchased from a gamekeeper on the estate of Lord Bradford in the early 1950s, at a time when there were only three or four chocolate breeders in the country. He was the son of the legendary 'Shropshire Bob', a dog famed at that time for his outstanding ability in the field, and his son, 'Brad' (as we had named him), was to follow in his sire's footsteps and in so doing, endeared himself to the hearts of everyone. To the family he became known as 'Brad, the King of dogs'. Some little time later when a title had to be found for the kennel, what better name could come to mind than 'Bradking', and so this affix came into being."

The two foundation bitches were Sandylands Carona and Sandylands Clove. Carona was the dam of their first Champion, Sh. Ch. Bradking Bonny My Girl, who in turn was the dam of a wonderful bitch, Eng. Sh. Ch., Am. Can. Bda. & Mex. Ch. Bradking Black Charm, who went out to Mike Beattie in Canada, in whelp to Sh. Ch. Balrion King Frost. She left behind her yellow son, Sh. Ch. Bradking Cassidy, a lovely typey dog.

Bradking Cassandra (two CCs), a sister to Cassidy, was to be the dam of the next Champion, Bradking Bridgette of Davricard, owned by David Craig. I had the pleasure awarding her a CC – a big roomy chocolate bitch, just the sort I like. Cassidy was also the sire of a good brood bitch, Keysun Ruling Star of Bradking, who in turn produced three Champion offspring in one litter, sired by Ch. Kupros Master Mariner. They were: Sh. Ch. Bradking Molly Mo, co-owned with

*Eng. Sh. Ch.,
Am. Can. Bda.
Mex. Ch.
Bradking Black
Charm:
Exported to
Canada.*

Oakley.

David Craig; Ch. Bradking Mike, in Canada; and Sh. Ch. Bradking Music Maker of Kingstream, owned by John and Neata Banner. Music Maker has had a spectacular show career to date, with ten CCs, a Reserve Group win at Bournemouth in 1992, and twice winner of the Pedigree Chum Champion Stakes, staged over three days at Championship shows.

There are a further four Bradking dogs with CCs or Reserve CCs, and five more Champions abroad. The Kelleys have the distinction of being the only kennel to have bred Champions in all three colours in the UK. As well as Labradors, they have an interest in Dalmatians, and they have made up two Irish Setter Show Champions.

Sh. Ch. Cambremer Madonna: Top Labrador 1992.

Heidl.

CAMBREMER: JOYCE & LESLIE BRABBAN

Although this kennel was founded in 1965, the first real success came in 1973 with the purchase of Braunspath Simona of Cambremer (one CC) and Glenarem Skyrocket, who became their first Sh. Ch., noted for his soundness and excellent movement. Mated together, these two produced the kennel's first-home bred Sh. Ch., Cambremer St Clair. She in turn produced the yellow brothers, Sh. Ch. Cambremer Countdown and Cambremer Celebrity (three CCs in Sweden), when she was mated to Sh. Ch., Am. Ch. Receiver of Cranspire.

St Clair was also mated to Ch. Fabracken Comedy Star, and from this litter Joyce and Leslie kept the black bitch, Cambremer Montclair, a winner of two CCs and three Reserve CCs. It was the quality of this bitch and the success of her progeny that made her the top brood bitch of 1989, 1990, 1991 and 1992. Montdair is the dam of Sh. Ch. C. Madonna, Sh. Ch. C. All That Jazz, Sh. Ch. C. Jazz Singer, Int. Ch. C. Du Valloon de Villard (Switzerland), Nor. Ch. C. Bianca, and the CC winners, C. Copy Cat, C. Classical Jazz, and C. Striking Midnight over Lawnwood – all these were black with the exception of Striking Midnight, who was yellow.

The yellow line has also produced C. Oh So Sharp (a grand-daughter of St Clair), who has won one CC and is the dam of Sh. Ch. C. Sharp Shooter and also C. Clancy (one CC). The kennel has had many good wins, but the most memorable was Crufts 1989 when they took the dog CC with Sh. Ch. C. Jazz Singer, and the bitch CC and Best of Breed with Sh. Ch. C. Madonna. This kennel has also been *Our Dogs*/Pedigree Chum Top Breeders for the years 1987, 1988, 1989, 1991 and 1992. I might add that the two 1992 wins, Top Brood Bitch and Top Breeder topped my own kennel by one point – Warringah was in the lead until right at the end of the year.

CARPENNY: PENNY CARPANINI

The kennel was established in 1970 with a Lawnwoods bitch. From the first litter, bred in 1975, a yellow bitch was kept, Carpenny Veuve-Cliquot. Cliquot's second litter to Sandylands Sovereign of Suddie produced Carpenny Camargue, a marvellous brood who Penny really considers to be her

Sh. Ch. Carpenny Bonhomie (left) and Ch. Carpenny Chevalier.

David Bull.

foundation bitch. Cliquot's third litter to my own Fair & Square, produced a yellow son, Carpenny Special Vintage. Although only lightly shown, Vintage gained three Reserve CCs.

Camargue proved to be a remarkable bitch, producing three Champions and five Junior Warrant winners to four different sires. She was predominantly a dog producer, giving only a token bitch in each litter. Her first litter, to Sh. Ch. Receiver of Cranspire, produced Ch. Carpenny Chevalier (ten CCs, fifteen Reserve CCs), and the N.Z. Ch. Carpenny Chateau Cranspire, owned by Ken Hunter in England, and gaining two CCs and two Reserve CCs before going to Lyn Cooper in New Zealand. Another successful mating was to Trenow Brigadier, before he became a Champion. From this came Sh. Ch. Carpenny Bonhomie, a young dog who has, to date, won fifteen CCs and seven Reserve CCs. Both Chevalier and Bonhomie have been used at stud. Chevalier has Champion offspring in the UK, Europe, USA, and Australia. His daughter, Sh. Ch. Audacity of Carpenny, brought in by Penny at seven weeks old, along with two littermates, is, she thinks, one of the loveliest bitches she has owned. Her show career started at eleven months old and she was made up to a Sh. Ch. by sixteen months of age. She joined Mme Paulette Laffitte in France shortly afterwards.

Chevalier is the sire of several well-known sires in their own right: Sh. Ch. Wishwood Shaft and his brother, Shuttle, based in Sweden, Ch. Crosscroyde Cotton on Quick, Aust. Ch. Authority of Carpenny (litter brother to Audacity), Ch. Gladlab Chase Me Charlie, based in France, and Dicconsons Cavalier of Carpenny, winner of one CC and one Reserve CC before going to Phillippe Lammen's in Belgium, where he awaits only his Working Certificate to become an Int. Ch. To date, Bonhomie has produced one Champion in America, a CC winner in France, and Reserve CC winners at home and in Holland – a good record for a relatively young dog.

By force of circumstance, Carpenny is a very small kennel, located in a town, so it is important that the dogs are quiet and biddable, and the maximum of one litter a year is carefully planned. As a practising registered osteopath, Penny believes that structure governs function, and that soundness and good conformation go hand in hand. The KC/BVA schemes for hips and eyes are used on all stock as valuable aids to breeding.

Pictured left to right: Charway Simona, Roseacre Hollyberry of Charway and Ch. Charway Little Sian.

CHARWAY: JANICE PRICHARD

Since the 1970s this kennel has been based on the best Ballyduff, Sandylands, and Timspring lines. Its aims have always been to produce good-natured dogs of excellent type and quality, and dogs which have an interest in working.

Janice started showing Labradors as a very young girl, and she bred her first litter in 1965. The kennel has always been kept small, usually no more than six adult dogs, usually black. There has always been an interest in work as well as show, some of the dogs being worked during the shooting season. Similarly, there has always been a keen interest in the breed's inherited problems, and Janice makes full use of the BVA/KC hip and eye schemes in order to select suitable dogs for breeding.

Ch. Charway Ballywillwill is the kennels best-known dog. He was *Dog World* Top Show Labrador in 1981, and top sire in 1984, 1985 and 1987. His top show award was winning the Gundog Group at the Welsh Kennel Club in 1981. The kennel's best brood bitches have undoubtedly been Roseacre Hollyberry of Charway, Charway Simona, Charway Sally Brown (two Reserve CCs), and Wetherlam Black Cherry of Charway, who have jointly been responsible for the kennel's many successes over the years. jCharway Champions made up in Britain are Sh. Ch. Charway Nightcap, Ch. Charway Little Sian, Sh. Ch. Charway Blackthorn of Follytower (owned by Margot Woolley), Ch. Charway Ballylinnet and, of course, Ballywillwill. Other kennel mates to gain high awards were Charway Uncle Tom (two Reserve CCs), Charway Sally Brown (two Reserve CCs) and Charway Black Magic (one Reserve CC). The Charway Champions abroad have left their mark with seven in America, one in Canada, two in Finland, two in Germany, two in Holland, and two in South Africa.

Cornlands Diant Mann in Black (left) Best in Show at Open Shows, and Ch. Cornlands Blonde Lady, BOB Crufts, 1982, pictured with kennelmate Cornlands Kindrum Clancy.

Fall.

CORNLANDS: PEGGY RAE

Passed to judge Labradors at CC level for more than thirty years, it was nearly thirty years before that Peggy was given her first Labrador as a girl on her parents' farm in East Anglia, only half a mile from where Cornlands is today. She bred her first litter in 1953, using a dark yellow bitch she had bought as a pup, called Flush of Cornlands. This bitch was mated to Ch. Diant Swandyke Cream Cracker, and her first Champion was born, Ch. Cornlands Peter So Gay.

A daughter of his, Cornlands Lady Be Good, was a winner of eight Field Trial awards and one CC. When she was mated to Ch. Cornlands Kimvalley Crofter (a 'gift' from the Becketts) she had two pups. Only one survived, and she turned out to be Ch. Cornlands My Fair Lady. Unfortunately, Lady Be Good died when in whelp for the second time to Crofter, in 1965, when she contracted Leptospirosis. My Fair Lady was a bitch of quality and strength, yet she was feminine all through.

She won so much for Peggy, including the top spot in the breed at Crufts in 1968 on the same day that her kennel mate, Ch. Cornlands Nokeener Highlight (brought in from Mrs H. Williams) took the dog CC. Peggy considers this her greatest achievement in showing, and the record of taking the double at Crufts stood for twenty-one years until the Brabbans broke it in 1989, with two home-bred Champions.

My Fair Lady took Best in Show at the Labrador Retriever Club Ch. Show in both 1969 and 1970, as well as winning a total of seventeen CCs. During her show career she also worked in the shooting season and suffered not one, but two cruciate ligament tears, first in one leg then in the other. It says a great deal for the University Veterinary Hospital at Cambridge, who treated her on both occasions.

Sh. Ch. Crawcrook Cavalier: Noted for his balance, outline and movement.

Anne Roslin Williams.

She had three litters, the most significant being to Ch. Timspring Mace which produced C. Lady Lavender, Cornlands Bay and Aust. Ch. C. Chive of Jaywick. In her litter to Eng. & Ir. Ch. Oakhouse Glenarem Classic, Cornlands Aristocrat was kept, and Cornlands Adonis went to Switzerland where he became a Champion. A daughter from the mating of Fair Lady to Highlight, C. Lady Rose, was mated to Ch. Timspring Mace and produced the first Labrador Champion in Israel, Ch. Cornlands Charlock.

Lady Lavender bred to Ch. Squire of Ballyduff, produced the very pretty bitch, Ch. Cornlands Blonde Lady, who, like her grandmother before her, went Best of Breed at Crufts in 1982. Other Champions have been: Ch. C. Westelm Flight (brought in from the Fountains), Sh. Ch. Cornlands Hamlet (bred by Sir Robert Lusty from a Cornlands bitch mated to Crofter), Ch. Cornlands Landy (a Westelm Flight son, sold to Mrs Rayment, Wishwood), and Ch. Cornlands Young Emperor.

CRAWCROOK: LINDA REDMILE

The kennel was established in 1971, and Linda had the sort of luck that everybody dreams of – the first bitch she owned went Best of Breed at Crufts, in 1977, at seven years of age. Sh. Ch. Crawcrook Princess was a very special lady, a beautiful old-fashioned bitch, with scope, and lots of drive on the move. Considering that Linda was a novice, she got the very best out of Princess, and went to the top with her. Princess produced CC winning offspring in Crawcrook Calhiban (one CC), and Champion grandchildren in Sh. Ch. Crawcrook Cavalier, Ch. Crawcrook Coronel of Oakrowan (owned by Hamish and Vera Lippe), and Champion great-grandchildren in Sh. Ch. Crawcrook Chianti of Mistywoods, owned by Winifred Fleming.

There are a further four Champions from this kennel in Europe, and two other dogs gaining CCs or Reserve CCs. Sh. Ch. Crawcrook Cavalier, winner of six CCs and three Reserve CCs, including one at Crufts in 1984, was an extremely well-known dog, noted particularly for his balance and outline, and grand movement. In his later years he dominated the Veteran classes at the Breed Championship shows. I watch his daughter, Ch. Warringah's Waltzing Matilda, striding out every day with the same effortless movement, so his memory lives on.

Ch. Fabracken Comedy Star: The male record holder with a tally of thirty-five CCs.

FABRACKEN: ANNE TAYLOR

The first Labrador came to Fabracken in 1966, and she was a yellow bitch from the Redvales kennel of Mary Rider. Anne was just a schoolgirl at the time, and Fabia was almost bigger than her. They started off in Obedience classes, graduating to Obedience shows, but when Anne discovered that successful Obedience dogs have to sit straight (I know what she means, they call it the 'Warringah Sit' at my classes), she moved over to Breed shows. In her only litter, Fabia produced the black bitch, Fabracken Georgie Girl, who became a Reserve CC winner.

Following school Anne attended Agricultural College, and by the time she had finished, her bitches were too old to breed from. She therefore acquired a Mark daughter from Didi Hepworth's Poolstead kennel, and this became Ch. Poolstead Pin Up of Fabracken. She proved to be a natural worker, and Anne says that Pin Up taught her more than she taught her. It was Pin Up who really started off her interest in the working side of the breed.

Pin Up was mated to Sh. Ch. Martin of Mardas, and Anne retained a black dog puppy, little knowing what he would grow into. He became Ch. Fabracken Comedy Star (the male CC record holder in the breed), winning thirty-five CCs, twenty-eight Best of Breeds, twenty-four Reserve CCs, and three Reserve Groups. He also sired Champions and Field Trial and Working Test award winners. Most of all, he had the loveliest of temperaments and was a joy to live with – everybody loved him. He even used to enjoy joining Anne on her windsurfing board, out on Lake Windermere.

Pin Up was then mated to Ch. Charway Ballywillwill, and produced the black bitch, Ch. Fabracken Dancing Shadow, winner of eleven CCs, seven Best of Breeds, and fifteen Reserve CCs. From Shadow's first litter, three gained their titles, and in her second she produced the yellow bitch, Ch. Fabracken Hello Sunshine.

Over the years Anne has become more interested in the working abilities of the breed, and now the Fabrackens spend their winters working. Only five or six dogs are ever kept at one time as they are part of the family, and a litter is only bred when a dog is needed to carry on the line. The aim is to breed a slow-maturing dog who, hopefully, is still capable of winning CCs and working as a veteran.

Margot Woolley pictured with four generations of Follytower Labradors left to right: F. Artemis, Sh. Ch. F. Augusta, F. Black Cherry and Ch. F. Silsdale Old Chelsea.

FOLLYTOWER: MARGOT WOOLLEY

Margot Woolley's famous kennel of Follytower dogs has been a great force on the British scene; they are well-known for their beautiful heads, their lovely reach of neck, and their stylish lines, and they are full of breed type. The kennel was started in 1963, and their foundation bitch was Ch. Follytower Silsdale Old Chelsea. Every Follytower dog has been descended from her.

Margot's most famous dog was Ch. Follytower Merrybrook Black Stormer, sired by Ch. Sandylands Tandy out of Follytower Old Black Magic (a Chelsea daughter). Stormer had a superb show career, winning fifteen CCs, numerous Reserve CCs, three Groups and two Reserve Groups, as well as getting down to the last three in Show at Peterborough, under Maurice Gilliat (of Holton fame). Stormer also took Best of Breed at Crufts in 1973, and the following year he won the dog CC.

He will long be remembered for the wonderful offspring that he sired. There were some wonderful bitches, including: Sh. Ch. Follytower Merry Go Round of Brentville (a chocolate bitch, owned by Peter Taylor), Sh. Ch. Follytower Augusta, Sh. Ch. Sandylands Sonnet of Knoboly (owned by Mr and Mrs Ellison), and Sh. Ch. Bradking Black Charm (Mr Kelley). Many of his sons were influential studs in their own right: Sh. Ch. Sandylands Stormalong (Mrs Broadley), Eng. Ch. Am. Ch. Lawnwoods Hot Chocolate (Mrs Satterthwaite), Sh. Ch. Thor's Lightning Boy (Mr Nicholls), Eng. Sh. Ch. Am. & Can. Ch. Sorn Sandpiper of Follytower, and Sh. Ch. Charway Blackthorn of Follytower.

As well as these Champions, Margot made up Sh. Ch. Follytower Poolstead Pinafore (bred by the Hepworths); she bred the Nightingales' Sh. Ch. Follytower Kirsty, and Angela Williams' Ch.

Follytower Black Cypress. Follytower Fudge gained one CC, Artemis (one CC, one Reserve CC), Spindrift (two CCs, four Reserve CCs), Kupros Moonriver of F. (two Reserve CCs), Willow (two CCs, eight Reserve CCs), and Follytower Pandora at Rocheby (one CC, one Reserve CC).

Abroad, the Follytowers have two Champions in South Africa, four in America, one American and Canadian Champion, plus one Champion each in Finland, Norway, Israel and Barbados. Margot is an International judge in Labradors, and she is held in high esteem both in the UK and overseas.

FOXRUSH: JUDITH CHARLTON
The kennel was established in 1968, and Judith's foundation bitch was Foxrush Sandylands Gaytime, born in 1967, who in turn produced the first Foxrush litter in 1969, in which Foxrush Bo-Peep gained her stud book number. Due to business commitments, very few litters have been bred over the years, but puppies brought in, especially from the Chapmans, have been very successful.

Ch. Croftspa Charlotte of Foxrush gained her title, and perhaps the best-known Labrador in the

Sh. Ch. Croftspa Hazelnut of Foxrush: Breed record holder with forty-five CCs.

Anne Roslin Williams.

UK is Sh. Ch. Croftspa Hazelnut of Foxrush. She is the breed recordholder with forty-five CCs, fifteen Reserve CCs, and one Reserve in the Gundog Group to her credit. Hazelnut was born in 1983, sired by Sh. Ch. Ardmargha Mad Hatter out of Foxrush Caprice of Croftspa (a daughter of Charlotte). She has had many spectacular wins, one of the most memorable, perhaps, being at the Yellow Labrador Retriever Club Ch. show in 1986 where she took the bitch CC, this being the second awarded to her by Gwen Broadley (which Judith considers a great honour). She was top winning Labrador in 1985, 1986 and 1987.

Ch. Aditis Becky of Foxrush was brought in from Norway as a young bitch, and she gained her title in the UK. She was a great, great, grand daughter of Charlotte, and was spotted by Judith when she was judging in Norway. There are two Foxrush Champions abroad, one in Norway, Foxrush Pioneer, and one in Sweden, Foxrush Silhouette. Nine other Foxrush dogs are in the Stud Book.

Sh. Ch. Heatherbourne Fisherman: Best of Breed Crufts, 1983.

Sally Anne Thompson.

HEATHERBOURNE: HEATHER WILES-FONE

The Heatherbourne Labradors, owned by Heather Wiles-Fone, were established in 1967 with the purchase of two bitches out of Ch. Sandylands Tandy. Four years later a lovely young bitch joined the kennel, and she was to become the kennel's first Champion, namely, Sh. Ch. Heatherbourne Harefield Silver Penny. She is behind all the present Heatherbourne dogs, and is really the foundation of the kennel. When mated to Sandylands Charlie Boy, she produced Sh. Ch. Heatherbourne Silver Czar, and when mated to Mark she produced Heatherbourne Moira.

The second Heatherbourne dog to gain his title was Ch. Heatherbourne Lawnwoods Laughing Cavalier, a most gentle dog who also qualified in the field. He sired Sh. Ch. Heatherbourne Top Tune, who won nine CCs and ten Reserve CCs. Moira was a great producer. When mated to Ch. Follytower Merrybrook Black Stormer she produced the black Sh. Ch. Heatherbourne Statesman, and when put to Sh. Ch. Balrion King Frost she produced Sh. Ch. Heatherbourne Fisherman (Best of Breed Crufts, 1983). Fisherman was a very stylish dog and had a successful show career, winning his first CC and going Best of Breed at only ten months of age. He also won two Gundog Groups.

Sh. Ch. Copperhill Lyric of Heatherbourne (a Silver Czar daughter, bred by Miss Startup) was a loving and faithful bitch, and so enjoyed her showing. A Group winner in her own right, she also produced three Champion offspring. These were Sh. Ch. Heatherbourne Court Jester and his sister Sh. Ch. Heatherboune Cinderella, sired by Sh. Ch. Bradking Cassidy, and Int. Ch. Heatherbourne Brown Sugar, in Switzerland. Court Jester and Cinderella took the double at the Three Ridings Labrador Club Ch. Show in 1984, with Cinderella going Best of Breed.

To date, Heatherbourne have produced eight Champions in the UK and ten abroad, spread over Australia, South Africa and the USA.

JAYNCOURT: JANE & PETER PALMER

Jane writes: "The first Labrador, Jayncourt Chicketta, was brought as a pet. She was was a 'Tandy' daughter, and when we eventually decided to mate her, we asked Gwen Broadley for advice. She suggested a young yellow dog who was later to become Aust. Ch. Diant Jaysgreen Jasper (a Tandy

Sh. Ch . Jayncourt Star Appeal.

son out of Diant Whisper). That was the first of many meetings with Gwen, and Sandylands has become almost a second home. The Sandylands stud dogs have been a very big influence within our kennels, and we still use them today – twenty-eight years later.

"Using Ch. Sandylands Midas to a yellow bitch, Jayncourt Michelle (from Chicketta's second litter to Jasper), we produced our first Champion, Sh. Ch. Sandylands Star of Jayncourt. Gwen brought the puppy from us when she was fourteen weeks old. Next time, Michelle was mated to Midas' litter brother, Ch Sandylands Mark, and this produced a lovely yellow bitch, J. Lucky Charmer. This bitch was mated to Sandylands Charlie Boy, and from the resulting litter we kept two bitches – J. Star Attraction and J. Star Misty. With the use of S. Charlie Boy, and later Sh. Ch. S. Garry and S. Charlston, we found the type for Jayncourt that I was looking for.

"We mated 'Star' to Sh. Ch. Sandylands Garry, and produced Sh. Ch. J. Star Appeal and Am. Ch. J. Star Performer. The litter sister, Misty, was mated back to her great grandfather 'Tandy' and so produced Ch. Novacroft Jayncourt Truly Fair and Sandylands Jayncourt Tallyho. When later Star Appeal was mated to Sandylands Charlston, she produced a most beautiful litter of seven pups, five bitches and two dogs. They were like peas in a pod. We kept J. Star Quality and J . Dancing Star, both were CC and Reserve CC winners.

"The kennel has bred ten Champions abroad, eight of them in America, one in Finland and one in Norway, the most famous being Am. Ch. Jayncourt Ajoco Justice (Ch. Ballyduff Marketeer – Am. Ch. Jayncourt Star Performer). who has been a huge influence on the breed in America – he is behind many of the top winning American dogs today. The litter was bred at Jayncourt, and Justice and his sister Magic went to the USA as twelve-week-old pups, followed by their mother, Star Performer some months later.

"We all have our special favourite dog or bitch – for me it will always be Sh. Ch. Jayncourt Star Appeal. The day 'Abbie' won her third CC at Bath Ch. Show she gave up being a kennel bitch and came to live in the house with the family and the 'oldies'. Abbie was my constant shadow – sadly no longer with us, but what wonderful memories I have."

*Kimvalley
Drummer:
Reserve CC
winner and
family
favourite.*

David Bull.

KIMVALLEY: DIANA & DON BECKETT

This kennel started in 1958 in the hope of substituting for their eldest son's imaginary dog! Their first two bitches were Kimvalley Maid and Kimvalley Guildown Cassandra, and all the dogs in the kennel today go back to Cassandra, who was, in fact, Don's all-time favourite. Cassandra, when bred to Ch. Sandylands Tandy, produced the two Champion dogs – Eng. & Am. Ch. Kimvalley Crispin, and Ch. Cornlands Kimvalley Crofter. Crispin was the best-known, and was a Group winner at Blackpool under Joe Braddon. He went to Mrs Clark's kennels in America, and he was the top-rated Labrador for two years until he met an early and untimely death going through ice on a pond. Sh. Ch. Brentchase Kimvalley Rosanna, bred by the Becketts and owned by Mrs Kinsella, also gained her UK title. Diana's most famous bitch was Eng. Sh. Ch. and Am. Ch. Kimvalley Picklewitch, bred by the Shobrooks in England. She was co-owned from a puppy with Mrs R. V. Clark Jnr of America; she gained her English title, and then had a marvellous career in America where she was in the sole ownership of Mrs Clark. The Becketts were in America for some years managing Mrs Clark's famous Springfield kennels. Picklewitch had the distinction of twice winning the Labrador National Specialty Show, and a third time going Best Opposite Sex at the grand age of eleven and a half years old.

Numerous other dogs in the kennels have attained high awards: K. Maid (Reserve CC), K. Kenbara Mr Softee (Reserve CC), K. Drummer (Reserve CC), K. Pearly Queen (Reserve CC), Kings Fancy of K. (Reserve CC), K. Rags to Riches (one CC). When he went to the United States, K. Kenbara Mr Softee was made up to a Champion. Diana says of him: "Of all the dogs we have owned – or ever will own – there will never be another 'Softee'."

There are two other Kimvalley Champions in the USA, as well as one in Denmark, and now there are two in Germany. Sh. Ch. Kimvalley Legend has just gone to his new owner, Michael De Kort, after being campaigned to his English title by Diana. Drummer now lives with the Beckett's daughter and her family. He did a great deal of winning, but in 1992 at Crufts suffered a severe heart attack. He is now retired from showing, and has a super life with Shelley, Tim and the girls.

Sh. Ch. Lasgarn Laudrup (Ch. Kupros Master Mariner – Lasgarn Lyric).

Anne Roslin Williams.

LASGARN: MESSRS E. G. & R. L. EDWARDS

The prefix Lasgarn was granted in the late 1940s, and the kennel showed Cocker Spaniels and Basenjis until 1963 when a yellow Labrador, Lasgarn Lash, was purchased from Cis Williams (Nokeener), who was a grand-daughter of Sh. Ch. Sandylands Sam. For a number of years the Labradors were only shown at local Open shows, but Lasgarn Louisianna, sired by Nokeener Newsflash, did a little winning at Championship shows.

In 1971 a yellow bitch, sired by by Sandylands Mark, was purchased from Mrs Williams, and she became Sh. Ch. Nokeener May Blossom of Lasgarn – a great showgirl. She started the kennel winning at Championship shows, even beating the great Ch. Follytower Merrybrook Black Stormer for Best of Breed when she won her first CC. Meanwhile, in 1972, Louisianna was mated to Mark to produce the first home-bred Champion, the black dog, Sh. Ch. Lasgarn Ludovic.

May Blossom did not prove to be a great brood. However, when mated to Sandylands Charlie Boy she produced Lasgarn Lineria, who, when mated to Sandylands Gay Boy in 1978, produced the yellow bitch, Sh. Ch. Lasgarn Leia – who won extremely well. Later a yellow male, Sh. Ch.

Lasgarn Livingstone, was made up; he was by Ch. Sandylands Newinn Columbus out of a bitch by Nokeener Welshman.

The first four Lasgarn title holders were all a mixture of Nokeener and Sandylands. Others of this breeding owned by Lasgarn included the CC winner Cathelmar Cabida and Lasgarn Lendl. Later, the Claytons kindly let Lasgarn have a black bitch, Ardmargha My Favourite of Lasgarn. She was superbly bred and is the grandmother of the black dog, Sh. Ch. Lasgarn Laudrup, sired by Ch. Kupros Master Mariner.

LAWNWOODS: MARJORIE SATTERTHWAITE

When Majorie's foundation bitch, Spinneyhill Lilac of Lawnwood, was mated to Nor. & Sw. Ch. Braeduke Silsdale Music Man, she produced Ch. Gay Piccolo of Lawnwood. This dog was handled to his Championship by Marjorie's young daughter, Pam, whose only previous experience had been with Lilac's first daughter, Hi-Bisto, sired by Sandylands Sam. Bisto joined Liz Clark at the Springfield kennels in the USA, and soon gained her American title.

Marjorie tackled the working side, and she decided that it was important that all her dogs were seen to be dual purpose. 'Pip' gained his gundog Working Certificate and ran in a few Field Trials, and his presence in the ring and his style at work gained him quite a reputation. When Lilac was mated to Rockabee Tobin (a son of Ch. Sandylands Tandy), another yellow male was kept, and he became Ch. Lawnwoods Fame and Fortune. He excelled in head and he had a superb front; he was a prepotent sire, a great gentleman and a joy to show.

The acquisition of Poolstead Personality at six months of age really sealed the fate of this kennel. It took them a while to convince her that she was as good as her litter sister, Ch. Poolstead Powder Puff, but then Personality went on to become a Champion and a marvellous brood. Mated to Piccolo, she produced Lawnwoods Laughing Cavalier, who later went to the Heatherbourne kennels where he gained his full title. His sister, Love in the Mist, was retained; she later went to live with Peter Taylor (Brentville).

Fame and Fortune was mated to Personality, and the result was two lovely bitches – Tapestry, and Fortune Teller. Personality was also mated to Ch. Follytower Merrybrook Black Stormer. The resulting son, Peppercorn, went to join Mithras of Lawnwood in Australia, where both gained their titles. Tapestry was mated to Stormer, and the outcome was the very well-known dog, Eng. & Am. Ch. Lawnwoods Hot Chocolate. 'Choc' was a dog with outstanding conformation and a wonderful dark coat. He won five CCs and many Reserve CCs before joining Jan Churchill in her Cesna aeroplane as co-pilot and touring the USA from coast to coast going to Dog Shows.

His daughter, Lawnwoods Hot Pants of Warringah, was my own foundation bitch and carried his name on in England. Fandango was a full brother to Choc by a repeat mating. He was a lovely rangey yellow (carrying no chocolate gene), and when mated to L. Starglow (a Mark daughter) the result was the kennel's next yellow Champion, L. Midnight Folly.

Sh. Ch. Tidesreach Neptune, bred by Noel Lewis, came to the kennels as a youngster and was campaigned to his title by Marjorie. When mated to Love in the Mist, he produced four wonderful Brentville daughters, and from one of these daughters (Brentville Marianne – Ch. Timspring Sirius) came his grandson, Secret Song of Lawnwood. Another of these daughters (B. Marcella) went to Warringah as one of our foundation bitches. Song was unlucky in coming up against two well-known black Champions campaigning for the CC record, and he failed to gain his title. However, he was unique in producing both a Field Trial Champion (Styleside Hawk), and the dual purpose Labrador, Ch Elowood Soul Singer, who competed in Field Trials as well as having a successful show career.

Ch. Lawnwoods Flight O' Fancy: A Champion and field qualifier at the age of two.

His name has been carried on by my own two bitches (who are sisters), Sh. Ch. Warringah's Hot Property and Sh. Ch. Warringah's Hot Favourite, Ch. Trenow Music Man (for the Floyds), and Follytower Sound of Music at Lawnwood, who have all produced many Champions, including a triple Champion in Sweden, Ch. Code of Conduct at Lawnwood in England (owned by Barry and Sue Edwards), and a Champion son, Trial & Error, in Australia.

Ch. Robabee Gretel of Lawnwood was brought in from Miss Thorpe and Miss Walker. Lawnwood-bred on both sides of her pedigree, she was a lovely bitch, full of type and quality. Then followed Ch. Lawnwoods Midnight Folly, slow-to-mature in head, a well-known and much-liked dog, a super showman, who gained his title, quickly followed by his famous son, Ch. Warringah Fair and Square. Both were wonderful-natured dogs, and very prepotent at stud, throwing their super type.

Folly's son, Cambremer Striking Midnight over Lawnwood carries on where Folly left off. In Germany he had an outstanding daughter in Ger. Ch. Floral Dance of Lawnwood; in Sweden he is represented by Ch. Lawnwoods Free and Easy, and in England by a black son, Wetherlam Storm of Lawnwood. Striking Midnight's claim to fame is in his daughters, Sh. Ch. Novacroft Lottie, and Ch. Lawnwoods Flight O' Fancy, a super bitch who gained her title on her second birthday and her field qualifier just three weeks later. She in turn has been mated to Sh. Ch. Sandylands Royal Escort, resulting in a superb bitch, L. Finlandia, and another Champion at two years, Ch. L. Free 'N' Easy (Faldo).

Marjorie feels that she has come full circle. Wetherlam Storm lives locally with Roll the Dice, and Marjorie has always been able to use him at stud. His offspring have included: Ch. Warringah's Flinders, her full-sister, Ch. Warringah's Adelaide, and her half-sister, W. Storm in a Teacup (one CC). Marjorie has kept a youngster out of his last litter to Fancy, and he is called Farewell.

Sh. Ch. Lindall
Bit Of Class
(Ch. Charway
Ballywillwill –
Lindall Classic).

David Bull.

LINDALL: LINDA & ALAN PORTER

The Lindall kennel really started in 1978 with the purchase of Morningtown Stormette, a very typey chocolate bitch (a daughter of Ch. Follytower Merrybrook Black Stormer), bought by Linda unbeknownst to Alan, using the saved-up holiday money. Linda put the bitch to bed in the sitting room the first night, and she came down the next morning to a room knee-deep in foam-rubber. Linda claims that they have not had a decent three-piece suite – or holiday – ever since!

Stormette was sold on condition that she would be shown, so they jumped in at the deep end and have been enjoying it ever since. For two complete novices, they did very well. Stormette was the first chocolate to win a Junior Warrant with all the points coming from Championship Shows, and she ended up winning one CC and one Reserve CC – a marvellous start.

When looking for a stud dog, Linda and Alan wanted one with clean lines to complement Stormette's rather compact lines, so they chose Ch. Charway Ballywillwill, who was still an untitled and leggy youngster at that stage. The outcome was Eng. & Am. & Can. Ch. Lindall Mastercraft, Lindall Miss Emma, and the Timms' foundation bitch, Lindall Miss Holly, who produced two Champion daughters.

Linda says that they still plan their litters in this way, trying to find a dog that complements the bitch, to improve on her. Others would not be able to do this because, through kennel blindness, they can see no wrong in their own stock. It has worked for the Lindalls – to date, they have bred two more Champions in Sh. Ch. L. Bit of Class (Lindall Classic to Ballywillwill), and Sh. Ch.

Lindall Rachelle (Ravone Girl Friday, Mastercraft daughter, to Sh. Ch. Balrion Kings Ransom), who is at present in the USA and is only a couple of points from gaining her American title.

Other kennel inmates have received high honours: Kupros Major at L. (Reserve CC), L. Personality (one CC, one Reserve CC), L. Pure Magic (one CC, two Reserve CCs), Boothgates Made to Match at L. (one CC, one Reserve CC), Rocheby Sugared Almond of L. (one CC, one Reserve CC), and L. The Right Stuff (two CCs, five Reserve CCs). Overseas, the Lindalls have four more Champions. The hard work that Linda and Alan have put into their dogs has paid off; they are dedicated to the breed and have taken the knocks as well as the good times, and they hope to leave the breed in good order when their time comes.

MARDAS: MARLENE & DAVID HEPPER

The kennel was started in 1969 with the purchase of one dog, Keithray Venturesome, and three bitches – Keithray Anthea, Bridget of Rosevilla, and Longley Tell Tale. The first three are behind all the Mardas Champions in the UK, with the addition of a double line of the Longley bitch in Samoori's pedigree.

The four Show Champions made up in England are the three black dogs, Martin of Mardas (Marketeer son), Mardas Master Mariner (Martin son), Mardas Samoori (Squire and Martin behind him), and the yellow bitch, Mardas Corndilly, who also gained a Reserve in the Gundog Group at the Three Counties Championship Show. She is a Martin granddaughter mated to Ch. Timspring Cleverly. Sh. Ch. Martin of Mardas' most famous son is the dog CC record holder, Ch. Fabracken Comedy Star.

The kennel is strongly based on the Ballyduff lines of the late Bridget Docking. Other dogs that have gained high awards are: Alocin Blue Tango of Mardas (Reserve CC), Mardas Clairissimo of Brandlesholme (one CC), Mardas Machiavelli of Alocin (one CC), Mardas Maritime Man (Reserve CC), Mardas Saphire (one CC), Mardas Semus (one CC, one Reserve CC), Mardas Simona (Reserve CC), and Special Edition of Mardas (one CC). This kennel has won Challenge Certificates in all three colours, and has six Champions abroad, covering America, Sweden, France and New Zealand.

NEWINN: ROSEMARY HEWITT

Rosemary was born into a dog family: her mother bred Shih Tzus and Poodles, and before going into Labradors, Rosemary had Wire Fox Terriers, Beagles and Pointers, all of which she showed. The first Labrador was bought in 1962 at the local cattle market, because Rosemary felt sorry for her. The bitch was six weeks old, pedigree-registered, and yellow. 'Devon', as she was called, was to be with Rosemary for the next fifteen years. She was shown with some degree of success, and had a litter to Landyke Lancer, producing some good pups in Newinn Wagtail and Newinn Mallard. During this time Rosemary married Michael, and two bitches were brought in as foundation stock at the beginning of the seventies, Newinn Sandylands Catrina (Charlie Boy's sister), and Poolstead Polyphoto of Newinn. Catrina is behind all of the kennel's Champions. When Catrina's daughter Amber was mated to Mark, she produced the famous dog, Sh. Ch Sandylands Newinn Colombus, who went to Gwen Broadley's kennels. Sh. Ch. Newinn Harmony of Peradon was the outcome when Amber's sister, Angelina, was mated to Mark. Angelina's daughter, Fleur, was mated to Ch. Keysun Teko of Blondella, and produced the well-known dog, Sh. Ch. Newinn Kestrel, who is in so many pedigrees today. When Polyphoto was mated to Newinn Natterjack (an Amber and Kestrel son), the lovely yellow Sh. Ch. Newinn Oasis was born, who went on to win ten CCs.

Rosemary Hewitt pictured with Sh. Ch. Newinn Oasis, winner of ten CCs.

Keysun Rhapsody of Newinn, brought in from Mrs Spencer (out of a Natterjack daughter to Sh. Ch. Bradking Cassidy), was the next to gain her title. Another dog joined the kennels (from another Natterjack daughter, Beltarn Princess Goda, who was bred to Ch. Kupros Master Mariner, by Mr Hadwen) and he became the next Champion – Sh. Ch. Beltarn Diuma of Newinn – a multiple CC winner, having gained fifteen to date. These last two Champions mated together have produced the latest Sh. Ch. in Newinn Greenfinch, a really beautiful black bitch; her litter sister, Goldfinch, has one CC and one Reserve CC.

A repeat mating has produced Newinn Clint Black, who has gained one CC and two Reserve CCs. Another youngster making his mark at present is Newinn Dwight Yoakam (Sh. Ch. Simandem Kings Neptune – Newinn Fire Imp, who goes back to Oasis), who has one CC and one Reserve CC. There are a further five Newinn dogs with CCs or Reserve CCs in Britain, four Champions in Sweden and one in South Africa.

NOVACROFT: DOROTHY I. GARDNER

'Dot', as she is affectionately known, has been a dog lover all her life, even to the extent of 'collecting' dogs on the way home from school – she claimed they were strays, although many were not! After leaving school she worked for a short time in an office to appease her mother, but after nine months she left and started work in a 'Westie' kennels. This gave her an excellent grounding in showing and presentation; strict discipline was maintained and Dot learnt a lot.

However, it was not until she had a home of her own that she was able to do her own breeding. Labradors were the first choice, and the kennel was started in 1959 with a Litchencroft bitch of working lines. A puppy brought in from the Jayncourt kennels (a Ch. Sandylands Tandy daughter) went on to become Dot's first Labrador Champion; her name was Ch. Novacroft Jayncourt Truly Fair. All the stock she has subsequently bred have come from a Lawnwoods bitch, L. Nereid (Sh. Ch. Tidesreach Neptune – Lawnwoods Tapestry), bought in the early seventies.

Sh. Ch. Novacroft Charles: Group winner, and winner of eight CCs.

David Dalton.

When bred to Ch. Gay Piccolo of Lawnwood, Nereid produced Novacroft Gay Rhapsody, who in turn was mother to two British Champions: the brother and sister Sh. Ch. Novacroft Charles, and Sh. Ch. Novacroft Chorus Girl. Chorus Girl was bred to her great nephew, Novacroft Senator, and produced Novacroft Savoir Faire, who in turn was mated to Cambremer Striking Midnight Over Lawnwood, and produced the gorgeous black bitch, Novacroft Lottie. Lottie's head should be studied by any one attempting to breed Labradors; it is quite classic – feminine, yet strong, wonderful eyes and neat ears – a far cry from the broad, cheeky, short-muzzled bitches that one sees in the ring at times today.

In America there are the Champions Novacroft Carlos and Novacroft Classicway Come Dancing, in Sweden the kennel is represented by Ch. Novacroft Arris, and in Bermuda by Ch. Novacroft Action Man. In the UK, Angolcroft William of Novacroft and Novacroft Nortonwood Amber have gained CCs, and N. Patrilia, N. Litchencroft Tin Tak, N. Abba, N. Startrend, N. Hinny Cake, N. Magnum, and Lasdalgin Live and Learn have all won Reserve CCs for the kennel. Dot has been busy in other breeds, having made up Champions in Miniature Bull Terriers, Sussex Spaniels and Whippets, and Reserve CC winners in English Springer Spaniels, and Curly Coated Retrievers. She judges the Gundog Group at Championship level, as well as seven breeds of gundogs, plus Whippets at the same level.

POOLSTEAD: MR & MRS R. V. HEPWORTH

'Didi' grew up in a home where there was always a Labrador as a shooting companion for her father. From those early days she can remember first a black bitch, followed by a yellow bitch, and finally a yellow dog bought in South Wales from a business colleague of her father's for her birthday in 1949. This dog's registered name was Cefn Glas Jasper, but she called him William. William was a marvellous dog, beautifully bred, a perfect gentleman, a good-looking dog, who worked well. Didi had him in mind when, in later years, she decided to look for a foundation bitch to breed from and show.

In 1955 she married Bob and they were given an English Springer Spaniel as a wedding present, named Trotter. William stayed at home as a companion and working dog with Didi's father (he had said he would rather lose his daughter than the dog), but when he died just a couple of years later, William went to join Didi once more. The following year, while buying dog meat in the pet shop, she saw a poster advertising Manchester Championship Show. She thought she would take Trotter and 'have a go'. She entered William, just for fun, in the Special Yellow Open Dog Class – he was nine-and-a-half years old, and neither she nor the dog had ever been to a show before. William took a third, and the Spaniel came fourth in Novice. Didi has never looked back. She went on showing William until he was eleven-and-a-half years old, and only once was he out of the cards. At ten-and-a-half years old he won the Limit class and challenged for the Reserve CC; the judge was Mrs Wormold.

Next on the agenda, now that she had been bitten by the 'show bug' was a bitch puppy to show, and later breed from. She eventually saw that Ann Wynyard had a litter due, sired by Sh. Ch. Landyke Stormer out of Ann's bitch, Diant Joy of Braeduke. Cheekily, Didi phoned her up and asked if she could come and see the bitch, and if she liked her, she might be interested in buying a bitch puppy to show. The final outcome was that they bought the only two bitch puppies in the litter, as she preferred one and Bob the other. They were Braeduke Juniper and Braeduke Julia; their famous brother was Joyful.

The prefix 'Poolstead' was the next thing acquired; it was the name of the woods surrounding their cottage and 'of Poolstead' was added to the two pups' names. Bob's bitch, Juniper, never produced a litter, but Julia proved to be a marvellous brood bitch, and from five litters (by four different dogs) she produced four English Champions, and one American Champion, and practically every dog in the Poolstead kennel goes back to her.

Two years later Kinley Willow was bought from Fred Wrigley. She was sixteen months old, and was to become the kennel's very first Champion. She proved to be a wonderful foundation bitch and a super gundog. At the first Field Trial that she and Didi attended, a Novice, they came second, as well as getting the best-looking dog in the stake – a memorable day. Unfortunately, she died at just six years old, having just whelped the litter which included P. Pussy Willow, and they had to hand-raise the litter. So Pussy Willow, mother of Sh. Ch. Poolstead Problem, was a very special little bitch – and lived to the great age of fifteen-and-a-half years old.

Didi says: "Problem was a very special dog for me, the only survivor from his litter – hence his name. He was my constant companion, a marvellous character and a great influence on the kennel – practically everything we have now goes back to him."

Some of the highlights in a breeding and showing career that has been studded with highlights are taking three CCs over four years at Crufts with Powder Puff, President and Pinnacle (all Julia's offspring), and winning the Gundog Group at Paignton with Preferential, son of Problem.

The strength of any kennel is in its brood bitches, and the Poolstead bitches have been quite superb: sound, typey, compact, and good movers that reproduced themselves to dogs from different lines, as well as their own studs. One of Didi's favourites is Positive Mystery who has produced five litters for her – and her last two Champions. When mated to Preferential, Mystery produced Sh. Ch. Poolstead Pipe Dreamer, who was Best of Breed Crufts 1991, as well as going Best in Show at the Labrador Club Championship Show the same year. In doing this she was awarded the kennel's one-hundredth CC. Her brother, Sh. Ch. Poolstead Pipe Smoker, was to become the kennel's twenty-fifth Champion. From the total of twenty-five Poolstead English Champions, twenty-three have bred by the Hepworths, the two exceptions being Ch. Poolstead Kinley Willow and Sh. Ch. Mansergh Sailors Beware, bred by Mary Roslin Williams and owned by Didi's son. There are many more Poolstead Champions abroad; the number is unknown, but most of the dogs exported have gained their titles in their respective countries.

Sh. Ch. Poolstead Problem: A great influence on future generations of Poolstead Labradors.

Anne Roslin Williams.

The dogs gaining their titles in the UK have been Chs.: P. Kinley Willow, P. Powder Puff, P. Pinnacle; Sh. Chs.: P. Porcelain, P. President, P. Popularity, P. Problem, P. Purdey, P. Pictorial, P. Mansergh Sailor Beware, P. Postal Vote, P. Preface, P. Preferential, P. Past Master, P. Match Maker, P. Pegg, P. Pearl Necklace, P. Pocket Picker, P. Pocket Money, P. Pipe Dreamer, and P. Pipe Smoker.

In other kennels there have been: Ch. P. Personality of Lawnwood, Ch. P. Pin-up of Fabracken, Sh. Ch. P. Pure Silk of Martinside, and Ch. Follytower P. Pinafore. The list speaks for itself.

ROCHEBY: DAVID & MARION HOPKINSON

The Rocheby kennel was established in 1966 with two Kinley bitches, Juno and Magic. Mr and Mrs Wrigley (Kinley) were unstinting in their help, advice and encouragement, as were the other established kennels. The success the kennel has had is down to their marvellous brood bitches. R. Spring Song (three Reserve CCs), a descendant of Kinley Magic, and Sweet Talk of R. (three Reserve CCs) are behind everything in the kennels today. R. Polished Oak (a Ch. Keyson Krispin of Blondella daughter, back to Sweet Talk) has been a strong influence in recent years, her daughter Acorn being their first Champion and Gundog Group winner.

The most influential dog to this kennel came with the purchase of Poolstead Pretentious at Rocheby from Bob and Didi Hepworth – he was Top Sire in 1990. Although never shown himself, his progeny have been outstanding. Acorn, when bred to Pretentious, produced an outstanding litter. In Britain the brother and sister Sh. Chs. R. Royal Oak (six CCs and Reserve Group winner) and R. Popcorn (ten CCs, Best of Breed Crufts 1992, and top winning Labrador bitch 1991) have had spectacular careers to date. In America their sister, R. Rippling Corn, has gained her title, and another sister in Sweden, R. Corn Flower, has three CCs. Popcorn, like her mother, Acorn, took

Marion Hopkinson pictured with Sh. Ch. Rocheby Popcorn (left) and her brother, Sh. Ch. Rocheby Royal Oak, sired by Poolstead Pretentious at Rocheby out of Sh. Ch. Rocheby Acorn.

David Bull.

Best Puppy in Show at both the National Gundog Ch. Show and the United Retriever Ch. Show – and surpassed her mother by going back the following year and taking both of the bitch CCs.

Champions overseas include: R. Top Hat in America, R. Jazztime of Follytower (Sweden), R. Rotarian (Germany) and R. Chancellor & R. Charity of Charway in South Africa. Other successful dogs in the kennels include: Follytower Charlotte of R. (two CCs, one Reserve CC), R. Fairy Tale (one CC, three Reserve CCs), Foxrush Almond of R. (one CC, three Reserve CCs), and Lindall Charmed at R. (Reserve CC).

STAJANTOR: VIC AND JANET COLE

The Coles interest in showing Labradors started in 1962 when Vic bought a yellow bitch puppy, Station Honeysuckle, from Mrs Townsend (Jaysgreen). Two years later, Stajantors Station Cindora was purchased, and then a yellow two-years-old, Lochranza Cherry Blossom (Lochranza/Sandylands) joined the kennel – these were the foundation stock that is in their lines today. Already at home were three black working Labradors that Vic went rough shooting with.

The first Champion for the kennel was from a mating of Cherry Blossom to Sandylands Charlie Boy, and this was the yellow male, Sh. Ch. Stajantors Honest John. He was the winner of three CCs, five Reserve CCs, a Reserve in the Gundog Group at Bournemouth, Best of Breed at Crufts

Sh. Ch. Stajantors Honest John: The Coles' first Champion.

Anne Roslin Williams.

in 1980 and down to the last six in the Group. Two years later he took the Reserve Dog CC at Crufts. The next Champion, made up in 1984, was out of a Cindora daughter mated to an Honest John grandson. This was Sh. Ch. Stajantors Dam Buster. Sh. Ch. Astrelettia Next Edition of Stajantor, bred by Mrs Clarke, was an Honest John son to I'm Lulu Belle of Diant (herself a Bitch CC winner at Crufts in 1981 – I remember it with great clarity as she beat W. Hot Property, and we got the Reserve CC). In 1992 Sh. Ch. Ballyduff Dawn of Bannerbridge was made up. This bitch was bred by Mrs Cuthbert (out of Stajantors Amy of Ballyduff), and she came to live with Vic and Janet when she was two years old, following her first litter.

Other dogs in the kennel that have attained high awards are: S. Matchmaker (Reserve CC), S. Slipper (one CC), S. Cinda (two Reserve CCs). Five others have Stud Book numbers. Both Vic and Janet judge the breed in Britain at CC level and internationally.

TIMSPRING: the late JOAN MACAN

Joan's Timspring kennel was started in 1961 when she moved out of London to Tims Spring near Berkhampstead, giving her the space to indulge her passion for dogs. Sandylands Tarna was brought in from Gwen Broadley (a Tan/Shadow daughter), along with Timspring Landyke Venus (a Landyke Lancer daughter). From this well-bred beginning Joan had some excellent yellow Champions, in Ch. T. Jubilant (out of Venus to Ch. Braeduke Joyful), Ch. T. Little Tuc (a Venus daughter to Tarna's full brother, Ch. Sandylands Tandy), and Ch. T. Mace (a Tarna son, bred to Ch. T. Jubilant).

Joan brought Eng. & Am. Ch. Ballyduff Seaman back to the UK, through quarantine, to join her kennels. When he was mated to T. Myrtle (a Jubilant daughter), he gave her the quality black dog and bitch litter Champions, Serendipity and Sirius. Sirius proved a good stud, and he sired the influential stud dog, Secret Song of Lawnwood. The next Champion the kennel had was Ch T. Tarf – always a favourite of mine. He was a Ch. T. Little Tuc son to a daughter of Sirius, and the lovely black bitch, Spark of Ballyduff. Another very typey yellow brood bitch was Little Tee of

Ch. Timspring Sirius: A quality black dog and an important sire.

Diane Pearce.

Timspring, a favourite of Joan's. She was a Tuc daughter, and when mated to Ch. Charway Ballywillwill, produced Ch. Timspring Cleverly, the last Champion Joan made up before her brutal death in 1988. Cleverley's brother Comfrey went to Australia, and Comely went to Canada, both becoming Champions in their new countries. Little Tee, when mated to Receiver, produced T. Russel, who gained a Reserve CC.

All of Joan's dogs were trained to the gun, and she greatly enjoyed taking part in Field Trials with her dogs. Joan published each year a book, at her own expense, on the hip scores in Labradors in the UK. This work has been taken on and continued by The Labrador Retriever Club as a tribute to her.

TRENOW: MAUREEN & TONY FLOYD
The kennel originated in 1973. The dog that first brought them to the forefront was Sh. Ch. Astonbrook Crusader, a Marketeer son out of Astonbrook Gemini, bred by Mrs Fisk. He joined the kennel as a pup and was campaigned to his title by Tony. He was a scopey, yellow, free-moving dog, with beautiful head – he was a joy to watch on the move. Roseacre Madonna of Trenow, a Madhatter daughter bred by Miss Nicola Hudson, joined the kennel and she was the dam of their first home-bred champion, Ch. Trenow Music Man, when bred to Secret Song of Lawnwood. A workmanlike dog, he proved his worth at stud and as a companion to the gun with Tony.

His sister, Minuet, was a valuable brood bitch, as well as gaining a Reserve CC. When mated to Joline Inkling of Follytower (a Crusader son with one Reserve CC) she produced two Champions in one litter – Sh. Ch. Trenow Briar Rose, a very beautiful pale-yellow bitch, and the dog, Ch. Trenow Brigadier. Brigadier attended his first show, the Labrador Retriever Clubs Ch. Show in 1987, at eleven months of age and went Best in Show. He was subsequently made up from five consecutive shows – the quickest Sh. Ch. to gain his title in the breed. He gained his field qualifier at the Midland Counties Labrador Retriever Club's Open Stake at sixteen months, becoming the

Ch. Trenow Brigadier: Best in Show at eleven months of age.

David Bull.

joint youngest full Champion in the breed. He is the sire of Sh. Ch. Carpenny Bonhomie who has gained fifteen CCs – and is still going strong.

Minuet, mated to Sandylands Rise and Shine, produced the newest star for this kennel in Trenow Flora. She has one CC and four Reserve CCs at the moment. Other dogs to receive high placings are Trentham Teal of Blondella (Reserve CC) and Trenow Secret Agent (Reserve CC). Although only a small kennel, with approximately eight dogs at any one time, the majority of dogs are gun-trained and have the opportunity to work on local shoots, plus rough shooting with Tony. The kennel has two Champions in Australia, T. Secret Agent, and T. Prelude, as well as Ch. Dolwen Ocean Belle at Trenow in America.

TREWINNARD: T.R. PASCOE

Tony was born of farming stock in west Cornwall, where both sides of his family were deeply interested in the exhibition and judging of all forms of livestock. It was, therefore, not surprising that Tony spent his early years going to shows with his father's pedigree cattle, and with his own riding ponies, rabbits and poultry. Tony thinks that much valuable experience was gained by tuition and competition in the Young Farmers Club stock judging during these early years.

Shortly after leaving school, he acquired his first Labrador, in 1953. This was the five-year-old bitch, Tuppence of Bonython, bred by the late Dora Lee. In 1959 Sandylands Tangle was brought in from Gwen Broadley, plus Braeduke James from Mrs Wynyard. Trewinnard Sandylands Tanita and Tondelayo joined the kennel in 1961. Tanita's son, T. Skiff (a Kinley Skipper son) sired their first Champion, Eng. Sh. Ch. & Am. Ch. T. Vagabond, in 1969, a yellow dog bred by C. W. Scott.

Sh. Ch. Sandylands Not Tonight of Trewinnard was bought in as a puppy from Gwen Broadley and was to become their next Champion, made up in 1978. She was out of Sh. Ch. Newinn Columbus to Sh. Ch. Sandylands Girl Friday. When she was mated to Sandylands Charlston, she produced two yellow dog Champions in 1979 – Sh. Ch. Trewinnard Not Likely, and Sh. Ch. Trewinnard Not Fussy of Crestlands, who was owned by Nan Leah.

Other dogs to gain high awards were T. No Credit (the CC at Welks in 1985) owned by the

Sh. Ch. Trewinnard Not Likely: Sired by Sandylands Charlston out of Sh. Ch. Not Tonight of Trewinnard.

Allens and T. Time For Tea (Ranchaven Rock Steady of T.– T. Startime), a lovely bitch and winner of a CC at Paignton 1990, plus five Reserve CCs. Owing to business commitments she was not campaigned a great deal, and she was unlucky not to gain her title. Trewinnard Anytime took Best of Breed at Crufts in 1988, plus a Reserve CC at Wales the week before his big win. Tony is a Gundog Group judge, currently passed to judge fourteen breeds in the Group, which he does in the UK and overseas.

WARRINGAH: DAVID AND CAROLE COODE

I can lay the blame at David's door – he bought me my first Labrador in 1967, as a first wedding anniversary present. We lived in Australia at the time, hence our Australian affix. The dog was a yellow male out of Candlemas Butterscotch. Within the year we had bought another yellow male (of similar breeding) – this time for David – for by this time we were hooked on competing in Obedience and showing. During the next seven years, both in Australia and then Malaysia, we continued showing and competing in Obedience, making up our first Champion with Malaysian Ch. Kanyanya Prince d'Or. We spent this time reading everything we could on Labradors, and we came back to England in 1974 with some pretty firm ideas of the type of Labrador we wanted to keep and breed.

We started our kennel with two Lawnwoods bitches, a two-year-old yellow, Brentville Marcella of Lawnwood, and a year later a black puppy, Lawnwoods Hot Pants of Warringah. These two were our foundation stock. We mated Marcella to Eng. Aust. & N.Z. Ch. Ballyduff Marshall, hoping for a black bitch – we got two black dogs, two yellow dogs, and eight yellow bitches! The yellow bitch we kept, W. Muffin, was mated to Ch. Lawnwoods Midnight Folly and produced our wonderful yellow male, Ch. Warringah's Fair and Square. He was an ambassador for the breed, with a kind, loving nature, wonderful conformation, and a noble head. He in turn proved to be a prepotent stud, leaving five Champion children behind him, and many other top winners.

Hot Pants was mated to Secret Song of Lawnwood, and produced two Champion daughters – Sh. Ch. W. Hot Favourite and Sh. Ch. W. Hot Property. These two lovely black girls in turn gave us

The Warringah Labradors (pictured left to right): Ch. W. Fair Dinkum, Sh. Ch. W. Hot Property, Lawnwoods Hot Pants of W., Sh. Ch. W. Hot Favourite (lying), Sh. Ch. W. Fair Clemency, Ch. W. Fore Square, Ch. W. Harlech and Ch. W. Fair and Square.
Anne Roslin Williams.

Champion sons. Favourite when mated to Fair & Square produced Ch. Warringah's Fore Square, who died at just eight years old from cancer. However, he left behind two excellent winners for the Reynolds (Carromer), and a Ch. son in Ireland, Ir. Ch. Rebel of Abelstown, owned by Kathleen Carvill. When Hot Property had her one and only litter, sired by Ballywillwill, she had eight dogs and one bitch. The dog was Ch. W. Harlech, a winner of eleven CCs, a Group, and a Reserve Group. One of those CCs and the Reserve Group was at Crufts in 1986 – a really memorable show for us. We had three Champions in the line-up in Open Dog: David went on to win the CC and eventually Best of Breed, and he let me take Harlech into the big ring where we were second to the Pointer.

We had put out two bitches on breeding terms: one was Harlech's sister, the other was a Hot Pants daughter. When put to Fair & Square they produced the two yellow girls, Sh. Ch. Warringah's Fair Clemency and Ch. Warringah's Fair Dinkum. Clemency, when mated to Wetherlam Storm of Lawnwood, produced the pretty pale-yellow W. Storm in a Teacup (one CC). Fair Dinkum has been a prolific brood – in only three litters she has produced eight Champions. In her first litter to Sh. Ch. Crawcrook Cavalier we had our own Ch. W. Waltzing Matilda, and her brother, Canadian Ch. W. The Wild Colonial Boy. In her second litter she was mated to Wetherlam Storm of Lawnwood, and we kept Ch. Warringah's Flinders. Other members of the litter were:

Am. Ch. W. Victoria; South African Ch. W. Bathurst; Int. Ch. (France) W. Banjo Patterson; and Warringah's Nullabor, winner of three CCs in Sweden. The third litter was a repeat of the second, and we have kept Ch. Warringah's Adelaide, at the time of writing our tenth and latest Champion. Another wonderful win was in 1990 at the Yellow Labrador Club Ch. Show when Flinders went Best in Show, and her full sister Adelaide took Best Puppy, under judges Mrs Satterthwaite and Mrs Wiles-Fone.

Flinders has had two litters. From the first, to Harlech, we have kept the two blacks, Warringah's Wallaroo (one CC, three Reserve CCs), and W. Whortleberry, who got her JW in just four Ch. Shows. At Richmond in September 1992 we took the double under judge Anne Roslin Williams, with Wallaroo and his mother, Flinders. Roo went Best of Breed and got down to the last six in the Group under judge Mrs Waring – another superb day. Roo and Berry are our hopes for the future.

RECENT SUCCESS STORIES
I have included the following three kennels, because their top dogs have made such an impact on the Labrador scene in the UK in the last few years.

CRANSPIRE: KEN HUNTER
Ken brought in the black dog Clayton Holt Hijacker of Cranspire (a Mark son), bred by Doreen Milne, in 1974, and this dog was to become his first Show Champion. Ken bred some excellent stock, many going overseas and becoming Champions in their new countries. In 1981 he brought in a yellow dog, bred by Coddington and Shortland, who was to become one of the most famous dogs in the last decade. This was Eng. & Am. Ch. Receiver of Cranspire (Dutch Ch. Cranspire Skytrain – Polly's Pride of Genisval, Newinn/Heatherbourne breeding). He was a clean-cut dog, an excellent showman, and he became a dominant stud, fixing his type on most of the litters he sired. Before he left for America he sired Ch. Carpenny Chevalier, Sh. Ch. Cambre-mer Countdown, Sh. Chs. Poolstead Pocket Picker and Pocket Money, and a grand-son, Sh. Ch. Tibblestone the Chorister (NZ Ch. Carpenny Chateau Cranspire – Sandylands Forever Amber at Tibblestone). In America he is the sire of numerous Champions. He has gone on to France where he is with Marc Gad, and his influence is felt over the Continent, where many of his Ch. children and grand-children abound.

Eng. Am. Ch. Receiver of Cranspire: A dominant stud, fixing his type on most of the litters he sired.

Ch. Crosscroyde Cotton On Quick: Best in Show winner, Bournemouth, 1991.

Alan Walker.

CROSSCROYDE: MR & MRS R. J. LAVELLE

From their first litter, in 1973, the Lavelles produced their first Champion, Sh. Ch. Crosscroyde Charlotte. She was out of their original bitch, Beaford Hope, mated to Ch. Heatherbourne Lawnwoods Cavalier. Charlotte's great granddaughter, mated to Ch. Carpenny Chevalier, has produced the great winner in recent years, Ch. Crosscroyde Cotton On Quick, or 'Harold', as he is known at home. Born in 1988, this dog has had a spectacular career to date, and he is still going strong. His wins include sixteen CCs, nine Reserve CCs, one Best In Show All Breeds Ch. Show (12, 000 plus dogs) at Bournemouth in 1991, two Group wins, two Reserve in Groups, Winner of the Champion Stakes at the National Gundog Ch. Show in 1992, as well as taking Best of Breed at Crufts in 1993 .

KUPROS: MARION & PETER HART

This kennel really started in 1973 with the purchase of Ballyduff Morella (Marketeer's sister), and all stock in the kennel descend from her. Previously the Harts had two dogs, out of Gay Piccolo of Lawnwood, that had been shown and trained to the gun, both gaining awards at Shows, Field Trials and Working Tests. Morella when mated to Stormer produced Kupros My Lady (one CC, two CCs, 3rd in Field Trial). She in turn was mated to her cousin, Ch. Squire of Ballyduff, in 1977, and this produced their first Champion, Ch. Kupros Lady's Pride. She was mated to her grandfather, Marketeer, and produced Kupros Bridget. When Bridget was mated to Eng. Am. & Can. Ch. Lindall Mastercraft she produced one of the most dominant sires of today, Ch. Kupros

Ch. Kupros Master Mariner: The most dominant sire in recent years.

Master Mariner. He is the sire of twenty-two Champions (eleven in the UK), and was the Top Labrador Sire from 1987 to 1992. At nine years old he added another CC to his collection. Peter is a part-time gamekeeper, and all his dogs are regularly worked to the gun. Five other dogs of Kupros breeding have attained CCs or Reserve CCs, and there are many Champions abroad.

BEST OF THE REST

There are other kennels that I wish I could cover in detail, only space does not allow me; but I should like to add those that have produced good dogs, making up some Champions, and that will be having an effect on the dogs coming along in the future.

These are David and Marilyn Nightingale (**Boothgates**) who have made up Sh. Ch. Follytower Kirsty and Sh. Ch. Boothgates Kountry Kurio. David Craig (**Davricard**) – two Bradking bitches brought in have been made up, B. Bridgette of Davricard and B. Molly-Mo. Shelagh Walton (**Gallybob**) is consistently producing good stock, and made up Ch. Gallybob Caraway. Diane Harris (**Insley**) took on Barona Pegasus (two CCs) when his owner Brian Cocks died, campaigned him to his title and has since bred the brothers, Sh. Ch. I. Iasis and Idas, who are Pegasus' great grandchildren. Mr and Mrs Timms (**Lejie**) have made up two Sh. Chs. in the U.K, Lejie Lucy and Lejie Ladys Slipper, as well as having three Champions abroad. Margaret Litherland (**Oakhouse**) consistently brings out good stock, but due to business commitments she only shows lightly; she made up Eng. & Ir. Ch. Oakhouse Glenarem Classic, bred by the Greenhalghs, and has six Champions abroad. Barry and Sue Edwards (**Subar**), based on Lawnwood lines, have made up the good black dog Ch. Code of Conduct of Lawnwoods; they have sound typey stock all trained to the gun. Molly Rayment (**Wishwood**) is producing sound stock: her first Champion was Ch. Wishwood Winston, in 1964 (from Cornlands stock), and she bred Sh. Ch. Wishwood Errant of Lyndham, in 1981, owned by the Elliots, and now Sh. Ch. Wishwood Shaft 1985, as well as having Champions abroad. Mr and Mrs Bedford (**Wynfaul**) have good dual purpose Labradors, and have made up Ch. Wynfaul Tobasco, a fox-red yellow dog, and the yellow bitch, Sh. Ch. Cricklecreek Camomile of Wynfaul, bred by Lorna Blackie.

Chapter Seven

THE LABRADOR IN THE USA

The Labrador Retriever is now the number one breed in the USA, with registrations close to 121,000 in 1992. This continues the upward trend in recent years with 95,768 registrations in 1990 and 105,876 registered in 1991. There are many reasons for this surge in popularity, but it is probably the all-round adaptability of the breed that has led to its formidable success. The Labrador excels as a working gundog, it has been adopted worldwide as a Seeing Eye dog for the blind, its marvellous nose makes it invaluable in drugs and arms detection, and most important of all, the Labrador is unrivalled as a family companion. Chris Wincek, secretary of the Labrador Retriever Club of America, highlights the outstanding qualities of the breed: "The hallmark of the breed is its temperament; its unconditional interest in pleasing. The Labrador displays such intense responsiveness and trainability. It will take such pressure in training, and yet remain so forgiving. It is these qualities which make the Labrador Retriever one of the greatest animals on earth."

The Labrador has made its mark in the show ring, and there are many important kennels producing top-quality stock. However, before looking at the present-day influential kennels, tribute must be paid to the Lockerbie kennel, owned by the late Jim and Helen Warwick. This kennel has had an enormous impact on the Labrador in America. Their judicious mix of English imports combined with the best American dogs produced a line that has left a great mark on the breed today. Their first Champion was bought from Mrs Curtis (Joan) Read, and this was Ch. Chidley Hocus Pocus. A yellow bitch, who was to become Ch. Ballyduff Candy, was imported from the Ballyduff kennel in the UK, owned by Dr Acheson and his wife, Bridget (later Docking). Candy was mated to two Ballyduff males, imported by Mrs S. Hallock Dupont. From these breedings came Ch. Lockerbie Blackfella, Lockerbie Lancer and Lockerbie Spanker.

In the early sixties, two puppies – littermates – were imported from Gwen Broadley's Sandylands kennel. They were Ch. Lockerbie Sandylands Tarquin, who was to become one of the great stud forces of the sixties, and his sister, Lockerbie Sandylands Tidy. With other good imports from a variety of English kennels, notably Sandylands Markwell, the Lockerbie stud dogs were widely used, and many kennels in the US carry their lines, or started with stock from them.

Both Jim and Helen enjoyed judging, and in the UK we used to look forward to Helen's trips over to England to judge our dogs. Helen also wrote a book on the breed, *The Complete Labrador Retriever* (published by Howell Book House), which was essential reading for Labrador enthusiasts on both sides of the Atlantic.

ALLEGHENY: CLARE SENFIELD
Clare, born into a farming family in England, moved with her American husband to the United

Allegheny's Cherry Blossom: Sired by Ch. Graemoor Bombay out of Am. Can. Ch. Kupros Midnight Frolic.

Ashbey Photography.

States in the mid-sixties. When they returned to England in 1971 for a four-year stint, they brought in Ellerthwaite Jay as their foundation bitch, bred by Nurse Rogers in Cumbria. This bitch was by Ch. Groucho of Mansergh out of E. Muscatel of Mansergh. She in turn was mated to her grandfather, Ch. Sandylands Mark, and two of the offspring went back with Clare to the USA.

The bitch Bezique soon finished her Championship. Bezique was mated to a good English import, Ch. Eireannach Black Coachman, and two pups were kept – Ch. Allegheny's Eclipse and his sister, Twilight. Eclipse did very well, especially at Specialty shows, as did his sister. Early on they both won their sweepstakes classes at the Potomac Specialty, and the following year both took their 'Bred-By' classes. Eclipse finished his Championship shortly after going to join Kendall Herr, but died from cancer within five years. In his short life he left his stamp on the breed, proving a good stud. His son, Ch. Marshland Blitz, was widely used at stud, producing good stock. Twilight earned 24 points – the second major was not to be – but she proved her worth as a super brood. Two of her daughters, Peppercorn and Nutmeg are still with Clare, enjoying their retirement. From Peppercorn's last litter (to Blitz) two pups were kept – Nicholas and Sugarplum, both showing a lot of promise. Looking back, 1978 was an important year, with the Coachman/Bezique breeding producing two dogs that were to play an important part in shaping the Allegheny line. Ch. Kupros Live Spark from the Harts in England joined the kennel the same year, and his input was to prove invaluable. He was a dog that was very much loved. He was a good Obedience dog, always willing to please, and he finished his Championship on his third birthday. He subsequently did well as Specialties, getting several Group placements as well as a Group 1 – quite a rarity, as he was owner-handled, with a full set of whiskers and not touched by the scissors, an achievement of which Clare is justly proud.

His son, Ch. Allegheny's McDuff (out of Bezique) made his own contribution to the breed. One of the highlights of his show career was going Winners at the National Specialty in 1981. He finished his Championship at that time, having only been shown in 'Bred-By' classes. He produced good offspring, and spent a fruitful year at stud at Jane Border's Braemar kennels in California. It was a thrill to see his granddaughter, A. Cricket, owned by Annette Watkins, go

Winners Bitch at the Potomac Specialty in 1992. A real stroke of fortune came in the shape of Am. Can. Ch. Kupros Midnight Frolic (litter sister of Ch. Kupros Master Mariner in England). This bitch had visited Live Spark to be mated, and Clare fell in love with her. However, it was nearly two years before her owner, Meira Wheeler in Canada, agreed that she could come to Allegheny. Like Live Spark, she loves doing anything you ask her, and she is as happy in the ring as she is retrieving ducks. She became an Am. Ch. very quickly, and then settled down to maternal duties, long lazy walks, and the odd day's hunting. An expert at puppy rearing, preferring to produce boys, she was always thought to be dominant black until the last litter where she produced five yellows. One bitch, Cherry Blossom (sire Ch. Graemoor Bombay) was kept, and she is a yellow version of her mother, always ready to go and full of life.

There have been others dogs that have meant a great deal to Clare, but those mentioned have been ones that marked turning points in her aim to amalgamate the best of two English bloodlines while developing her own. Success for Clare means looking back with a sense of achievement, and feeling that, perhaps, in some small way she has made some beneficial contribution to the breed.

AVALON: PAUL & JEAN NELSON

The kennel was established in 1965 when a year-old bitch was brought in; she was to become Am. Can. Mex. Ch. Zodiac Kashmir CD, WC. Kashmir finished with three five-point majors and was Specialed as a Veteran of eleven years, winning many BOBs. She is the great-great grandmother of Ch. Avalon's Invincible, who was Nationally rated in the Top Ten for three consecutive years.

So far, the kennel has bred over twenty-five Champions in three countries, and in all three colours. Primary emphasis is put on soundness, particularly fronts and rears, good otter tails, broad heads, and good side gait with reach and drive. Unless a dog has these qualities, it does not remain in the kennel. The Labrador is first and foremost a sporting dog, so soundness and stamina are all-important.

Paul and Jean feel that anyone starting out in Labradors should study Ch. Sam of Blaircourt very carefully, as he is depicted as the example of the Breed Standard. They also believe that if a

Ch. Avalon's Invincible: Nationally rated in the Top Ten for three consecutive years.

Labrador does not come up to scratch, it must not be used for breeding. Their maxim is: 'Think ahead before you breed'. Do not just look at the stud dog, but at the generations behind him, and think to the future, planning the right mixture of lines to produce the best possible puppies.

Avalon dogs have followed numerous professions: Obedience, working, and drug detection. Avalon's Jingo was one of the first heroin detection dogs in the US – the underworld put a bounty of $10,000 on him dead or alive!

AYR: NANCY MARTIN

Nancy writes: "As with many breeders, my interest in Labradors began with a wonderful old pet. Then I went through several Labs bought as show dogs – a few made it, a few did not. In the sixties I was lucky enough to have had Ch. Lockerbie Olivia (Ch. Sam of Blaircourt – Sandylands Tidy) and Ch. Great Scot of Ayr (Ch. Lockerbie Sandylands Tarquin – Sandylands Spungold). It was a thrill to win Winners Dog at the LRC Specialty Show in 1967 with old 'Great Scot' under the dean of judges, Percy Roberts.

"Later I was very fortunate to have Ch. Sandylands Morningcloud, from Gwen Broadley (from the last litter by Ch. Sandylands Mark – Sh. Ch. Sandylands Longley Come Rain), and from Mrs Docking I acquired Ballyduff Sparkler (Ch. Timspring Sirius – Spark of Ballyduff), dam of three Champions. Today I am working on the eleventh generation from these early Labradors.

"In over thirty years I have kept an average of six dogs at a time, having one or two litters a year. They are all house dogs, and all have passed their Working Certificate Tests, because we have a lot of fun doing field work. I have a group of friends who train once a week, and it's great to see the youngsters' progress. Two of my current bitches, Ayr's Lollapalooza and Ayr's Real Humdinger have gained their Junior Hunting Title (AKC), and one dog, Ayr's Real McCoy CD, JH, (Ch. Dickendall Ruffy SH – Ayrs Mollywog of the Sea), co-owned and trained by my friend Joanne Summers, is almost ready for the Senior Hunt Test level, and he has ten points towards his Championship.

"Over the years I am very pleased to have had eleven Champions, but I am mainly happy about producing the wonderful family pets, the good shooting companions, several guide dogs for the blind, and some therapy dogs, too." Although too modest to mention it herself, Nancy is well-known for her excellent book *Legends in Labradors*, published in 1980, which profiled some of the great early kennels, both in Great Britain and America.

BEECHCROFT: MARY & MICHAEL WIEST

Mary writes: "Michael and I started breeding Labradors in 1969. We tried many different lines, never producing what we really wanted. However, a trip to England, a visit to Ballyduff, and we found the type of dog we wanted. The Beechcroft line is founded on one very special bitch, Am. Ch. Ballyduff Lark, who was by Eng. Ch. Timspring Sirius out of Spark of Ballyduff, and, incidentally, a full sister to Nancy Martin's Ballyduff Sparkler.

"Lark's impact on the Labrador breed in the United States is nothing short of incredible. Not only was she a producer, but her children and their children continue her legacy. When Lark passed away at ten years of age, she had fifty-seven Champions that went back to her, and a number of working titled dogs as well. This number continues to grow. She was co-owned with Chris Kofron, but lived with us. Lark not only produced quality puppies, but as importantly, she never produced a bad-hipped dog or any dogs with eye problems.

"Lark was only bred to English imports: Ch. Jayncourt Ajoco Justice, Ch. Powhatan Black Badger, Ch. Strinesdale Black Rod, and Ch. Eduny Jubilee Squire – each of these dogs line-bred

The Beechcroft type, typified by Ch. Beechcroft's Clover of O'Henry, dam of Ch. B. Triolum.

with her. We have doubled, even tripled, on her, producing the Beechcroft line of Labradors. Over generations we have brought in other lines, but always go back into our own lines to maintain our style of dog.

"The Beechcroft dogs have done extremely well at Specialties. We have generations of Specialty winners. Most of the Specialty shows are judged by breeders, usually from England. The entries are huge, so to get the nod is always a great honour. The working ability of our line has been proven in the Obedience ring, as well as in the Hunting Retriever tests. Many of our dogs are leading the blind. There have been twenty American Champions made up or bred by us, and the number in Canada and abroad is unknown. The kennel is kept to about ten to twelve dogs that are easily manageable by one person – the dogs run together during the day and all happily get on with one another. Now that we have moved to New England, there is more space to run the dogs on the property and to swim them in the pond, which is an added bonus."

BLACKTHORN: BARBARA SHAW
The kennel was established in 1970, and since that time eighteen American and two Canadian Champions have been made up. Barbara writes: "Blackthorn Labradors really came to life with the purchase of one special black dog, named Am. Can. Ch. Monarch's Black Arrogance CD, WC. He was able to win in the Specialty breed ring and produce Specialty winners. His offspring have won Regional and National Specialties consistently under American and foreign breeder judges alike. He has sired forty-plus Champions.

"Other dogs who have made a big impact on the Blackthorn kennels are Ch. Blackthorn Flaxenfield Ruby UD, WCA (my personal favourite bitch who could do it all) and Ch. Sailin' Cajun's Casanova CD (Ch. Monarch's Black Arrogance – Ch. Elysium's Sailin's Cat Ballou), co-owned with G. and S. Huntzinger, and sire of ten Champions to date. There have been several good brood bitches who have come to live at Blackthorn, but none quite so good as a yellow daughter out of Black Arrogance, named Ch. Starpoint Blackthorn Blonde CD. Every dog she has been bred to has produced beautiful Championship quality puppies. She is truly a chip of the

Ch. Starpoint Blackthorn Blonde CD: She has produced ten Champions to date.

prepotent block of her father. She finished her own Championship in three shows, and has produced ten Champions to date. Most recently her daughter, Blackthorn's Simply Irresistible, won Best in Sweeps at the 1992 Nationals (owner Judy Geist). Last but not least, my young yellow dog, a double grandson of my Black Arrogance, named Blackthorn's Imminent Thunder (co-owner Robert A. Gilchrist), will help keep the style and type true to the course."

BRIARY: CEYLON & MARJORIE BRAINARD
The kennel was established in 1966, with the purchase of Lockerbie Shillelagh (Ch. L. Sandylands Tarquin – Princess of Marlow), a bitch from Helen Warwick's Lockerbie kennel. The following year they returned to the same kennel to buy a black dog puppy, who was to put them on the map for all time. He was Ch. Lockerbie Brian Boru (Ch. L. Kismet – L. Pebblestreet Dinah).

Marjorie writes: "Both were outgoing – Brian had great dignity, whereas Sheila had none." She adds: "I must make it clear that both Brian and Sheila were from the Lockerbie kennels. The fact that they produced so well can only be attributed to Helen Warwick's discerning eye and devotion to the true Labrador. My success, whatever it was, was entirely due to her breeding. I was extremely lucky, and must confess that my role was to see that Brian was used well, and I think I did that."

This was a dog that was accepted early on by discerning breeders, on his own credentials. He was never campaigned to any great extent or publicised and promoted, as some are in print. To quote from C. Bede Maxwell in her tribute to him when he died, aged fifteen: "He was the good wine that needed no bush." He became the sire of over sixty Champions, just about equally split male, female, black and yellow. He was a dog who never wasted his time attempting to breed a bitch that was not to his mind 'ready'. The offspring from the Brian/Shillelagh matings were amazingly sound, passing all OFA and PRA testing. For this reason Marjorie has never hesitated to breed back into their line and double up on them.

Anther dog that had a hand in forming the kennels was Ch. Spendrock Anthony Adverse. When bred to Ch. B. Floradora (Brian/Follytower Cressida), there were only two survivors of the litter and they were Ch. B. Abbey Road and B. Allegra (Marjorie's personal favourite), who were very influential in future breedings. The dog, Ch. Lockerbie Stanwood Granada was another dog that had a strong influence on the kennel. Kennels that based their foundations on Briary have been: Finchingfield (Marilyn Reynolds), Elysium (Irene and Stuart Sprickman), Glencoe (Kim Livingston & Marynada Pohi), Sailin' (Beth & Art Davis).

Ch. Lockerbie Brian Boru: One of the most prolific and prepotent sires, with over sixty Champions to his credit.

BROADWAY: MARYANN & GENE CZERWINSKI

The kennel was established in 1976/77 with the purchase of Ch. Devonwoods Dolly WC (Poolstead/Springfield breeding). She was not only their foundation bitch and first Champion, but also their first Labrador. Dolly produced Champions from three of her four litters, as well as Obedience title-holders, and dogs trained to the gun. One of her sons, Ch. Broadways Shenandoah WC was BOS at LRC Potomac in 1985 – the same day he was photographed for the AKC video on the Labrador Retriever in which he is featured. His son, Ch. B. Oklahoma (out of Beechcrofts Golden Chance) finished his Championship at a very young age and was one of the youngest Labradors to receive a Group 2 (Point Show) placement, at the tender age of nine months.

Dolly's second litter, to Ch. Poolstead Private Member, produced Ch. B. Pajama Game and Ch. B. Sugar Babies (co-owned with Judy deSombre, becoming the Chester Valley Labradors' foundation bitch), and both became Champions before the age of two. 'PJ' had three litters, and a daughter, B. My One and Only, from Ch. Receiver of Cranspire (the only bitch to survive a litter of ten), resides with Maryann and Gene.

From Dolly's third litter, by Ch. Lawnwoods Brand Hatch, came two lovely black girls, Ch. B. Foxfire (co-owned with Eileen Trasmontana), and B. Dreamgirls – I awarded her Reserve Winners Bitch. She was retired shortly after that having gained 12 points to her Championship.

When Sugar Babies was mated to Ch. Caballero Tango, she produced two Champion bitches in Ch. Broadways Hallelujah Baby (co-owned with Maryann DeBalko), and Ch. Chester Valley Sugar Krystle, bred by Maryann and Judy deSombre. She was BOS at Potomac in 1990.

In 1988 the kennel imported a puppy, Ch. Martinstide Mass Appeal (Sh. Ch. Poolstead Pocket Picker – Sh. Ch. Polstead Pure Silk at Martinstide) from the Sidaways in England. Since his arrival Peal finished his American Championship, was BOS Sweepstakes at the LRC National in 1988 at

Ch. Chester Valley Sugar Krystle (left) and her full sister from a repeat mating, Ch. Broadway's Hallelujah Baby.

eleven months of age, and took the MJLRC Specialty BOB two years running, in 1990 and 1991. His progeny are starting to make their mark. In 1991 a four-year-old black male, Ch. Belnaboth East of Eden's Rex (a Beechcroft Edgewood Tomarc son), joined the kennel, and he is already making his mark at Specialties.

A total of fifteen Champions have either been bred, co-bred, or owned by the kennel, and they are always owner-handled. The kennel has been based on Poolstead stock from Didi Hepworth's kennel in England. Litters are only bred to add to their stock each year. Both Gene and Maryann have ensured that dogs are shot over, will retrieve a bird, and enjoy swimming and retrieving in the water.

CACAO: EDNA PILLOW

Edna is known to many as 'Mrs Chocolate' or 'The Chocolate Lady'. However, her first Labrador, 'Ace', from Trollgaard Kennels, was not chocolate; his dam was – and from the moment she saw the bitch, Edna was sold on the chocolate colour. It took three years before a chocolate pup was available, a male called 'Deuce' from Jo de Besche. A chocolate bitch from the Could Be kennels in Missouri eventually joined them. She was Could Be's Flaming Rock: of good pedigree, sound and delightful temperament, she went back to two dogs imported by Jean Willey from Mrs Cairns (Blaircourt, UK). These were Ch. Indian Valley Rob Roy and Ch. Indian Valley Raed Wulf – the latter being the first chocolate male Champion in the USA.

Flaming Rock's first litter was to Deuce, and a male pup called Jake was kept. He did quite well in the show ring for the times, and needed only three points to finish his Championship. This represented encouraging progress, as on one previous occasion she had been told by the judge: "the Chesapeakes are not being judged in this ring" – that was at one of her first Point shows with a chocolate. She was often confronted by people saying: "It looks like a Lab, what breed is it?", and she was often the only person exhibiting a chocolate, even at Specialty shows. However, Edna remained determined to have a chocolate Champion, and it has paid off. To date, she has had six chocolate Champions. For the next litter Flaming Rock was bred to Helen Warwick's Ch. Lockerbie Sandylands Tarquin; the pedigrees tied up nicely on the Blaircourt line. Cacao's Chief WilleyWulf (a double Raed Wulf grandson) was also purchased at this time. Willey was shown

Cacao's Mr Personality: One of Edna Pillow's many successful chocolate Labradors.

Chuck Tatham.

and acquired nine points, and is grandsire of Ch. Cacao's Chief Mini-Willey. Chief Willey did a lot to help the breeding programme. Through Helen Warwick, Edna was able to buy Ch. Puhs Miss Swiss Miss ('Flicka') from Britt Marie Brulin (Puhs) in Sweden. She was a beautiful bitch and quickly gained her Championship. Follytower Augustus was brought in from Margot Woolley (UK). He never quite finished his Championship, but he was the sire of eight chocolate Champions, and the sire of Anderscroft Brown Sugar, who was a very valuable brood bitch.

Over the years Edna has brought in new bloodlines and combined them with the original lines, and it has paid off. She has found it a great challenge and has been rewarded by the impact her kennel has made on the breed in the chocolate lines. It is her feeling that chocolates have made great strides in coat, tail, eye colour, substance and bone.

CAMPBELLCROFT: DON & VIRGINIA ('GINGER') CAMPBELL

Ginger writes: "The Campbellcroft Labradors have always done it all – it just took them some twenty-plus years for them to teach us! It started with 'Daisy', Ch. Agber Daisy of Campbellcroft CD, WC, of East Coast breeding. We had good advice as to who to mate her to out on the West Coast, and we used a yellow son of Brian Boru, Ch. Briary Trace of Brian CD, WC. We kept a yellow bitch who was to become Ch. C. Pede CD, WC. Her first litter was back to her grandsire, Brian. That litter produced Annie, a black bitch, who took Winners Bitch at the 1981 Golden Gate Labrador Retriever Club Specialty, and a black male called Angus, who nobody wanted, but he turned out to be Am. Can. Ch. C. Angus CD, WC! 'Gus' took BOB the day his sister took WB, while their grandmother, Daisy, took Veteran Bitch. Angus proceeded to win two more BOB at the GGLRC Specialties, as well as BOB at numerous other Specialties, including BOB at the National Specialty from Veteran Dog Class at nearly ten years old. He also turned out to be a great sire.

"When he was mated to a Group placing bitch, Ch. Breton Gate Omega Boom, we decided to have a puppy and went to choose from the five black bitches in the litter. I chose a yellow, but Don liked the black bitch that kept trying to retrieve my sock – with me in it – so we came home with her. She became 'Carrie' – Ch. Breton Gate Cairngorm CD, JH, WC. In 1989 and 1990 she was

The Campbellcroft Labradors with Don and Virginia Campbell: (front row, left to right) Carrie, Angus and Daisy; (back row) Topper, Pede and Piper.

top ranked conformation bitch in the nation. She has turned out to be a great lady, winning many BOB at Specialties, following in her father's footsteps. As a brood bitch she has produced a Specialty BOB winner, and has taken the Brood Bitch classes at so many Specialties – who knows what the future holds as she enters her Veteran years?

"We feel we have had incredible success with our Labradors – I would love to know why, but I suspect it is just dumb luck. We breed one or two litters a year, some years none, but have been favoured with beautiful, sound, loving companions."

CEDARWOOD: GARY A. & DIANN SULLIVAN

Diann writes: "The kennel really started in 1977, and so far seven American and nineteen Canadian Champions have attained their titles, with more dogs just needing minor points. Cedarwood Labradors began as a quest to selectively produce quality, sound dogs that would be prepotent producers. Our initial seven years was a search for quality foundation animals. Most of the early purchases attained Championship titles, Field and Obedience certificates, but lacked soundness or necessary type, and therefore did not become part of our breeding programme. Ultimately it was based on combinations of Am. Can. Ch. Monarchs Black Arrogance CD, WC, Ch. Lockerbie Brian Boru WC, and the Ballyduff line.

"Our foundation bitch is Sailin's Cedarwood Pride, who is a daughter of Arrogance, and a granddaughter of Brian. She has produced good sound offspring from line-breedings that were gradually tightened. She herself, and then her daughters and granddaughters were crossed to Ch. Cedarwoods Clearlake Classic, who is a half-brother and half-sister on a son of Ch. Ballyduff Johnson (UK import). Temperaments are full of attitude and very willing to please, retrieving ability is all there, as are the good coats with the hard feel to the hand, that is improving with each generation. Our policy of being selective with animals joining the breeding programme has paid off with soundness and type coming through. Our dogs have worked as companion gun dogs and handicapped assistance dogs as well as Obedience competitors. Produce have been awarded Specialty Winners Dog & Bitch, BOB, Best Puppy in Show, Sweepstakes Winners, and Obedience

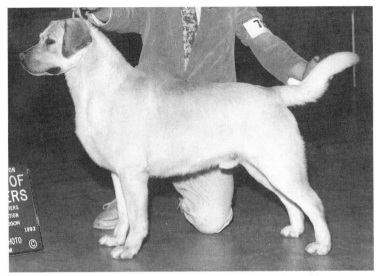

Am. Can. Ch. Cedarwoods Clearlake Classic. A typical Cedarwood Labrador shows sound temperament, good coat, and always has the ability to retrieve.

Callea Photo.

High-In Trials. Our hope for the future is to assist newcomers to the breed through sharing learned information, and to encourage the improvement of the breed."

CHELONS: CHERYL & LON OSTENSON

This is a small kennel, established in 1978. Cheryl and Lon keep no more than nine dogs at a time and breed just two or three litters a year, but they have produced eighteen Champions to date. The prime aim is to breed a good-looking Labrador that goes as well in the field as in the show ring – beauty plus brains. 'Nikki' was their foundation bitch (Cobbs Yellow Frenzy CDX, WC); she excelled in field and in Obedience and proved to be an excellent brood bitch.

She was bred four times, producing twenty pups, and nine went on to become Champions. Nikki's offspring include: Am. Can. Ch. C. Firestorm WC (National Specialty BOB Winner), Ch. C. Cascade Hunter CD (National Specialty Best of Winners), Ch. C. Columbia Ice WC (Regional Specialty Winners Dog), Am. Can. Ch. Vallivue Chelons Mr Levi WC, CD (a multiple Group 1 winning dog), and Ch. C. Sleepless Knight CD, JH, AWC (a Specialty BOB Winner). All were nationally ranked in the top ten. Nikki was listed as a top-producing brood for 1990 and 1991.

The line has continued with Nikki's children, grandchildren and great-grandchildren. For example: Ch. Chelons Sleepless Knight has produced two Regional Specialty BOB Winners; his daughter, Ch. C. Satin McCoy, produced four puppies from her first litter who went to a Regional Specialty, and all earned placements, one going Reserve Winner Dog, and one going Best Puppy in Show.

CHUCKLEBROOK: RED & DIANE PILBIN

Chucklebrook was established in 1967 and founded on a bitch called Ch. Spendrock Bohemia Champagne. She was a daughter of the famous Ch. Spendrock Banner WC, a bitch of Sandylands breeding. Chucklebrooks have made up approximately twenty Champions since then.

Champagne was well-known in her own right as a showgirl, and later as a producer. She won at such prestigious events as Westminster and the National Shows, and became the Top Producing Bitch in the US in 1976. Today every Labrador bred in the kennel can trace back to her. Champagne was first bred to Eng. Am. Ch. Ballyduff Seaman. That breeding produced Ch. C.

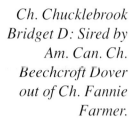

Ch. Chucklebrook Bridget D: Sired by Am. Can. Ch. Beechcroft Dover out of Ch. Fannie Farmer.

Helen, who combined beauty and hunting ability. This clarified the direction the kennel was to take, breeding on Ballyduff and Sandylands lines. The next generation produced the kennel's first chocolate, Ch. C. Fannie Farmer (Ch. Sandylands Markwell – Helen). She completed her Championship at just sixteen months, at a time when winning with a chocolate was very difficult. Fannie produced very well, and when bred to Mary Wiest's Ballyduff-line bred dog, Am. Can. Ch. Beechcroft Dover, she produced Ch. C. Danmark and Ch. C. Bridget D, both Specialty sweeps winners. Another quality chocolate, C. Mousefeathers, was produced when Fannie and Eng. Am. Can. Ch. Lindall Mastercraft breeding was used. The yellow side of the family relied heavily on Sandylands breeding, through some of the better known American producers such as Markwell and Brian Boru. In 1980 Ch. Follytower Singalong was purchased from Margot Woolley (UK). He was a bit of an outcross – a sound dog, who eventually became the top USA sire in 1985.

Chucklebrook today tries to maintain a small kennel where each dog receives its deserved individual attention. This means trying to keep to twelve dogs, and producing three or four litters a year. The Chucklebrook Labs now serve as guide dogs, therapy dogs, sniffer dogs, hunting companions (and trialers), as well as adored family members.

EDGEWOOD: MARK & MARY HAUSMAN
Established in 1976, this kennel's unusual foundation was based on a stud dog as opposed to a brood bitch. This was Ch. Beechcrofts Edgewood Tomarc. Every dog in the kennel is either a child or grandchild of his. As the house dog, Tomarc starts taking care of the puppies at a very young age, and while Mark cleans out the box, Tomarc is tending the pups! Tomarc marks his offspring with his excellent personality and good looks. So far he has produced breed Champions, Obedience Champions, tracking title holders and gun dogs, in all three colours. With such good-looking children Tomarc has won numerous Stud Dog Classes and Brace classes, particularly with Am. Can. Ch. Belnaboths Tom of Edgewood.

Currently in the kennel are the stud dogs, Tomarc, Tom of E. Full Tanker, and the brood bitches Dickendalls Raz-Ma-Taz, Beechcroft Believe-It, Poppyfields Tina of Edgewood, E. Black

Ch. Beechcrofts Edgewood Tomarc: The foundation stud dog of the Edgewood kennel, pictured after a day's hunting.

Shimmeree and E. Wild Lady Rose. All exhibit the type and personality of Tomarc, and all have been shown successfully in the breed ring, with placements at major Specialty shows in both the USA and Canada. Most of the kennel is major-pointed in the USA. In addition, all the dogs perform well in hunting situations, preferring duck hunting where they can swim throughout the day – and no matter how cold the water or long the retrieve, they always get the job done.

FOLKLAUR: LAURA DEDERING

Folklaur started in 1978 with the arrival of a promising nine-week black pup bitch from Marilyn Reynolds, who became Ch. Finchingfield Folklaur CGC, TDI (Ch. Briary Brendan of Rainell – Ch. Briary Bustle). It took Lorna six years of studying pedigrees and watching at shows before she

Ch. Finchingfield Folklaur (Ch. Briary Brendan – Ch. Briary Bustle): Arrived at the Folklaur kennels as a nine-week-old pup.

chose her puppy 'Raven', as she was called, and this bitch finished her Championship at the LRC of Greater Boston Show, winning her third major. In 1992, at the age of fourteen years, she has gained her AKC Canine Good Citizen Award and Therapy Dog International Certification.

Raven became the foundation of the Folklaur line, producing four breed Champions, a Specialty winner, and other pointed offspring. One of her daughters, Ch. Folklaur Pandora, was my Winners Bitch at the LRC of Central Connecticut when I judged there in 1986. Her other Champion offspring were: F. Aurora, F. Orion of Talmarc, F. Echo of Wingfeather. Aurora (Raven – Ch. Sandylands Markwell of Lockerbie) was the first home-bred Champion and is the dam of Ch. F. Barry of Rainell. F. Luna (Raven – Ch. Northwood Sandman) is proving to be a good brood, being the dam of Ch. F. Moonlite.Several of Laura's dogs have been donated to the Seeing Eye and are currently working with their blind owners. Starting in 1991 the first Folklaur to Folklaur breedings took place, producing several promising youngsters as a result of doubling up on her foundation bitch, who remains a tribute to the Briary, Lockerbie and Sandylands lines behind her.

HARBORTOP: NINA MANN

Nina writes. "My kennel was established in 1977, only keeping six bitches and two dogs, and until recently only breeding one or two litters a year. I have, to date, made up eleven Champions. I was very lucky in the quality of my two foundation bitches, Am. Can. Ch. Follytower Jenny and SHR Chucklebrook Western Magic CD, WC. Magic gained both her majors, but was prevented from finishing by an elbow injury.

Rocheby Joseph's Coat JH: Now winning well for the Harbortop kennel.

"Both bitches have produced excellent type, temperament and field ability. Their progeny have been in demand for good-looking hunting dogs. One of Jenny's grandson's will finish his Master Hunter title this year. I am now breeding fourth generation offspring of both bitches, staying with similar backgrounds, in particular the Kupros and Lindall lines that are over here. Three years ago I purchased from the Hopkinsons (Rocheby, UK) a young chocolate dog of similar lines, Rocheby Joseph's Coat JH, who I feel will complement my line."

HENNINGS MILL: JOHN & DOROTHY (DOT) GALVIN

Started in 1973, the kennel is based on the typey chocolate bitch Bradking Beverly (Ch. Fabracken Comedy Star – Bradking Cassandra) imported from Mr Kelley in the UK. She went on to be the

Scartho Frost: Known as 'the Boss', sired by Eng. Ch. Simandem Kings Neptune out of Eng. Ch. Scartho Briar Crest.

dam of four Champions, and three of her daughters and one son live at Hennings Mill today.

From Anne Taylor, John and Dot next imported a dog, known as 'Czar', who was to become Ch. Chafern Court Star of Fabracken (Eng. Am. Ch. Receiver of Cranspire – Fabracken Daydreamer). Czar was the number two producer of Champions in 1990, second only to his sire, who now resides in France. Czar's influence is now seen all across the country. Crossed with Beverly lines, he has produced some good dogs for the kennels, namely H.M. Crown Jewel 'Cloney' and four of her offspring, H.M. Crown Comic, Black Comedy, Crown Comedian and Credible Comic. Cloney is also responsible for H.M. Hunt Club Hanna and Ch. H.M. Sommit Ruff Gem.

When Czar was bred into the Eng. Am. Can. Ch. Lindall Mastercraft lines through Lindall Miss Holly, she produced Ch. H.M. Caruso, who is making a name for himself. Her daughter, H.M. Witchcraft, when bred to Czar produced Ch. H.M. Centre Court Ashley. When Miss Holly was bred to Ch. Jayncourt Ajoco Justice, the outcome was Ch. H.M. Justus. H.M. Capricious Lady (Justice – Balrion Wilful Lady) produced Ch. Falon of H.M. and H.M. Talimar Tessa, who have gone on to produce strength and soundness, encouraging John and Dot to pursue this combination of lines further through the 'Boss', Scartho Frost (Eng. Sh. Ch. Simandem Kings Neptune – Eng. Ch. Scartho Briar Crest), and they look forward to seeing what he will produce.

The original older lines have combined well with the UK lines to produce approximately twenty Champions bred by H.M., going back to their top producer Ch. Country Place O'Hennings Mill to the latest Ch. H.M. Czar Trooper. Ch. Hampshire Calypso (Eng. Ch. Sandylands Newinn Columbus – Novacroft Melting Moment) produced Ch. H.M. Royal Calif, Ch. Valleywood Romany Riannon CD, and Ch. Valleywood Corker O'Tabatha. Thus Calypso will be found in foundation pedigrees of other kennels in the USA.

HIGHLANDS: GEORGE & LILLIAN KNOBLOCH

George and Lillian share their love of Labradors. They believe in a good-looking, genetically sound dog that can both work and show, and this they have achieved. Twelve Champions have been made up since they started in 1976.

They have had great success with their chocolates, nationally ranking their first chocolate Champion, Ch. Highlands Bronze Chieftain, who was number one chocolate dog in the USA in three different years. It was his chocolate son, Am. Can. Ch. Highlands Chivas Regal who was

Ch. Coalcreek's Gimme A Break: Number One Labrador (all systems) in 1988.

Winners Dog in 1991 at one of the largest East Coast Specialty shows under Margot Woolley (Follytower). George and Lillian's desire to work with yellows led to the purchase of 'Tanker' – Ch. Coalcreek's Gimme A Break – who within a short time of coming to Highlands became the number one Lab (all systems) for 1988. He produced several Champions, including a daughter, Ch. Highlands Break of Dawn, who was the number one Specials Bitch for 1989. Tanker has also sired many guide dogs for the blind. I was pleased to award him BOB when I judged him at Old Dominion Kennel Club in 1988. Highland have had several black Champions including Ch. Sir Keith of Kimvalley, who was the number one black dog in 1985, and sire of their top-winning Obedience Trial Champion, Highlands Uptown Girl WC, Can. CD.

JANROD, JANWOOD: JANIS I. GRANNEMANN

The kennel's first Labrador was purchased in 1973, but it was not until 1979 that the first litter was bred and the first Champion made up – since then a further twenty-two Champions have followed. It is unusual to have two kennel names, and this is because Janis shares the dogs with "two wonderful men". One is her husband, Rod, and the other is US and Olympic National Shotgun Coach, Lloyd Woodhouse. The primary goal is to produce a typey working dog. Rod likes the easy-going, good-looking family dog and 'Woody' wants the dog that can really hunt. After many hours of research they settled on two lines – Ballyduff and Shamrock Acres. They feel the time was well spent, and they could not be happier with the temperaments and working ability that they are getting in their dogs. The foundation bitch, JanRods Sunhill Cindra, was a cross of both

Ch. JanWood's Secret Agent: BISS Winner.

American Shamrock Acres line and the English Ballyduff line. She was a granddaughter of Ch. Shamrock Acres Light Brigade, and a great granddaughter of Ballyduff Powhatan Gale. They continued to breed on both of these lines. Four generations of Specialty winners have come from Cindra. Three Specialty winners came from Cindra and Ch. Franklin's Golden Mandigo (a Light Brigade son). A daughter of this breeding, Ch. JanWood's Lady Perkins WC, was bred to their Swedish import Ch. Mallard's Flying Cloud of JanRod WC. 'Zack', as they called him, is a Ch. Ballyduff Fergus son. This breeding produced the BISS winner Ch. JanWoods Secret Agent. JanRod's Lady Solitare was Best in Sweeps at the Southern California Specialty at ten months. She is out of Ch. JanWood's Mountain Mist WC – a sister to Secret Agent – and Ch. Beechcroft's Citadel. Citadel is from Mary Wiest's kennel, which is based on the Ballyduff line.

KELLYGREEN: SALLY KELLY
The two original black bitches were bought in 1964 as family pets/hunting dogs, but in 1969 came the first chocolate. Although the kennel produces all three colours, the chocolates have always been a challenge. Although pleased with the versatility of her Labs, Sally wanted to improve type and get a more out-going temperament. In 1982 she went on her first trip to England – to Crufts – where she met Janice Prichard (Charway) and booked a pup from her chocolate bitch Sally Brown,

Ch. Charway Maverick: Imported from the UK.

and so Charway John Brown came to America. Sally feels he made an important contribution to upgrading the chocolate Labs in the USA. Since then over thirty dogs have been imported from the UK, and many have been important to the kennel. They include: Ch. Charway Maverick, Am. Can. Ch. Charway Crofter, Ch. Barnaby of Charway, Blondella Beau Ranger, Rocheby Straw Boater, and Balrion Red Alert.

The kennel has twenty-five retired dogs (of 8-14 years), twelve English Bred Stud dogs, and about twenty young pups and bitches. They all run together loose on their 110 acre farm. Pups are raised in the home, and all adult dogs come in and they all get on beautifully together.

Kellygreen Labs are actively involved in all jobs that the Labrador does, and the hope is to continue to breed sound, typey dogs as close to the Standard as possible. The kennel, to date, has made up ten Champions.

Ch. Killingworth Thunderson: Sire of twenty-seven Champions.

KILLINGWORTH – LORRAINE ROBBENHAAR-TAYLOR

The kennel originated in 1959 on Field Trial lines, and over the next few years developed an interest in show dogs that could work. From that time, the foundation stock for all the Killingworths were Am. Can. Ch. Annwyn's Jack O' Diamonds (chosen because his pedigree contained a number of English lines and several early Field Trial Chs.), and Ch. Windrow's Samantha. Samantha was only bred once, and a son, K. Black Brant, was kept. A daughter of Samantha's, Snipe, was also only bred once in 1970, and when mated to Ch. Torquay's Scorpio (a Jack O' Diamond's grandson) the litter included the dog who was to do so much for the kennel, Ch. Killingworth's Thunderson. Thunderson was determined not to be sold – he always hid under bushes or under the couch when potential purchasers called. However, he became a Champion by fourteen months of age. In fact, he was not keen on the show ring; he would only go around the ring once, and he was known to occasionally play 'dead dog' in the ring. But he loved to work and adored puppies, dropping tennis balls into their box for them to play with. He was the sire of twenty-seven Champions. He was also a very special dog to Lorraine. He was only ten years old when he died in 1980, and is still sorely missed.

Ch. Clemmsen of Killingworth was the only chocolate to win the Breed at Westminster. This dog was conceived at an airport (Jan Churchill had flown in with Eng. Am. Ch. Lawnwoods Hot Chocolate) and was whelped in a hurricane (no power for three days, pups whelped in front of the fire), but he proved a real winner for the kennel. A devoted companion, he was important because he is behind all Lorraine's chocolates and some of her blacks. He produced several foundation bitches for others, including the outstanding Ch. K Clementine (Sue Ostermuller).

Ch. Kupros Spartacus was brought in from the Harts (UK) in 1981, and he has proved an important and prepotent sire over the past decade, passing on his type, soundness, and outstanding temperament for show and work. He is the sire of fifteen American Champions, with some still to finish. His bloodlines have been woven in with Thundersons with great success, and he has also mixed well with Clemmsen lines. A great show dog, a Specialty winner, and a wonderful companion, he also sired one of the first bitches to attain her Master Hunter title.

Lorraine recently started judging the breed. She has, therefore, cut back on breeding, but she has kept several young dogs going back to Samantha through Thunder and Spartacus. To date, thirty-five Champions carry the Killingworth prefix, and the studs and broods have been responsible for well over one hundred Champions not carrying the 'K' prefix.

Ch. Lobuff Missouri Breaks: Number Two Lab in the US in 1987.

LOBUFF: COL. & MRS J. H. WEISS, LISA & EUGENE AGRESTA

Lisa writes: "As a family, the first two dogs we owned were from Ann Carpenter; a black male in 1963 called 'Lobo', followed in 1966 by a yellow male, 'Buffy' – their breeding went back to Joan Read's Chidley line. They were shown and we had lot a fun, as well as becoming hooked on the sport. All of us Weiss sisters – and there were five of us – enjoyed the junior showmanship classes. Tragically, the two dogs were killed in a car accident in 1969, but are still remembered in our prefix, 'Lobuff'.

"In 1969 Ch. Gunslingers Tawny Boy was bought in from Bill Metz (he was out of his top winning Ch. Lewisfield Gunslinger) and we purchased a black bitch from Jan Churchill. She was to become Ch. Spendrock Cognac (Ch. Lockerbie Goldentone Jenser – Ch. Spendrock Banner WC), our foundation bitch. The first Lobuff homebred Champion, Ch. Lobuff's Dandy Lion, came from these two. Cognac was bred twice to Ch. Spendrock Heatheredge Mariner (a Ch. Sandylands Mark son), and these breedings produced Ch. Lobuff Sea Faring Banner and Ch. Lobuff Tequila Sunrise. Almost every dog we have today goes back to these two.

"Cognac was bred five times and produced Champions from every litter. Ch. Lobuff's Gandy Dancer (by Ch. Almars' Bobo Quivari) was Reserve Winners bitch at the Labrador National in 1977 under Mary Roslin Williams. Ch. L. Tequila Sunrise and Ch. L. Sea Faring Banner were very special to my father, and they produced some wonderful offspring. Ch. L. Missouri Breaks was number two Lab in the US in 1987 and a Specialty winner. She was best Puppy LRCP under Jo Coulson in 1985. Her sister, Ch. L. Sundown at Kerrymark (co-owned with Cavan and Karen Acheson), was also a Specialty winner (both sired by Ch. Northwood Sandman). Banner bred to Ch. Beechcroft Skylark produced Ch. Beechcroft C'Brook Seaworthy, a Specialty Winner, and Ch. Beechcroft-Lobuff Sky Chief. Father and both sons have been top producers for the guide dogs for the blind. In 1992 Ch. Lobuff's Bare Necessities, sired by Ch. Dickendall Ruffy SH (also a Banner great-great-grandson), was the number two Labrador in the US. He was the 1991 National Sweepstakes winner. "Lobuff is still a family project. We are a small kennel, usually keeping eight to ten dogs. Nowadays, only my Dad and I go to the shows to judge and exhibit, but we couldn't do it without the help and support of my mother and my husband who take care of the children and dogs left at home – it's a real team effort. Twenty-three Champions have been made up since we started."

NORTHWOOD: KAREN & CHARLES SCHULTZE

In 1975 a black bitch was purchased as a family companion; the family enjoyed showing the puppy at matches and so decided to buy two more bitches in. As they had just moved to a wooded area on the north shore of Long Island, the kennel name "Northwood" was chosen as it seemed appropriate. In the first four years of showing Karen and Charlie made up three Champions: Briary Birch, Williston Jollymuff Jubal, and Finchingfield Fantasia. Charlie trained Birch and Jubal towards their Working Certificate, and the two Schultze daughters, Janet and Patti, competed in Junior Showmanship with Jubal and Fantasia. Both Jubal and Fantasia are Specialty winners, and Jubal is a Group winner. Fantasia was bred twice to Ch. Sandylands Markwell of Lockerbie, and produced a total of five Champions. From her other four litters she produced four more Champions. One of her sons, Ch. Northwood Sandman, was Best of Opposites in Sweeps at the Mid-Jersey Specialty, at ten months of age, and he finished his Championship with three majors, at seventeen months old. He has sired numerous American and Canadian Champions and many Specialty winners, as well as having over thirty of his progeny working as guide dogs. During the years the kennel has had other stud dogs from Canada and the West Coast, and they have all made their mark on the Labradors that have been bred. The most recent is Am. Can. Ch. Cedarwoods By Design, who is co-owned with Susan Ostermuller. An impressive black, at only two years old he is a breed and Specialty winner. His offsp-ring look most promising. To date, the kennel record stands at fourteen Champions made up from fifteen litters.

Ch. Northwood Sandman: Sire of numerous Champions, as well as providing over thirty guide dogs for the blind.   John L. Ashbey.

SIMERDOWN: ROB & LINDA VAUGHN

Linda writes: "We established Simerdown Labradors in 1970, and our small kennel of around twelve dogs is made up mostly of bitches. We bring males in from lines that interest us, as I enjoy showing males, and, being in a somewhat isolated part of the country, it is good to have males to

Ch. Simerdown's Wanda: Representing the kennel's aim to breed sound, good-looking Labradors with the brains and temperament to work in the field, or as service dogs.

use without having to ship out all the time. My goal is to breed a sound, beautiful, lovable Labrador, who should be able to work in the field, or as a service dog, or be a wonderful pet – and be handsome enough for the show ring.

"I have used basically American lines, such as Lockerbie, Brian Boru, Monarchs Black Arrogance and others, and I have added such English names as Sandylands, Marbra, and Ballyduff, over the years. I line-breed most of the time and outcross to dogs that are line-bred for the features my line lacks. We are now on the fourth and fifth generation of Simerdowns. I only add to my kennel when I have a bitch puppy that is a definite step forward, or when I buy a stud dog prospect. Thirty-seven Champions have been bred since we started in 1970."

TABATHA: CAROL HEIDL
Carol writes: "The Tabatha kennel was established in 1969. Through the years, striving for the conformation I preferred, we did Obedience and Tracking. One of my girls, Ch. Tabatha's Dodena of Franklin CD, TD, WCX, tracked and found a lost retarded child eight hours after he had gone missing. Hunting requires an athletic dog, and this helped me to establish the temperament I love. As with others starting a kennel, I went through many dogs that I dearly loved but were not the calibre to base a kennel on.

My two most influential bitches were a black, Ch. Tabatha's Corker O'Valleywood WC (by Ch. Hampshire's Calypso), and a yellow, Ch. Tabatha's Valleywood Decoy WC (by Ch. Driftswoods Celebration). Both of these bitches were bred by Christine Kofron and were out of Ch. Valleywoods Kannonball Kate (Ch. Jayncourt Ajoco Justice – Ch. Ballyduff Lark). Corker and Decoy were Specialty winners and have produced multiple Specialty winners for me. Now their grandchildren and great-grandchildren are winning Specialties. All in my kennel, save one, go back to these two retired girls. I have one English import, Cambremer Roxanna, from Les and Joyce Brabban, who has done extremely well at the US Specialties."

Ch. Tabatha's Revelry WC (Ch. Borador's Ridgway Reflection – Ch. Tabatha's Sparkler WC).

TERACROFT: SALLY SASSER & BEVERLY SHAVLIK

As breeders, Teracroft is a relatively new venture, although both Sally and Beverly have owned and loved the breed for twenty-five years. In the early eighties they decided to pool their resources and build a modern kennel facility, which was completed in 1985. Firstly, they imported a yellow bitch from the Palmers (Jayncourt, UK). Penny was bred to Ajoco Justice, but unfortunately only had one pup. Later they imported the black dog who was to become Ch. Jayncourt the Professor (Ch. Kupros Master Mariner – Jayncourt Earth Angel), and the yellow bitch, Ch. Jayncourts Dolly Bird, sired by the Professor out of Jayncourt Peace. So far, 'Prof' has four Champions to his credit. In 1989 Ch. Aroscas Sophisticated Lady joined the kennel, imported from Gunilla Andersson in Sweden. 'Sophie' was Winners Bitch at Miami Valley Specialty under Heather Wiles-Fone (Heatherbourne, UK). Sophie was bred to Ch. Dickendall's A'Hoy (Ch. D. Moorwood Tiger CD, JH – D. A-Ha), who was purchased from Kendall Herr. Puppies from this litter look most promising. To date, eleven Champions have been bred by this kennel.

Ch. Jayncourt The Professor: Proving to be a successful sire.

Ch. Valleywood Nighthawk (pictured as a puppy): A multiple Specialty BOB winner.

Ashbey Photography.

VALLEYWOOD: CHRIS KOFRON

The foundation of this kennel centred around two bitches, Ch. Valleywood's Kannonball Kate (Ch. Jayncourt Ajoco Justice – Ch. Ballyduff Lark) co-bred with Mary Wiest, and Chucklebrook Cassandra (Ch. Sandylands Markwell of Lockerbie – Ch. Chucklebrook Champagne Mist, bred by Diane Pilbin.

Chris writes: "Kate produced offspring very similar to herself – very balanced; good movers, who were sound and showy. Three of her offspring were Specialty winners. Cassie produced lots of substance, coat, angulation and pretty heads. The majority of my dogs today go back to these original two through Katie's grandson, Ch. Valleywood Kodiak, and Cassie's daughter, Valleywood Crow Haven Fiddle (Ch. Elysium's Citizen Kane – Chucklebrook Cassandra). Among them are my favourites Ch. Valleywood Nighthawk (Ch. Marshland Blitz – Valleywood Crow Haven Fiddle), a multiple Specialty BOB winner, and his daughter, Valleywood Nightmoves (who is out of Valleywoods Catch The Spirit). Since the kennel started in 1977, approximately twenty-five Champions have been made up."

VENETIAN: CHARLOTTE VENEZIANO

Since the kennel bought in its first Lab in 1964, some thirteen Champions have gained their titles. The first Labrador, Venetian Lady, was primarily a family pet and hunting companion. Her lines were based on Diant (English) and Chidley (American) on her sire's side, and on Whygin (American) on the dam's side. As fate would have it, a neighbour was heavily involved in showing German Shepherds, and, impressed by 'Lady', he persuaded Charlotte to attend some dog shows. The more Charlotte learned, the more interested she became in attempting to breed her bitch, and Venetian's Lady is behind all the bitches that she is presently showing.

Venetian's Mijan Drummer Boy: Best Winners and BOB at the Mid-Jersey Specialty on the same day that he finished his Championship.

Wm. Gilbert Inc.

Living on the South Shore of Long Island poses limits on the number of dogs that can be kept in harmony with the surroundings. Therefore, only one or two dogs are run on at a time. This takes a lot of patience because they do not always live up to their early promise, and time marches on. Charlotte is a speech therapist, and all her dogs work as therapy dogs for handicapped pre-school children. Both the staff and the children enjoy her visits with the dogs.

One of Charlotte's favourite dogs was Ch. Venetian's Mijan Drummer Boy, a beautiful black, who finished his Championship by taking Winners Dog at the Mid-Jersey Specialty Show, and crowned the day by going Best Winners and Best of Breed. He is behind the bitches that are currently being shown. Probably the most prepotent stud dog in the kennel is Ch. Hennings Mills Master Blend, bred by the Galvins. He is a sturdy, typey chocolate who gives himself to his kids, and is the sire of the bitches that they are presently showing.

WINDFALL: ANNIE & RON COGO

A relatively new kennel, it got going in 1985 with the purchase of two young bitches. The first was a three-month yellow from Chris Kofron (Valleywood), who was to become Ch. Valleywood Windfall Chelsea (Int. Ch. Sandylands Rip Van Winkle – Valleywood Crow Haven Fiddle). Chelsea has been a prolific brood bitch, producing forty-six pups from four litters! The second acquisition was a black bitch, Ch. Tabatha's Windfall Abbey (Ch. Borador's Lord Travis – Ch. Tabatha's Valleywood Decoy WC). Abbey went through some awful stages on the way to adulthood. At one stage her nickname was 'Gator' – she had such a long muzzle; but finally it all came together, and at eleven months she took her first points, a four point major.

The rest is history. Abbey's career took off with her finishing her Championship at the Potomac Specialty, and going on to win numerous Best of Breeds at Specialties. She has produced three Champions from two litters, to date. Her daughter, Ch. W. Hurricane Karla, has a son out of English import Lindall Chase, who won the Bred-by class at Mid-Jersey; later the same month, at only fourteen months of age, he took a four point major first time in the All-breed ring. His name is Windfall's Black Bart.

Ch. Tabatha's Windfall Abbey WC, WCX, JH: A multiple BOB winner at Specialties and has produced three Champions to date.

Chuck Tatham.

Ch. W. Profit for Sunspots, an Abbey son, is now working for his JH and Obedience titles with his owners Lisa Keplar and Frances Davis. Abbey's third Champion is Ch. W. Carbon Copy, owned by Celeste Arpke. A fourth daughter, W. Win Storm (Ch. Beechcrofts Citadel), has both majors and three legs towards her Junior Hunter title.

Chapter Eight

THE LABRADOR IN CANADA

By Pat and Mike Lanctot

The Canadian Labrador Retriever owes a great deal to its early breeders and enthusiasts, and honourable mentions must go to Frank Jones (Annwyn) of Minesing, Ontario, Hugh Crozier (Crozier) of Winnipeg, Manitoba, and Bob Blythe (Blythe) of Cobourg, Ontario. Without the forethought of these knowledgeable and dedicated individuals, the breed would not be where it is today. In the following pages we have credited a few of the many breeders who have made significant contributions to the promotion of the breed in Canada. To accomplish this we will travel from coast to coast, starting appropriately with the Atlantic east coast and Newfoundland. Newfoundland was the home of the controversial St. John's Waterdog which many believe to be the origins of the Labrador Retriever.

NEWFOUNDLAND

In St. John's the WATERDOG Labradors are owned by Mike and Lynn Woods. Established in 1972, their foundation consisted of two dogs purchased from England, Am. Can. Champion Powhatan Black Badger, CDX and Ch. & Ob. Trial Champion Ballyduff Storm, UD, WC. The pride of the Woods' kennel is their homebred Am. Can. Ch. Waterdog's Raine Storm, CDX (a Storm daughter) who was owner-handled to Best of Breed at the Mid Jersey Labrador Specialty in 1981 over an entry of 220. Another dog of note from this successful kennel is Am. Can. Ch. Waterdog's Raine Dancer (a Raine Storm son). In the nineties the Woods have cut back considerably on breeding, as Mike has become a popular licensed judge and has been spending much of his time judging Labrador Specialties in Canada, the US and Europe.

NOVA SCOTIA

Moving westward from Newfoundland to Fall River, Nova Scotia, is our own EBONYLANE kennel. Established in 1974, the Ebonylane foundation consisted of Best in Show winner and producer, Am. Can. Ch. Shamrock Acres Ebonylane Ace CDX, WC. The most cherished award won by Ace was the Neville trophy, awarded in 1980 by the Labrador Owners Club for the top all round Labrador in Show, Field and Obedience.

Best in Show winner Am. Can. Ch. Hollyhock Sam (an Ace son on lease to Ebonylane) was Top Labrador in Canada in 1980. Ch. Ebonylane's Shadow (an Ace daughter) when bred to Australian import, Ch. Astroloma Joshua (line-bred on Ch. Sandylands Tan) produced our pride and joy, Am. Can. Ch. Ebonylane's Aslan – Canada's top-producing sire of all-time with over one hundred Champions to his credit in fifty breedings. Aslan was instrumental in Ebonylane becoming the top

*Am. Can. Ch.
Ebonylane's Aslan,
sire of over 100
Champions. He is
the top Champion-
producing sire of all
time in Canada.*

*Am. Can. Ch.
Ebonylane's
Buccaneer Gold, the
top winning
Labrador of all time
in Canada*

Champion producing kennel of all time in Canada. This combination of Josh and Shadow also produced Am. Can. Ch. Ebonylane's Midnite Bandit (multiple Best of Breed winner at Specialties in the USA), Am. Can. Ch. Ebonylane's Caviar (winner of the Puppy Sweeps at the American National Labrador Specialty in 1981), and Am. Can. Ch. Ebonylane's Northern Trooper CD (a back-to-back Group winner in the USA). Of special pride to us is that we produced the Top

Labrador in Breed in Canada in 1984 (Am. Can. Ch. Ebonylane's Buccanneer Gold) and the Top Labrador in Breed in the USA in the same year (Am. & Can. Ch. Ebonylane's Yellow Poplar). Both these top dogs were out of the same bitch, Am. Can. Ch. Ebonylane's Cotton Candy Bucky was sired by Aslan, and Pops was sired by Bandit. In 1983 we purchased Ch. Waterdog's Raider of Ebonylane, CD. Raider bred to Aslan daughters produced many Specialty, Breed and Obedience winners, including multiple High in Trial winner Ch. and Obedience Trial Ch. Ebonylane's Kira Am. UD WCI, who was top Obedience Labrador in Canada in 1991.

We operate a small kennel of eight to ten adults, and we have produced sixty-five litters over eighteen years. We attribute much of our success to the co-operation and support received from our puppy owners. Since our move from Hemmingford, Quebec, to Fall River, Nova Scotia in 1989, we have semi-retired from breeding to allow more time for travel and judging.

NEW BRUNSWICK
Moving westward to Hampton, we find the HUNTSDOWN Labradors, owned by Anne Fiona Mugglestone. Established in 1977, mainly on British lines, the cornerstone of this kennel is Am. Can. Bermuda Ch. Eduny Jubilee Squire Am. Can. CD, sire of Am. Can. Ch. Huntsdown Jubilation (winner of three all breed Best in Shows), Am. Can. Ch. Huntsdown Valleywood Spice (Winners Dog at the Miami Valley Labrador Retriever Specialty) and Am. Can. Ch. Huntsdown Buddha Beechcroft (winner of the 1986 Can. National Labrador Retriever Specialty and Best of Breed at the Labrador Retriever Club of Greater Boston Specialty.

Another dog of note from a different line was multiple Best in Show winner Ch. Covehead Mack. These and many other Huntsdown dogs have won numerous awards at Canadian and American Specialty shows. There are also many Seeing Eye and Arson detection dogs bearing the Huntsdown prefix.

QUEBEC
In La Bell Province at St-Gilles (county of Lotbiniere), we find the CHABLAIS Labradors, owned by Madeleine Charest and Jean-Louis Blais. Established in 1979, their breeding program is focused mainly on British, American and Ebonylane lines. Their foundation bitch is Ch. Lindenhall's Olan de Chablais (a daughter of Am. Can. Ch. Ebonylane's Buccaneer Gold CD). Olan bred to Am. Can. Bermuda Ch. Bradking Mr Chips produced a wide base which has generated many of the Specialty winners of the early nineties. Chablais has been very active, winning more than their fair share at Specialty shows in both Canada and the USA.

Some notable Chablais Labradors are: Am. Can. Ch. Venetian's Blender de Chablais CD, and multiple Best in Specialty and Best Puppy in Specialty winner Am. & Can. Ch. Chablais Myrtill. Ch. Chablais Rigodon was Best in Sweepstakes at the Labrador Owners Club Specialty in 1988. Can. Bermuda Ch. Chablais Barnabe was Winners Dog and Best in Sweepstakes at the 1990 Labrador Retriever Club of Canada National Specialty, under Arthur Kelley (Bradking). A couple of up-and-coming dogs at Chablais are Chablais Romance and Chablais Cargo.

The RANBOURNE Labradors are based in Ste. Justine de Newton, established in 1982 by Martin and Valerie Walters. Their most memorable Labrador is Am. Can. Ch. Shadowvale Jill at Ranbourne, bred by Huguette and the late Mike Beattie. Jill was Winners Bitch and Best of Winners at the Labrador Retriever Club of the Potomac Specialty Show in 1987, under Dorothy Gardner (Novacroft) and the late Joan McCann (Timspring). The very next day Jill went Winners Bitch at the Old Dominion Kennel Club show, under Barbara Nowak (Broyhilkl). In 1989 at the Labrador Owners Club Specialty show she was Winners Bitch, Best of Winners and Best of Breed under Debra Lynn McKinley (Fantasy).

Jill's first litter by Am. Can. Bermuda Ch. Bradking Mr Chips produced Ch. Ranbourne This Bud's For You, co-owned with Robert Gibson (Fieldenshow). In 1989, Buddy had notable success as a puppy: Best of Opposite in Sweepstakes at the 1989 Labrador Retriever Club of the Potomac Specialty, Best in Sweepstakes at the Labrador Owners Club Specialty, under Dr Mike Woods (Waterdog), and Best in Sweepstakes at the Labrador Retriever Club of Central Connecticut Specialty, under Barbara Barfield (Scrimshaw). In 1992, under Bob's guidance, Buddy went Best of Breed at the Labrador Retriever Club of Canada National Specialty, under Janet Cole (Stajantor). To complete a perfect day, Jill placed Best of Opposite Sex and Buddy's daughter Ch. Shadowvale Designing Woman went Best Puppy. Ranbourne is a small kennel, nevertheless they have several young puppies, going back to Jill and Buddy, that are now starting their show careers.

ONTARIO

Moving further westward, at Ste. Anne de Prescott, is the home of the SHADOWVALE Labradors. Established in 1974 by Huguette and the late Michael Beattie, Shadowvale is dedicated to breeding true English type Labrador Retrievers. All their present day Labradors are descendants from their original imports, International Am. Can. Bermuda Mexican Eng. Ch. Bradking Black Charm CD WC, and Am. Can. Puerto Rican Ch. Heatherbourne Forget Me Not.

Black Charm won Best of Breed at the Labrador Retriever Club of the Potomac Specialty, was twice Best of Breed at the Labrador Owners Club Specialty and Best of Opposite Sex at several American Specialties, including Winnebago, Mid-Jersey, Miami Valley and the Potomac. From her first litter in Canada, Black Charm produced three American Best in Show winners. Faye Faye (Forget Me Not) also produced many Specialty winners, among them Am. Ch. Shadowvale Just So, Am. Ch. Shadowvale Aaron at Greystone, Am. Can. Ch. Shadowvale Beddington Vine, Ch. Shadowvale Just Reward and Am. Can. Ch. Shadowvale Jill at Ranbourne.

Shadowvale are fortunate to have two Specialty winning males standing at stud, Am. Can. Ch. Bradking Rangeways Mr Chips and Am. Can. Ch. Bradking Mike. Their value as sires has been undeniable in both Canada and the USA.

In Napanee we find the LINDENHALL kennel, owned by Wayne and Peggy Donovan. The kennel was established in 1977 with the purchase of several Labradors from strong Field lines. In 1982, after trying unsuccessfully to show their Field dogs, a yellow male puppy was purchased from Ebonylane, as they say, the rest is history. The puppy grew up to become multiple Best in Show winner Am. and Can. Ch. Ebonylane's Buccaneer Gold, CD – the top winning show Labrador in Canadian history. Bucky passed on his winning ways to his sons: Ch. Rathamill Angus at Lindenhall, CD (winner of the Canadian National Specialty in 1989), Am Can. Ch. Beaumans Gold Chip at Lindenhall (No. 1 Lab in Canada in 1988, 1989, and in 1990 was top Sporting Dog) and Am. Ch. Lindenhall's Grand Quest Rebel (one of the top Labs in the USA for 1992). All the Labradors at the Donovans, with the exception of two chocolates, are related to Bucky. The two 'browns', Jacxon Browne and Georgia Browne are from the Sandledge kennel in the USA. Lindenhall has produced over forty Champions, and many others with Obedience titles and WCs as well as several guide and therapy dogs. With each new generation, Lindenhall's aim is to breed some multi-purpose Labrador Retrievers. In Shelburne we find the AMARANTH Labradors, owned by Joan Calder. Established in 1978 their foundation stud dog was Ch. Northriding Raleigh CD WC, whose dam was a South African Field Trial Ch. from Zelstone and Sandylands, and whose sire was from Wimberway, Liddly and Castlemore lines. In 1986 Ch. Amarantha's Tailsman CD WC was breeder-owner handled to No. 2 Labrador in Breed in Canada with a Third in Group win at the very prestigious Credit Valley show in Toronto. He became the No. 1 Labrador in Breed in 1987 and No. 5 Sporting Dog. That same year Obedience Trial Ch. Amarantha's Silver Moon, Am. UD became Canada's top Obedience Labrador and No. 4 Sporting Dog in Obedience. Top Labrador Owners Club Puppy in 1990 was Ch. Amarantha's All Of Me. To date, Amaranth has produced over forty breed Champions and three Obedience Trial Champions. Amaranth have continuously tried to produce show dogs that would rather retrieve.

The OAKLEA kennel is based in Simcoe, owned by Eileen and Ken Grant. The Grants emigrated from the UK in 1967 and began breeding Labradors under the Oaklea prefix in 1972. The major interest of the kennel has been attending Labrador breed shows throughout North America, where they have had some success. Some of the more notable wins were the Best of Breed at the US National and Canadian National Shows with Am. Can. Ch. Oaklea Gala and Jancroft's Jamie at Oaklea respectively. Their stud dog, Am. Can. Ch. Finchingfield Ivan of Oaklea, won two major breed Specialties – both from the veterans class. One of their bitches, Selamats Oaklea Yellow Rose, won the breed at the Labrador Owners Club Specialty in Canada. The Grants have both judged sweepstakes classes at American Specialties.

MANITOBA

The RICKWAY Labradors are based in Selkirk, owned by Lorne and Joyce Love. Established in the late 1970s, this small kennel usually only has ten residing dogs at any given time. It has produced a steadily improved stock from Australian, British and American lines. The first dog of major impact on this kennel was Ch. Ferntree's Front Runner, acquired from Australia's Ferntree kennel. The next import, from the Lachinvale kennel of Australia, augmented the distinct look that has hallmarked these dogs in Western Canada. Can. Ch. Rickway's Sun Raider was the kennel's first dog of notoriety. He was No. 3 Labrador in Canada in 1987 and No. 4 in 1988 and 1989. At seven years of age he captured Best of Breed at the Canadian National Labrador Retriever Specialty and quickly followed with Reserve Winners Dog at the American National Specialty over an entry of 266.

Prior to this, Am. Can. Ch. Rickway's Tuscaroura (a Sandylands Rip Van Winkle daughter) completed her American Championship with almost back-to-back majors. She was one of the top Labrador puppies to be shown in the USA in 1987. Her granddaughter, Am. Ch. Breezy's Whirlwind JH, was awarded Best of Breed at the American National Specialty, under J. Pritcharu. A recent import from Arthur Kelley's Bradking line is now making his mark. Rickway is the proud winner of the 1992 Pedigree Pal Award for the most Labradors to complete their Championships in that year.

ALBERTA

In western Canada, at Okotoks, we find the BEAUTAWN kennel, owned by Bill Gugins. Bill's involvment with Labrador Retrievers began in 1966 while living in the Calgary area. His first acquisition of a registered Labrador Retriever was in 1970, purchased as a hunting companion and family pet. After the passing of this first Labrador, the move to Okotoks coincided with the opportunity to purchase a daughter of Am. Ch. Lockerbie Brian Boru – and this was the true beginning Beautawn Labradors. In 1981, Beautawn's first bitch, Ch. Springfield Native Fancy CD was bred to Am. Ch. Braemar's Oakmead Dillon CD WC, producing Beautawn's first homebred brood bitch – Beautawn's Brandy On The Rock CDX WC. Among Brandy's many impressive achievements, the most notable was winning the Dam and Progeny class at three Regional Specialties and the Labrador Retriever Club of Canada's National Specialty, and each time with

Beautawn's Brandy On The Rock, an outstanding brood bitch for Bill Gugins.

different offspring. Two of Brandy's progeny have done her extra proud, Ch. Beautawn's Inside Information Can. Am. CD WC (No. 3 Labrador in Canada 1990) and his litter sister, Ch. Beautawn's Instant Replay CDX WC (Best in Specialty at a Regional Specialty). Another of Brandy's progeny, Ch. Beautawn's High Country Taffy, was a multiple Group placement winner, Best Puppy in Show winner, and No. 2 Female Labrador in Canada – all while she was still under ten months of age. The influence of Brandy on the Labradors of Beautawn is still very evident in the Labrador puppies produced there today. Brandy has consistently produced type, temperament, trainability and the Labrador that does it all. These are the traits that will always remain the goals of the Beautawn breeding program.

In Calgary, the WINDANNA kennel is owned by Charles and Judy Hunt. They acquired their first Labrador in 1975, a fox-red bitch puppy named Gemini's Anna (Ch. Halsinger's Laddie – Ch. Wimberway's The Treasured Tam). Their kennel name, Windanna, was registered in 1977 and was permanently registered in 1984. As of 1993, they have produced over fifty homebred Champions, thirty-two Companion Dogs, ten Companion Dogs Excellent and two Obedience Trial Champions. On the Field side, Windanna has produced twelve Working Certificates, one Working Certificate

Ch. Windanna's Opus Won, a representative of the versatile Windanna kennel.

Intermediate, plus seven NAHRA started. Windanna encourages their puppy owners in all phases of the Labrador as they believe the Labrador is a truly all-round dog. Their present line goes back to Best Puppy in Show winner, Ch. Windanna's Snow Queen CD (Ch. Ghillie's Jeep – Gemini's Anna CD), who produced seven Champions in two litters. Her daughter (by Am. Ch. Raintree Braemar Bailiff CDX) was Best Puppy in Show winner Ch. Windanna's Betsy Paramore, who produced four Champions including a third generation Best Puppy in Show winner. Betsy's daughter (by Ch. Finchingfield of Oaklea), Windanna's Pallas Athena CD, produced eight Champions and a Best Puppy in Show winner. Athena's daughter (by Am. Can. Ch. Oakmead Magnum Force), Group placing Champion Windanna's Molly Melody, produced eight Champions in two litters. Windanna believe in sending their bitches to the best possible stud dogs who complement their lines. Windanna was very proud to be awarded the Pedigree Pal Top Breeder Award for 1991. Charlie and Judy were founding members and on the past executive of the Labrador Retriever Club of Canada. They are also members of several Labrador Retriever Clubs in Canada, the USA and in the UK. Both Charlie and Judy are licensed Canadian Kennel Club Group 1 judges, and they are active organisers of Regional Specialty Shows in Alberta.

The SPRINGFIELD kennel is based in Cochrane, owned by Frank and Shirley Costigan, who started breeding Labradors in England in 1962. Honey of Medbrun, bred on Sandylands Bob, was their foundation bitch. She was bred to a Scottish dog from Ballyduff lines, resulting in a litter of twelve. The Costigans moved to Calgary, bringing Honey and the pick male from this litter with them, and established the Springfield kennel. They became involved in Field Trials, Obedience and later in conformation. They have continuously strived to maintain the hunting ability in their dogs. Two of the top females bred by the Costigans are: Ch. Springfields Fanny Sweet Adams WC (top-producing female in Canada for three consecutive years, with fifteen Champions from five litters) and her granddaughter, Ch. Springfield's Meadow Muffin (Best of Breed at the 1987

Canadian National Specialty, and the dam of nine Champions from three litters). Two stud dogs have been important in Western Canada. They are Am. Can. Ch. Springfield's Uhuru (Specialty and twice Best in Show, All-Breeds) and his half-brother, Ch. Springfield's Northern Justice (No. 1 Lab in Canada in 1979). Both these dogs have sired many Champions, and they are sons of Fanny. It is not possible to name all of some seventy Champions bred by the Costigans, but Ch. Springfield's Under The Rainbow – No. 2 Labradorin Canada in 1988, and the sire of many Champions – deserves special mention. He is producing happy, typey and eager gun dogs.

The RANCHMAN kennel is located in Medicine Hat, and it is owned by Marion Reid. Established in 1968, Ranchman is a small kennel, and the aim is to consistently breed dogs that are true to type, capable of meeting all needs – show, Field, Obedience or treasured pet. Their first Labrador in Canada, Annwyn's Glenavon, was bought from their dear friend and mentor, Frank Jones. This dog became Bob's hunting companion and the children's friend.

Over the years they have acquired the following Labradors: Killingsworth Tarbinavon, Can. Am. Ch. Killingworth Squire (Best in Specialty Show), Can. Am. Ch. Harbortop Ranchman's Jasper and Ch. Harbortop's Ranchman's Jasmine. Shown by daughter Hilary, Jasper won the Canadian National in 1983, under breeder/judge Nancy Martin. A daughter of the chocolate UK import, Ch. Boothgates Krazy Kaper (Alex), Boothgates Kountry Kurio, holds the record in the UK for the most wins by a chocolate Labrador. Two up-and-coming Labradors from the Ranchman kennel are Boothgates True Design and Rickway's Ranchman's Master Key. Both Jasper and Alex have produced many Champions in both Canada and the USA. Ranchman's Rogue Nero was top Junior Field Trial Dog in Canada in 1982. Jasper was No. 2 Labrador Retriever in Breed competition in Canada in 1983, Squire was No. 3 in 1981. The Ranchman kennel strives to breed brains with beauty and good companion all-round dogs. All their dogs that are used for breeding are cleared for elbow and hip dysplasia (OFA), eyes checked yearly and VWB. Every puppy is sold on a non-breeding agreement until it has passed these requirements. They strongly believe that with these clearances they can in some small way help to eradicate these genetic inheritances.

BRITISH COLUMBIA

On the Pacific coast, situated in the heart of Vancouver Island, the relatively small CASADELORA kennel was established in 1969 by Walter and Mary Brown, and they have achieved noteworthy success. Founded on Sandylands lines, they later introduced Ballyduff and Briary to their breeding program. The foundation bitch of this kennel was Ch. and Obedience Trial Ch. Trollheimen's Golden Sol, a granddaughter of Ch. Sandylands Tweed of Blaircourt. The pride of this kennel was Am. Can. Ch. Casadelora's All Spice CD WC, who was top Labrador in Canada in 1981 and 1982, and No. 2 in 1980 and 1983. Sam was also the first dog to earn an 'All Around Labrador' award from the Puget Sound Labrador Retriever Club. Sam is gone now but his legacy lives on in his offspring. Casadelora has always strived to produce trainable all-purpose Labradors, and to this end has achieved many Obedience titles and Working Certificates. Ch. and Obedience Trial Ch. Casadelora's Atlanta, owned and trained by Pauline Gaudette, was top Labrador in Obedience in Canada in 1985. Ch. Casadelora's Sea Fury, Can. Am. CS WC was Canadian National Ch. on wheels 60-80 pound class in weight pulling competitions, sponsored by the International Weight Pull Association. His personal best pull was 2650 pounds. Casadelora's Play'n Jane, owned and trained by Jim McFarland, established a new point record in winning Field Trial Puppy in British Columbia for 1991. Casadelora has bred and finished over fifty show Champions. The kennel is striving to produce dogs of sound body and mind, who typify the characteristics and temperament of the breed.

Chapter Nine

THE LABRADOR IN SWEDEN

The Labrador is very popular in Sweden. In the Top Twenty List of Popular Breeds for 1991, the Labrador was placed fourth, and there are between 2,000 and 2,500 Labradors registered every year with the Swedish Kennel Club. Sweden is widely recognised as one of the leading producers of top-quality Labradors.

REGISTRATIONS

If you want to have your Labrador puppies registered with the Swedish Kennel Club, you have to abide by certain rules that the Kennel Club have made concerning the parents of the litter. Both parents must have had hips X-rayed and have had their eyes checked for Progressive Retinal Atrophy (PRA) in the year prior to the mating. The Labrador Club in Sweden also asks for elbows to be X-rayed to show if the dogs are free from osteochondrosis dissecans (OCD). If this is not done, it will not prevent you from registering your puppies with the Kennel Club, but it is now considered the correct thing to do. There is also a *Breeders Magazine* published, which includes details of:

1. All litters being born and their parents.
2. Eye results.
3. X-ray results (hips and elbows).
4. Show results.
5. New breeders.

All this information, readily available, does help enormously to plan a breeding programme. The Kennel Club registers for 1991 in Sweden reveal that the hips of 1378 Labradors were X-rayed. Of these 1112 did not show any sign of hip dysplasia (HD), 256 dogs did show some degree of HD. In Sweden the degree of HD is split into four categories numbered one through to four. Number one is 'not very much' and number four is 'bad'. The 256 dogs with some degree of HD were placed as follows:-

Score	Number of dogs
1	129
2	84
3	31
4	1

The statistics for elbow X-rays show that a total of 1021 were examined in 1991. The vet was looking at this group of young dogs for signs of arthritis: 859 were clear and some 149 had some degree of arthritis; these were split into three groups: Not very bad: 96 dogs, Medium: 29 dogs,

Bad: 24 dogs. Dogs must be over one year of age to be permanently registered and scored. There is only one vet in Sweden checking all the X-rays so a consistent level is achieved.

THE SHOW RING

At Swedish shows there are normally between fifty and one hundred dogs in attendance for the Labrador judge to go over. Each dog gets a written critique, hopefully of fifty words or more, and is given a quality evaluation. The dogs given an 'excellent' evaluation are called back into the ring after all the individual class entrants have been assessed and are then placed one to four. To become a Swedish Champion you need three CAAs given by at least two different judges. One of the CCs must also be awarded to the dog when he is past twenty-four months of age (i.e. from Open Class). To become a Champion, a Labrador must also win a Field Trial award, which makes it very difficult. In Sweden it is not possible to amass CCs, because once a dog has won three CCs, the Kennel Club prohibit competition for further CCs, although the dog may compete for Best of Sex, or Best of Breed. The judge is permitted to award as many Reserve CCs as he or she wishes.

SCANDINAVIAN TITLES
SUCH: Swedish Show Champion.
SJCH: Swedish Field Trial Champion.
SFUCH: Finnish Show Champion.
NUCH: Norwegian Show Champion.
Int. CH: International Champion.
NORD UCH: Northern Show Champion.

FIELD TRIALS
These are divided into four classes:
Young Dogs 9-24 months; Special Beginners 24 months and upwards; you must then graduate to the Open Class; after winning first prize in the Beginners Class, and after winning two first prizes in the Open Class, you must move up to the Master Class. To become a Field Trial Champion a dog requires three first prizes in the Master Class, given by at least two different judges. An award must also be gained in the show ring, to confirm that the dog has correct conformation.

LEADING KENNELS

INGE SON THOOR: KAMRATS
Inge started in the breed thirty-five years ago, when he contacted Mary Scott of the Branhope Labradors. She helped him to buy his first English dog from Yvonne and Arthur Pauling of the Cookridge Labradors. The Cookridge type appealed immensely for type, size, expression, temperament and the interest to work, and this was to be the grounding for the Kamrats kennel. The dogs had to be dual purpose, being both good workers and top winners in the show ring. So far, this kennel has bred fifty Champions. Two dogs have been Champions in three different areas: Show, Field Trial, and Obedience, and ten dogs have been Champions in two areas, both Show and Field. Inge's first imported dog was called Cookridge Rajah of Hazelhill. HA mated his bitch of Liddly Hassan and Blackbird of Ide. That resulted in his first litter. In 1960 the chocolate bitch, Cookridge Cola, joined the kennels and she was the base of all his chocolates, as well as the chocolates in the Puhs kennel. In all, ten dogs were imported from England, and they all became Champions. The most widely known was Powhatan Sentry, imported from the Aikenhead's

SUCH Kamrats Jolly-Bob: Carrying on the ideal.

Powhatan kennel in England. He came out as a three-year-old in 1971, and in that same year he became a Champion, and the Gold Dog of 1971 (the Dog of the Year, All Breeds). The following year he became a Field Trial Champion.

From his own breeding, favourites have been the three-times Champion Kamrats Buse, and Kamrats Frida. Kamrats Buse's mother, Ramah Chocolate Chips, came to Sweden in whelp to Ch. Sandylands Mark. Chips had five puppies, and three of them stayed in the kennel. They were the bitches Kamrats Angel and Jeaney, and the dog, Buse. They all became International Champions, they are still valuable to the strength of the kennel. Ch. Kamrats Buse was outstanding, both in looks and his keenness to work, symbolising a dual-purpose Labrador. The Champions of the nineties include Kamrats Magic-Man, Tilda and Jolly-Bob, and they carry on the ideal of a sound Labrador that does well in both the show ring and at Field Trials. Kamrats Jolly-Bob is reckoned to be a copy of his Grandpa, Kamrats Buse.

MAJVOR NASMAN: ALVGARDENS
Majvor Nasman started breeding Labradors in 1969. Her first bitch was the English import Sandylands Twanah, bought from another Swedish breeder. Twanah was eighteen months old at the time, and already had one CC. She was out of Sandylands Tweed of Blaircourt and Sandylands Tanita, and had good hips. She became a super brood bitch, although she was only bred from twice as there were not many good stud dogs available that suited her lines. Her first litter was by Int. Swedish Finnish Ch. Puhs Grabb, and the second was by Int. Swedish Finnish Ch. Black Eagle of Mansergh, who had been brought in from Mary Roslin-Williams' famous Mansergh kennel in England. Eagle was four years old when he came to Sweden, and became a strong force in the breed, giving his offspring good bone and excellent coat.

From Twanah came several Champions and double Champions. The most famous was Int. Northern Ch. and Swedish Field Trial Ch. Alvgardens Midnight, who was also a carrier of the chocolate gene. The breeding of Eagle and Twanah gave some very good results. Both parents were awarded the Swedish Kennel Club's special award for being 'Good Carriers', and thanks to

Int. SUCH SFUCH Gun-Smokes Eliza: Dam of sixteen Champions.

them Alvgardens kennel was awarded the Breeders Prize from the Swedish Kennel Club – the first of a total of ten such awards and nine 'Good Carriers' awards – the most any one Labrador kennel in Sweden has received.

Since 1976, all puppies and progeny have been invited to a special-get together at the kennel, every other year. Notes are compared and nothing is hidden. A contract is signed with buyers that encourages them to X-ray hips and elbows, and check the eyes on their dogs. In this way, a check can be kept if any problem occurs, and breeding programmes can be planned accordingly.

During the seventies Int. Ch. Nord. Ch. Alvgardens Black Eve and her daughter, SUCH & SFUCH & SJCH Alvgardens Jet, and SUCH SFUCH Alvgardens Black Mammy were a strong force in the kennel. Twanah's granddaughter, Int. SUCH & SFUCH Gun-Smokes Eliza was the main brood bitch during the eighties. She was the mother of sixteen Champions, which is a great record for a Labrador bitch. Since Eliza, SUCH & SFUCH Alvgardens X-princess has given several Show and Field Trial Champions. The chocolate sisters SUCH & SFUCH Alvgardens Baroness and Int NORD SUCH Shoshone, have won several Best in Shows and Best in Groups.

Majvor Nasman prefers to show her dogs under judges who care how a good Labrador is made. She believes that a dog should do well in the show ring one day, and do equally well in the Field the next. Dogs should not carry excess fat, and should move with drive and purpose.

YVONNE WESTERLUND: SMART FELLOWS
In 1972 Yvonne Westerlund purchased her first Labrador as a pet. This was a black male who was sired by Triple Ch. Kamrats Buse. In 1977 the black male, Attikonak Mister MacCloud, bred by Gunnilla Ek, joined the kennel and became an International and Northern Champion. He was a grandson of the famous Ch. Sandylands Mark. The first litter the kennel bred was in 1981, and, so far, twelve litters have been produced. The yellow bitch Minnows Lucinda, bred by Charlotte Lindell, was by a Mark son to a Mark granddaughter, and she arrived in 1982. This bitch, together with the black bitch Stowlodge Quintette, bred by Mr and Mrs Beven and imported in 1985, became the foundation of this successful kennel. All dogs carrying the Smart Fellows affix today,

Stowlodge Quintette: Foundation bitch of the Smart Fellows kennel.

E. Rasehorn.

have one or both of these bitches in their pedigree. Another valuable dog is the black male, Stowlodge Stoddart, a full brother to Quintette. He has taken ten Best of Breed awards, Best Veteran In Show at a Kennel Club Championship Show, and he has sired nineteen CC winners. Stoddart and Quintette go back on Sandylands, Ballyduff, Cornland and Wishwood breeding.

When Minnows Lucinda was mated to Ch. Attikonak Mister MacCloud, she produced the top winning black bitch, Smart Fellows Just Splendid, who won no less than twenty-seven Best of Breeds, was Group placed at Championship Shows and Best In Show winner at Spaniel and Retriever Club Championship Shows. When Lucinda was mated to Stowlodge Stoddart, she produced the yellow, Smart Fellows Believe It Or Not. This bitch was a Championship Novice Stake winner, who, in her turn bred to a Quintette son, Smart Fellows Order From New York, produced three CC winners. Quintette has been a marvellous brood bitch, from three litters her progeny have won thirty-six CCs and her grandchildren to date have won thirty-nine CCs. She herself is a CC and BOB winner.

Four Quintette children have been Group Placed at Championship Shows. They are Smart Fellows Order From New York, Smart Fellows Our Dream Of Mite, Smart Fellows On The Cool Side and Smart Fellows With Class & Style. Class & Style is a successful brood in her own right, and offspring from one litter have so far won ten CCs. Another Quintette daughter, Smart Fellows Once In Never Out, is now competing in the Master Class at Field Trials.

The highlight of this kennel's successes occured at the big international show at Stockholm in 1988. The Best of Breed winner, sired by Stowlodge Stoddart, was placed fourth in the Gundog Group; the veteran dog, Smart Fellows Storm Cloud, won Best Veteran in Show; and – the icing on the cake – the kennel won the Best Breeders Group in the show.

PIA RAZERA-BRULIN: WINNIES
It was love at first sight when Pia Razera-Brulin saw her first Labrador in 1968. He personified the ideal dog, one leg in each corner, no fussy coat, ears and tail as they should be, ideal size and substance and, above all, the temperament that you could see in his eyes – once seen never

SUCH Winnies Kliche: Top winning Labrador for many years.

forgotten. At this time Labradors were few and far between in Sweden, and Pia was often asked if the dog was a crossbreed.

Pia worked as a kennel maid at Puhs kennels during the school holidays, and she knew from the start that Labradors were the breed for her. She started to look for a suitable bitch for breeding and in 1973 she bought Puhs Artiga Marta, a yellow daughter of Cruston Wapanachi of Trewinnard, and a black dog, Puhs Black Thunder. Tweed was a great grandfather on both sides. The dog became a Champion. He got his first CC from Mrs J. Harvey, with Best of Breed, and was placed in the Group – a wonderful way to remember your first CC.

The two were subsequently mated, and result was one dead puppy. At the second attempt three pups were delivered by caesarian, and all three were kept by the kennel. The black dog became S SFU Ch. Winnie's Art Director; he was a very keen worker and was the sire of some Field Trial Champions in Sweden. Pia rated the yellow bitch as a stunner, but she failed to be placed in the show ring. Then in 1978 Gwen Broadley – one of the best Labrador judges in the world – was invited to judge at the Stockholm Show, and she awarded the bitch a CC! The black dog who took the dog CC later came to England and gained a CC in the ownership of Mrs Broadley. On the third occasion, Puhs Artiga Marta was mated to Ballyduff Maroon, and a typey black bitch with the Ballyduff stamp was kept – this was Ch. Winnies Folio Bold.

When Ch. Baronor Phoenix, a yellow Mark son, was imported to Sweden he provided the perfect match for Ch. Winnies Actress. They produced a yellow litter, and Ch. Winnies Kliche was kept. She was the type of bitch that you could show under any judge – everyone loved her. She was the top winning Labrador for some years, winning Best of Breeds until she was eight years old, under such prestigious judges as Mrs Hepworth, Mrs Crook, Eva Mjelde and Anne Liland.

Crawcrook Calhiban was imported from England, and he sired Ch. Winnies Kliche's first litter, which contained both Champion and Field Trial Champions (with CCs). Her second litter was to a Lichitas Blizzard son, and produced Ch. Winnies Wide Type. In the big Stockholm show in 1985 she was judged by Mrs Hewitt and Keith Hart. Winnies Wide Type was Best of Breed and Winnies True Love was Best in Show – a highspot for any breeder.

Novacroft Arris was imported from Mrs Gardner in England, and when mated to Winnies Kliche produced nine puppies, all of them winners. Two became Finnish Champions, Winnies Keep Sake and Winnies Kajal. I awarded Winnies Knick Knack Best of Breed, and this award was also given under such notable judges as Mrs Charlton and Mr P. Iversen. Winnies Kame, a black bitch, and the black dog Winnies Krock Odill were kept in the kennel. When Odill was mated to a granddaughter of Winnies Folio Bold, the result was Winnies Dreamline, a young black bitch who as a junior has already one CC and three BIS to her credit. In 1990 Novacroft Buster was imported from Mrs Gardner in England, and his progeny will soon be seen in the ring.

The Winnies kennel has always aimed to breed dogs that look like Labradors and nothing else, with good breed characteristics in tail, feet, coat and expression, as well as being sound and typey.

BRIT-MARIE BRULIN: PUHS
After a visit to the Kamrats kennel, Brit-Marie Brulin bought her first Labrador in 1961, called Kamrats Puh, and it was this dog that was to give her the kennel name Puhs. In 1963 she purchased her first Labrador from England, Guildown Aussie, who became an Int. Sw. Fin. Show Champion. In 1963 the first 'Puhs' litter was bred.

When Brit-Marie had visited the Kamrats kennels, she was deeply impressed by the first chocolate import to Sweden, Cookridge Cola. When Mr and Mrs Thoor mated Cola to the Finnish and Norwegian Show Ch. Diant Dobrudden Breydon, Brit-Marie bought the chocolate bitch Kamrats Careena, who went on to become International, Swedish and Norwegian Show Ch. and Field Trial Champion. This bitch, together with the English imports Cookridge Ramah and Sandylands Geoff, were to become the foundation of her internationally known chocolate kennel. Three chocolates of Puhs breeding have become Champions in America, with Am. Ch. Puhs Superman being the most well-known. This dog became the first chocolate to go Best in Show at a Labrador Specialty Show in the United States. To date, Brit-Marie has bred twenty-two chocolate Champions, with the latest being Int. Ch. Ger. Austrian Ch. Puhs Brown Autumn.

GUNILLA ANDERSSON: AROSCAS
Gunilla Andersson was born into a family that was interested in dogs, and she was given a Boxer bitch when she was seven years old. She entered dog shows and had moderate success with this

Int. Ch. Ger. Austrian Ch. Puhs Brown Autumn.

Int. Nord. Ch. Sw. Ft. Ch. Aroscas Fight.

bitch. In 1965 she decided to choose Labradors as her breed, and she bought her foundation bitch from Brit-Marie Brulin. This bitch was never going to set the world on fire with her looks, but she was sound and healthy, and became a brilliant brood bitch. She was dominant black, and the kennel has now produced the fifth generation home-bred bitch Champions from her. In 1969 she imported a beautiful black bitch, Sandylands Mamba, from Gwen Broadley's Sandylands kennel She turned out to be a beauty, and was also a great worker, especially in Field Trials. In 1972 she was the top winning Retriever in Field Trials, eventually becoming Ft Ch. Swedish and Finnish Sh. Ch. Gunilla's interest in field work had earlier been aroused when a yellow bitch, Puhs Piglet, was bought in from Brit-Marie Brulin. A chocolate dog was also purchased from the Puhs kennel, Puhs Atos. He was the first Field Trial chocolate male in Scandinavia. He was also a great show dog, winning three Groups and Reserve Best In Show all breeds in Finland. He ended up as Int. Nord. Ch. Sw. Ft. Ch. Puhs Atos.

By the end of the sixties Gunilla had mated her first homebred Champion bitch to Sandylands Alpha, and from that litter come Int. Nord. Ch. and Sw. Ft. Ch. Aroscas Fight. He had several Group wins and was six times Best in Show. One of his most memorable wins was in Norway at the Norwegian Kennel Club Show all breeds. Unfortunately he had to be put to sleep at only six years old. Gunilla mated Mamba to Fight and produced two Champions in the litter – Int. Ch. Aroscas Moondust and Ch. Aroscas Moonbeam. Moonbeam was inseminated with sperm from Sandylands Charleston from England, and the outcome was three puppies. One went to Aud Preshus in Norway; he became a Champion and BIS winner all breeds; his litter sister went to Denmark and did a lot of winning on the Continent. In 1971 Sandylands Midnight Maestro was imported from England. He sired many great workers and became Int. and Nordic Champion. He is the father of Int. Nord. Ch. Aroscas Country Song and Swiss/German Int. Ch. Aroscas Mr Swede. In the mid-seventies Rocheby Sea Witch joined the kennel. She was inseminated, at a later date, with sperm from Sandylands Blaze, and the litter gave her the BIS winner Ch. Aroscas I'm Queens Blaze. Gunilla is now on the third generation down from her.

Looking back over the past twenty-seven years, the Aroscas kennel has kept the same strong line going throughout, and has bred thirty Champions, five Field Trial Champions – four of these being Field and Show Champions.

Chapter Ten

THE LABRADOR IN AUSTRALIA

HISTORY OF THE BREED

One of the strongholds of the Labrador Retriever in the southern hemisphere is the continent of Australia, where the breed is held in high esteem in all States. The first documented evidence of Labradors in Australia was in 1929 when Mr and Mrs Austin of Mortlake, Victoria imported a black dog, Liddly Acorn, and two black litter sisters, Liddly Cowslip and Liddly Celandine. Acorn was bred by Mr M. Gilliatt (Holton), and was chosen for Australia by Mr and Mrs Saunders who added their 'Liddly' prefix before exporting him.

Between 1933 and 1955 Miss Hilda Lascelles, who is acknowledged as making an enormous contribution to the breed in Australia, imported seven dogs from the UK, most of which were Liddly breeding, carrying Banchory, Whatmore and Winterhill lines. From these early beginnings the Labrador spread throughout the States and Territories of Australia, and in the last thirty years a combination of outstanding imported dogs and clever breeding by a succession of enthusiasts has seen a strong breed type established.

Among the most influential imports from the UK were Ch. Wendover Jonah (Mr G. Head), Ch. Sandylands Tan (Mrs D. Such), and Ch. Poolstead Pioneer (Mrs A. Spanswick). Descended from these imports are three dogs who have made a significant contribution to breeding programmes in Australia in the last twenty years. They are Mr H. Scott's Ch. Lindhills Bobo Beck sired by Tan; his grandson Mrs E. Gent's Ch. Gunnislake Stormer and Guy Spagnolo's Ch. Amansi Badri Singh, sired by Pioneer. Between them, this trio sired more than one hundred and thirty Champions, in addition to the one hundred and fifty sired by Tan himself. The influence of English breeding is borne out by the fact that in the last decade, when English specialist judges have been engaged, Best in Show winners at Labrador Championship Shows have invariably been by English sires. Overseas specialist judges reiterate that the top Australian Labradors could compete with the best in the world, and breeders are working hard to ensure that this situation continues.

Each Mainland State of Australia has a Labrador Club, all of which conduct Championship Shows, Obedience and Retrieving and Field Trials. If you consider that England could fit into New South Wales a number of times, the vast distances that Labrador enthusiasts need to travel will be appreciated. The Sydney exhibitors are best situated, as they can drive the 700kms to Melbourne in eight hours or 900kms to Brisbane in thirteen hours. Other distances from Sydney are Adelaide 1300kms and Perth 3300kms. The largest entries are usually at Breed Championship Shows, or at the Royal Shows held in each State annually. In national registrations the Labrador is always in the top six, but, in recent years, the economic situation has seen the demise of a number of large kennels and a decrease in the number of litters whelped, thus reducing the overall number of dogs.

Ch. Sandylands Tan: A highly influential import from the UK.

Australian breeders are very aware of the hereditary problems in the breed, particularly in relation to hip dysplasia, and most breed clubs conduct regular eye clinics.

TITLE QUALIFICATIONS

BREED CHAMPION: A total of one hundred points has to be gained at four or more different shows under four or more different judges in order for a dog to become a Champion. Five Points are gained for going Best of Sex, plus one point for yourself, and one for every other dog you have beaten, over six months old of the same sex. No more than twenty-five points can be gained at any one show. Both Best Dog and Best Bitch gain points at a show in the breed. As in the UK, the youngsters have to compete with established Champions to gain their title.

FIELD TRIAL CHAMPION: In order to become a Field Trial Champion, a dog has to gain eight points, which can be made up as follows: Novice: 4 points 1st place, 2 points 2nd place. Open Stake: 4 points 1st place, 2 points 2nd place. Championship Stake: 8 points 1st place, 4 points 2nd place. The judge may award a first place, but if, in his opinion, the work is not of sufficient merit, he may withhold the Champion points.

DUAL CHAMPION: To become a Dual Champion a dog has to be both a Show Champion and Field Trial Champion.

NON SLIP RETRIEVING TRIAL CHAMPION: A dog has to gain twelve points, which can be made up as follows: either two wins in All Age, or one Championship win. All Age: 6 points 1st place. Championship: 12 points 1st place, 6 points 2nd place.

OBEDIENCE TRIAL CHAMPION: A dog has to gain passes in Obedience Trials; more than one dog at a trial will be able to pass, as you are aiming at getting above a set score. I think this is a fairer system than we have in Britain, and certainly in my time in Australia I enjoyed entering Obedience Trials because it was just my dog and me against the score. To gain the various Obedience Titles you will need: 3 passes in Companion Dog: CD. 3 passes in Companion Dog Excellent: CDX. 3 passes in Utility Dog: UD. 2 passes in Tracking Dog: TD. 3 passes in Tracking Dog Excellent: TDX.

LEADING KENNELS
FRANK KEYS AND KEITH PRIOR: WAINTREE *(VICTORIA)*.

Frank Keys from Melbourne bought his first Labrador in 1943. This was a black male called Alamein Samson, who died from the dreaded scourge of the time – Distemper. He was replaced by a yellow bitch of Liddly breeding. His show career started in 1947 with moderate success. Frank fell in love with the Diant/Rookwood bloodlines through reading English magazines, and in 1957 he imported Rookwood Nutcracker, shortly followed by Diant Victoria. Both gained their Australian titles with ease, and went on to be both Group and Best in Show winners. All occupants of the kennel are now in direct bitch line down from Nutcracker.

In 1981 Frank came to England and, in partnership with Keith Prior, he bought Aust. Ch Rookwood Blonde Boy, Aust. Ch. Balrion Knight Errant and Balrion Wayward Lad. Blonde Boy and Knight Errant are both multiple Group and Best in Show winners. The kennels are now based on these bloodlines which are working very well. In the last two years, two of his latest Champions have taken the Best in Show at the Labrador Club of Victoria Championship Show – in 1990 Aust. Ch. Waintree Talking Boy and in 1992 Aust. Ch. Waintree Capangown.

The critique from the *Labrador Quarterly*, America, from the judge of the 1992 show, Mary Wiest (Beechcroft, America) reports: "My dog CC came from the Australian Bred Class. He is Ch. Waintree Capangown by Ch. Sandylands Mastermind and Waintree Madamin Black. He is a lovely black dog, quality from head to tail, excellent rear with good coat and tail, lovely expression, nice brisket, well balanced, and moved well." Reporting on the Bitch Reserve CC she writes: "My bitch Reserve CC was Waintree Rap Dancer by Ch. Waintree Madams Boy and Larelar Midnight Dancer. This lovely bitch is also owned and bred by Mr Keys and Mr Prior. She is a lovely yellow bitch who is very well put together, with excellent quarters, good coat, nice head and movement anyone would enjoy watching." Since its conception in the late forties, this kennel has produced many Champions, of consistently good type, and forty-five years on from its start, it is still a force to be reckoned with.

JILL McMASTERS AND WAYNE POHOLKE: KADNOOK *(VICTORIA)*.

The Kadnook kennel was established in 1969 after six years of exhibiting. The first Kadnook litter arrived in 1969, and the aim has always been to breed dual-purpose Labradors – that is, show dogs

Ch. Waintree Talking Boy (Ch. Rookwood Blonde Boy – Ch. Waintree Madam Mouth).

that work, and workers that win in the show ring. The foundation sire of the kennel, Ch. Oakbank The Signalman, was a classic combination of Ch. Sandylands Tan, Ch. Wendover Jonah and Ch. Rookwood Nutcracker – a mix which helped establish many Australian Labrador kennels.

The first Kadnook Show Champion was made up in 1974, and the first Kadnook Field Trial Champion in 1980. Since then a steady number of both show and working Champions have followed, culminating in the ultimate achievement of Triple Champion Kadnook The Prophet (Show Ch., Field Trial Ch. & Retrieving Trial Ch.). This dog, in turn, has produced Kadnook The Blakcameo AOC (Aust. Obedience Trial Ch.), thus making Champions up in all competitive aspects of the dog world available to Labradors in Australia.

Ch. Kadnook The Prophet (Proph), was purchased as a young pup by a great trainer and handler of working gundogs, Charlie Ball. He was purchased from show lines to prove that a show dog could work. Charlie was told not to expect too much as 'the Proph' would develop slowly and not be at his best until he was four years old. Under Charlie's guidance, Proph won a Novice Field Trial as a youngster, and had a brief introduction to shows, but was a typical awkward teenager. He gained his Field Trial Title in his first season, and was runner-up in the KCC Field Trial Championships in 1981. After a couple of years further development, Proph embarked on a serious show campaign, handled by his breeders. The week before he turned four, he won his first Group; he quickly won his show title and finished his serious show career with the reserve challenge at the Melbourne Royal in 1983. Charlie now set Proph for Retrieving Trials. He was

Triple Ch. Kadnook The Prophet CM (Strangeways Statesman – Ch. Kadnook The Silhouette).

very consistent in his work, and at trials from May 1983 to April 1985 earned Certificates of Merit, and won the Victorian Gundog Club Retrieving Trial Dog of the Year in 1984. So at just six years of age Proph became the first Australian Triple Champion, a remarkable feat by any standard, but one so richly deserved by Charlie Ball, one of the great gundog trainers and a true dog man. In 1986 Proph came home after the untimely death of Charlie Ball. Proph has proved a wonderful producer, siring Show Champions, Retrieving Trial Champions, many Obedience titled progeny, and some good Field Trial winners, as well as a large number of Guide Dogs and Guide Dog breeding stock. Truly a great dog. At Kadnook today, there are several multi-titled dogs and bitches to carry on the tradition of dual purpose Labradors into the future.

GUY SPAGNOLO: DRIFTWAY (NEW SOUTH WALES).

The foundation of Driftway coincided with Guy's move from Western Australia to Sydney in 1972. Good fortune enabled him to acquire Amansi Badri Singh (Ch. Poolstead Pioneer – Econpal Oopak), a black dog who became his first Champion and an excellent producer. Shortly afterwards Ch. Ballyduff Carol joined the kennel; this was made possible by Anna Spanswick, who imported the bitch from England. Carol was a bitch of impeccable breeding and quality, and she proved herself invaluable in establishing a rock solid foundation for the line. The first litter from these two

Ch. Driftway Sailors Lass (Ch. Driftway Captain My Captain – Ch. Driftway Dynasty).

foundation stock produced a pair of outstanding specimens. The dog, Ch. Driftway Damien, went to Western Australia, and in the hands of Duncan Scanlon, became the top Gundog in that state for several years. The bitch, Driftway Dusky Dreamer, stayed at home, and had a spectacular show career including Best Gundog Puppy Sydney Royal 1975, Best Gundog Sydney Royal 1977, plus notable wins at Specialty and All Breeds shows under local and overseas judges.

Dusky was also a producer of quality puppies to several sires. Her most notable litter was by Ch. Longley Speak Easy (imp. UK), and included five Champions, all of which feature prominently in the present-day winning stock in Australia and New Zealand. Three stayed at Driftway: the yellow bitches Ch. Driftway Dynasty and Ch. Driftway Olivia, and the black dog Ch. Driftway Statesman, a breed record holder and an invaluable sire. The bitch, Dynasty, gave the kennels seven Champion bitches from different sires, the most noteworthy of these being Ch. Driftway Destiny, sired by Ch. Jabiru the Etruscan, and Ch. Driftway Sailors Lass, sired by Ch. Driftway Captain My Captain. Late in 1988 the black Australian and New Zealand Ch. Balnova Maelstrom came to the kennel, and his quality English lines have combined successfully with the Driftways. His winning progeny so far include Ch. Driftway Rainbird, and the two black brothers Ch. Driftway Dancing Brave and Ch. Driftway Desert Storm, accounting for major wins at Specialties and Royals Australia-wide. Today the Champions Driftway Stephanie, Captain My Captain, Sailors Lass, and Pride 'n Joy, with the two young black brothers, fly the flag at Driftway.

ANNA SPANSWICK: CAMBEWARRA *(NEW SOUTH WALES).*
Anna Spanswick started breeding under the Cambewarra prefix in 1962. She had access to the very best of the many English imports that came into Australia, and was lucky to acquire dogs that bred true to type down through the generations to the present day. The first litter bred in 1963 was Ch. W. Kerry to Aust. Ch. Sandylands Tan (UK imp.), owned by A. and D. Sutch.

A few years later, in 1967, Aust. Ch. Poolstead Pioneer was acquired from Mrs Hepworth in the UK. His illustrious career spanned many years, and through his prolific son, Aust. Ch. Amansi Badri Singh, he is still leaving his mark on dogs today. It is interesting to note that when the late Fred Wrigley came to Australia to judge the Labrador Club of NSW Ch. Show in 1971, he gave Poolstead Pioneer Best in Show, and on the same day recommended the mating that produced Amansi Badri Singh. This dog was purchased as a puppy by Guy Spagnolo of the Driftway

Ch. Cambewarra Ripple (Driftway Sandpiper – Ch. Cambewarra A Bounty).

kennels. In 1968 the late Mrs Docking sent out Aust. Ch. Ballyduff Carol, to join the kennel – a really lovely typical black bitch, who was also a prolific producer. A combination of Pioneer and Carol produced stock which still has a bearing on the breed today. Two well-known dogs from these lines were Ch. Cambewarra Gannet, also a grandson of Tan, and Ch. Driftway Dusky Dreamer, both winners of Gundog Groups at the Sydney Royal Show under International judges. It was in 1978 that two more Poolsteads came to the kennel from Mrs Hepworth: a dog, Aust. Ch. Poolstead Public Speaker, and a bitch, Aust. Ch. Poolstead Popular Choice – both yellows as Pioneer had been. Both produced good winners who subsequently also produced successfully.

In 1982 the lovely bitch, Ch. Driftway Fine 'n Dandy, was bought in from Guy Spagnolo. She not only proved her worth in the show ring, but was a great producer. When Fine 'n Dandy was mated to Ch. Strangeways Sorrel she produced Ch. Cambewarra Fife 'n Drum, who has notched up fourteen Challenges at Specialty Shows, with five Best in Shows at All Breed shows. When later mated to NZ Ch. Poolstead Puzzler (imp. UK), owned by Mr and Mrs Oscar in New Zealand, she produced Ch. Cambewarra Peggity, a fine bitch who is still a great asset to the kennels. When mated to Aust. Ch. Authority of Carpenny (imp. UK) she produced a bitch, Ch. Cambewarra A Bounty, and a dog, Ch. Cambewarra A Ringer. 'A Bounty' was put to a son of Ch. Poolstead Public Speaker, Driftway Sandpiper, who was also a grandson of Ch. Ballyduff Carol. This mating gave yet another beautiful bitch, Ch. Cambewarra Ripple, who was titled at just over twelve months of age. Authority was sent to Australia by Penny Carpanini in 1988, and he has consistently stamped his lovely type on his progeny. He has been a winner of Challenges at Specialty shows, as has his daughter, Ch. Cambewarra Nutmeg. All the dogs mentioned, except Ballyduff Carol, were yellows, and in the attempt to find a good black, Tsavo Olympic Hopeful (a granddaughter of my own Fair & Square) was imported in-whelp to Eng. Ch. Keysun of Blondella from Mrs L. Lacey. In the resulting litter was the black dog, Ch. Cambewarra Blondella Buff, and the yellow Ch. Cambewarra Blondella Sun. Both dogs have had some good Specialty and All Breed wins, and their offspring, to date, are showing similar promise.

ELIZABETH & HUGH GENT: GUNNISLAKE *(NEW SOUTH WALES).*
Shortly after emigrating to Australia in 1963, the Gents obtained their foundation bitch, Lindhills Khoyla, from Harry Scott of the Lindhills kennels, who was, at that time, exerting a very strong

Ch. Gunnislake Stormer (Ch. Strangways Buff – Ch. Lindhills Sally): Sire of thirty-six Champions.

influence in the breed. Khoyla was a daughter of Ch. Diant Woodpecker and her dam's sire was Ch. Diant Leading Light. Mated to Ch. Mallardhurn Juan, Khoyla produced the first homebred Champion, Ch. Gunnislake Woodpecker CDX. He produced a number of Champions, and his son, Ch. Kimbawood Golden Rajah CD, was one of the popular stud dogs in the seventies.

A most important acquisition was a yellow bitch, Ch. Lindhills Sally, who was the start of a very strong line of yellow bitches. A granddaughter of one of Australia's most influential imports, Ch. Sandylands Tan, Sally whelped a black dog, Ch. Gunnislake Stormer, in 1974, who was to become one of the most prolific and effectual sires in Australia. Mated to a wide range of bitches – many from leading kennels in Australia and New Zealand – he sired thirty-six Champions, and he can be found in the bloodlines of many of today's leading kennels. Another leading stud dog was his grandson, Ch. Gunnislake Shamrock, who was sired by Ch. Poolstead Public Speaker.

In 1985 the chocolate dog, Ch. Lawnwoods Kapitan (Int. Ch. Lindall Mastercraft – Lawnwoods Crepe Susette) was imported from Mrs Satterthwaite in England, and his influence is now being seen in the second and third generations. Although only a small kennel, in the twenty-nine years since its conception, it has owned and bred twenty-six Champions.

Ch. Gunnislake Stormer was Best in Show at a number of All Breeds Championship shows, twice BIS at the Labrador Retriever Club Ch. Show, BOB, and BOS in Group at the Sydney Royal Show. His daughter, Ch. Tarka Storm Cloud, followed in his footsteps being twice BIS at the Labrador Club Ch. Show, and was Best Opposite Puppy All Breeds at the Sydney Royal in 1979, under Hans Lehthin. A line of yellow bitches descended from Ch. Lindhills Sally provided continuous winners: Ch. Gunnislake Suraya, Ch. Gunnislake Charade, and Ch. Gunnislake Fern all made their mark, winning major awards. In recent years the Gunnislakes have had a successful run, especially under British breed specialists at the prestigious Labrador Breed Club Ch. Shows, taking Reserve BIS and BIS, with Ch. Gunnislake Shamrock and Ch. Gunnislake Peppercorn under such judges as Sue Hill (Evelege), Judith Charlton (Foxrush), and Dorothy Gardner (Novacroft). The judicious mix of Australian and English bloodlines will see the Gunnislakes continue as a breeding and showing force in years to come.

Aust. NZ Ch. Strangways Sorrel, a son of Ch. Glowlight My Fair Lady.

Michael M. Trafford.

PAT DUNSTAN: STRANGWAYS *(NEW SOUTH WALES)*.

Being a keen shooter, Pat Dunstan purchased her first Labrador as a retriever companion in 1954. Entry into the competitive dog world came in 1965 with the purchase of Aust. Obedience Champion Larkhall Jonah CM as a puppy – an early Ch. Sandylands Tan, Ch. Wendover Jonah combination. The first litter arrived in 1971 from the line bred Tan bitch, Ch. Glowlight My Fair Lady. Lady proved to be a prepotent brood for both type and work. Some of her descendents of note include: Ch. Strangways Buff, Strangways Statesman (sire of Triple Ch. Kadnook the Prophet), Ch. Berida the Admiral, and the outstanding dog Aust. NZ Ch. Strangways Sorrel. Dual Ch. Strangways Top Hat CM fulfilled the aim to breed typical, good-looking, sound Labradors with all-round working ability. In 1985 Ch. Timspring Comfrey was imported from the late Joan Macan's Timspring kennel in England. He has proved another great producer, and a dog that has given much pleasure. Other imports followed: two in partnership with New Zealand – NZ Ch. Carpenny Chateau Cranspire (who had gained two CCs before leaving England) and Cranspire Revenue – plus Pat's own Ch. Timspring Penny Post. The tradition continues with NZ Obedience Ch. Strangways Stardust, and the young retrieving trial star, Strangways Goshawk, and his sister, Strangways Bellbird. The kennel has been to the fore in the fight against hereditary diseases, and has also worked closely with the Royal Guide Dogs for the Blind, providing breeding stock and puppies.

MRS N. M. (Gilly) GILBERT: JAYWICK *(QUEENSLAND)*.

'Gilly' has owned Labradors since 1949, starting with a yellow bitch, with Liddly, Sandylands and Poppleton breeding, who emigrated with the family to Australia in 1952, and had her first litter in 1953 when the prefix was registered. From that date, through the next forty years, a long record of breeding, showing, training and boarding ensued. Gilly started judging in 1959, and was judging All Breeds by 1965. Over the years, twenty Labradors have been imported from England, and these include: two Diants, two Rookwood, one Liddly; two Cornlands, one Tibshelf, one Ardmargha, one Candlemas, and one Courtcolman – most of these going back to Tweed. The

Courtcolman bitch, Courtcolman Ceri CM (a show and working bitch, with three Certificates of Merit at Field Trials in the UK) deserves a special mention.

She was imported in-whelp to Ch. Whatstandwell Coronet. This was a repeat mating, planned because Gilly had been so impressed by the progeny from the first litter which she had seen while on holiday in England. In fact, it became a race to get her to her new home before she whelped, as she had to make the journey by sea because of quarantine regulations. However, the boat was delayed, and the pups were born on the high seas. Gilly's daughter met the boat, and was most impressed by the way the 'wharfies' lowered mum and puppies in their kennel to the dock, four standing by to steady it. Then it was off to quarantine in Brisbane, where they were able to get some goodies into the mum and pups. They went out of quarantine the next day to go to Brisbane Royal and took Best Litter. Later two of the pups won the Challenges there. Over the years

Aust. N.Z. Ch. Diant Piper of Jaywick (left), imp. UK, and daughter, Jaywick Xanthe.

the kennel has bred or owned sixty-eight Australian or New Zealand Champions, countless Obedience titled dogs and five Retriever Champions. All stock purchased has been from show and working kennels in the UK. Gilly is still showing dogs, but is not, alas, in the ring herself now.

Highlights in the show ring include many Challenges at the Brisbane Royal, and one at Sydney Royal. Perhaps the most successful dog, show-wise, has been the kennel's last import, Aust. NZ Ch. Diant Piper of Jaywick (imp. UK), born in Scotland in 1983, who came out as an eighteen-month-old from Louise Wilson Jones. He has won multi Best in Show All Breeds in New Zealand and Australia, and the Labrador Club of Queensland. He was Top Show Dog of the Labrador Club of Queensland in 1986, 1987, 1988 and 1990 (in 1989 he was runner-up beaten by one point!). He has handed his terrific temperament down to his progeny, and is still Gilly's much-loved and devoted companion in the house.

Chapter Eleven

STARTING A KENNEL

PLANNING AND LAYOUT

Once you own more than three or four dogs, especially if they are Labrador size, it really becomes a necessity to have outside kennels and runs. I can only speak with authority on what has worked well at the Warringah kennel.

Start off by making a plan – if possible, allowing scope for future extensions. We started with three double kennels (two dogs per kennel), and we now have a run of six kennels. These were built in three stages, over the years, all facing south to catch the sun, and are just about perfect for our requirements. Having worked for the Guide Dogs for the Blind Association for a time, which gave me a marvellous training and grounding, I had pretty strong ideas on how I wanted my kennels to be. I drew up the plans and my husband, David, built them (having a civil engineer for a husband is very useful!).

The need for space and light played a large part in my plans, with the other essentials of providing draught-free, cosy beds, and facility for me to see the dogs, and to be in contact with them, from the house. Consequently, I can look out on some part of the kennels, the concrete run, or the long pebble run from any one of the four windows in my kitchen The kennels are located just across the patio from us and we eat out on most fine days from spring to autumn, so the dogs have fairly constant human contact, and this is not just confined to feeding and walking times, which is the case for many kennel dogs.

The first three kennels we built had inside compartments of 6ft x 4ft. They were 6ft high at the front, sloping to 5ft 6ins at the rear, to make easy access for cleaning. The two internal walls between the kennels are solid walls up to a height of 3ft, with weld mesh for the remaining 3ft. This enables the dogs to see through to each other, it gives more light, and it keeps the air circulating. The outside runs of these three kennels are split into two. One is 12ft x 12ft, in front of kennels one and two, and the other run measures 6ft x 12ft, in front of kennel three. The provision of a smaller and a bigger run has proved invaluable. The dogs tend to use the bigger run by choice, as they like to be together, but if I have some youngsters that I do not want to be bumped about, they go into the smaller run. This is also useful if I have bathed a dog prior to a show, and I do not want all my work undone with the dog digging into the grey, sandy soil of the pebble run.

The first litter we bred, which was twelve pups, convinced us that a 6ft x 4ft kennel interior was not big enough to house a litter. So Stage Two of the building plan was built. This was a 10ft x 4ft kennel with a 10ft x 12ft run. It proved to be a little on the chilly side for puppies (all construction is in painted breeze blocks and concrete floors). So our wooden (and insulated) puppy kennel and run came into existence at a later date. Stage Three entailed the construction of the last two kennels, taking us up to a run of six double kennels, filling up the existing space to the wooden boundary line, bordering with a bridle path. Both these kennels are 8ft x 4ft, and they share a run 16ft wide by 12ft long. Again, the internal wall between the two is solid up to 3ft high, and weld mesh for the remainder.

The run of six double kennels has a passage running along the front of the runs, a double check that no dog can escape. All the concrete runs are roofed over with see-through fibre-glass corrugated roof panels, and this means the runs can be used 365 days of the year, no matter what the weather throws at us! Inside each kennel is a wooden whelping box, 4ft x 3ft, with aluminium edging to stop chewing. We use shredded paper as bedding all the year round, as it is clean, hygienic, easy to burn when the bedding is changed, and it keeps the dogs' coats in good order. Each kennel has a stable-door, an opening window – I like to have fresh air wafting through the kennels – and a small electric space heater is fixed on the wall, which takes care of any condensation in the winter months. There is an electric light in each kennel, all the runs are illuminated, and the all-important bowl for fresh water is provided in every kennel and run.

KENNEL MANAGEMENT
As soon as the dogs are let out of their kennels in the morning, I shut the bottom half of each door, leaving the window and the top half of the door open to air the kennel. The dogs are not allowed to go back into the sleeping quarters until they go to bed at night. Each run is provided with large wooden packing cases (we came back from Australia and the Far East with them eighteen years ago, and they are still going strong), or else we use wooden platforms 2½ft x 3ft, raised from the floor by side and middle supports. The dogs can get inside the boxes or on to the platforms and be off the concrete and out of draughts. Water is available in all outside runs, at all times. We run all our dogs and bitches together all day. All three breeds get on well together – the twelve Labradors, two German Shorthaired Pointers and two Sussex Spaniels. Good temperament is a must, and we do not have any trouble breaking out among them. As far as the dogs are concerned, I am 'Top Dog', and they do as I say.

After morning walks, the dogs have the use of a 44ft x 12ft covered concrete area, as well as a 25ft x 110ft long pebble run. This was originally grass, but as it was worn away we replaced it with a mixture of the 20mm and 10mm standard gravel; it is approx 4in deep and drains freely. It makes the dogs use their feet, and it is easy to pick up and keep clean. All kennel runs and fences, except the one that borders the bridle path which runs through our property, are 6ft weld-mesh. The other fence is made of closeboard wood, to stop the dogs from seeing the people, dogs, horses etc. on the bridle path, and vice versa.

We are lucky to have four and a half acres in all, so five times a day the dogs have access to a three-quarter acre paddock. I rarely if ever get a mess in the concrete runs, and only occasionally in the pebble run, due to the use constant use of the grass paddock. All areas are picked up three times daily. It is most important to ensure that all areas are kept free of droppings – dirty kennel areas are taboo to me.

I have found the use of a kennel kitchen very helpful. We have a wooden shed, 10ft x 14ft, in which all the dog food is stored. We have the dog fridge/freezer out there, plus bins to store biscuit and storage space for tinned meats, the dog medicine cabinet, cleansing materials for the kennels, bowls, collapsible cages and newspapers for the puppy kennel floor etc. The biscuit bins are stored underneath a high trestle table, which we use for preparing the meals. This job is done, one day in advance, usually as soon as the dogs have just eaten. I find that with Labradors, who are renowned 'trencher men', that the wait while sixteen meals are being prepared can be just too much for them

– and certainly too noisy from my point of view. So meals are made up a day in advance; packets of meat are taken from the fridge/freezer, and then all the food is covered to keep off any flies etc. At feeding time the next day all that remains to be done is to measure out the meat and add the stock to each feed. Unfortunately, we do not have water laid on to our 'kitchen', so the bowls have to be taken into the house, where I use the utility/laundry room instead of my own sink so that all dog bowls are kept separate.

THE DAILY ROUTINE

The kennel day starts between 7am and 7.30am. when we let out all the dogs into the grass paddock. This includes the 'oldies' in the kitchen (from eight years old, they become house dogs), and the youngsters from the kennel. The kennels are tidied up (fluffing up the paper and changing the water in the bowls), and we check that all runs are free from any mess. We pick up in the garden, and then go round the paddock, picking up any mess from late the night before or that morning. The dogs then go back into the kennel area or the kitchen, depending on status. Breakfast is provided for the puppies, and all the dogs are given a biscuit.

At 9am the walks start, four dogs going out at each session. Three walks are taken in the woods – behind our house is 160 acres of National Trust woodlands, which is why the house originally appealed to us so much – and there is one road-walking party (for legs, feet, pasterns and nails etc). A different group is road-walked each day, so that every dog is road-walked once a week. Each walk is between two to three miles. Walks are over by noon and the dogs are fed. Most of the dogs are only fed one meal a day, and then they go out into the grass paddock for a few minutes to relieve themselves. They then return to the kennel and run areas, or the kitchen, to snooze the afternoon away.

At 3pm we usually given them another couple of minutes in the grass paddock, and again at 5pm, when the puppies are given tea. At 7pm (excluding the winter) the dogs have a run in the paddock before either going to bed or coming into the house for the evening. It is not unknown for us to have sixteen dogs in the sitting room of an evening; they all lie down quietly and behave themselves. The dogs have one final run, and then, with a biscuit for all, they are ready to settle into their sleeping quarters.

The dogs are walked four days a week. One day is spent scrubbing the kennels from top to bottom, and at the weekends we rest. In fact, the dogs are quick to learn this routine because the lane by our house is busy during the rush hours on weekdays, and the quiet of the weekends lulls them into sleeping in an extra hour, and we can often go to 8am before we hear any sound from them.

Dogs like routine, and I find that mine respond very well to this schedule. Perhaps, by other people's standards, my dogs are cossetted, but I would be unable to leave them alone for too long a time – four to five hours is my maximum. Everyone has to do what is right for them. For the last ten years, I have been fortunate in having help in the kennels, and that enables me to enjoy my hobby of showing and judging at the weekends, with a clear mind.

To summarise: the requirements for a good kennel are light, a dry atmosphere, a good bed with deep bedding, and a reasonable run to move around in (mine are quite large, I know, but length is more important than width). It is important to have a sensible kennel routine; dogs have an excellent in-built time clock, and they do not like change. Exercise is essential for a fit and healthy animal – cold will not hurt a Labrador, but avoid damp and draughts, which are not good for any dog.

All our kennels face south, and are shielded from the prevailing westerly winds by the house and the garage (as we are on the north west side of a hill, this is important). This arrangement is extremely good for nearly all of the year, but if there is a spell of very hot weather, the two large trees in the pebble run do not provide sufficient shade. America has come to my rescue here, and on one of my trips, I purchased a large green, close-woven nylon mesh, which I can tie over the kennel-run roof during the summer, and this cuts out a great deal of sunlight. On really hot days I utilise 'space-blankets', which are shiny aluminium on one side, and coloured on the other. I hang the blankets, shiny side out, along the kennel passage to take the full force of the sun. This leaves the kennel run area very cool and shady, and the dogs make full use of it.

I have found space blankets are a boon – I always carry one or two in my car. In the summer they are useful for tying over the roof and side where the sun is striking your car. As long as the windows are open a few inches all round, and the tailgate is up, dogs can be left inside a cage in the relative cool. However, it is still essential to take every precaution on a hot day to ensure that your dog does not overheat and suffer from heat exhaustion. In the winter, a space blanket is equally useful to keep in the car in case of a breakdown in bad weather. The coloured side should face outwards this time, silver-side inwards – and wrapped in this you will maintain your body heat, which just might save your life.

THE ISOLATION KENNEL
If you get to the stage where you are keeping stud dogs as well as bitches, then an isolation kennel is a very good idea. We have found ours a great help. It was originally yet another wooden garden shed, 10ft x 8ft, used as a workshop by my husband. When a new and bigger workshop was built over the garage, I commandeered the shed before it was turned over to storing garden furniture and barbecues! It is now used for in-season bitches and has had an 8ft x 10ft run added. The entire inside is insulated with fibre-glass mats between the wooden beams, on the walls and ceiling, and covered in plywood to give a smooth surface. It also proved invaluable when we had an outbreak of kennel cough. I kept the three infected youngsters isolated for six weeks, and this prevented the spread of the infection to the other dogs, which included a bitch and her week-old puppies. The in-season bitches go round the corner of the house to the isolation kennel, away from the males, and are run separately after them in the paddock.

Keeping a kennel well-run is not easy – it requires a lot of hard work. But well-exercised and properly-fed dogs, housed in clean kennels and runs, do bring great rewards – not the least being that you are keeping your animals fit, healthy and happy.

Chapter Twelve

BREEDING LABRADORS

If you have been bitten by the showing bug, and had some success, you may well decide that it would be nice to have a litter and show something of your own breeding, under your own affix. People sometimes say to me: "Oh, I am not a breeder, I just want one or two litters from my bitch." Anyone who breeds a litter is a breeder, and should give the matter as much careful thought and consideration and take all the necessary measures, as someone who has been in the breed for years. If you find it is too expensive to carry out all the various health tests on your breeding stock, you do not have the breed at heart, and you are not being fair to the prospective buyers of your puppies, who will be taking them into their homes and hearts for the next twelve years.

Breeding a litter is a serious step to take, and it is essential to have a thorough knowledge of your breed. You should study the Breed Standard (and I do mean 'study'), and you should attend at least a couple of Championship shows to see some good, winning bitches. You must then make an objective assessment of your own bitch. You cannot expect a rather mediocre bitch to produce sparkling puppies, no matter how good or prepotent the sire is. So, if she is not a good specimen, do not breed her – we already have enough unwanted puppies and older dogs in dogs homes, or left as problems for the Breed Rescue organisations to deal with. However, if you have bought a good bitch from a breeder of renown, you may have an animal that is suitable for breeding.

There is another important consideration before you embark on breeding a litter. When you have bred a litter, you do not relinquish responsibility for the puppies when they leave you as babies. We have more than our share of hereditary diseases in Labradors, and if a problem should show up in the pups as they grow, you as the breeder must be prepared to return the money paid, or to help out in paying for operations to alleviate the problem, or even to re-home the pup or older dog. I am not trying to throw a wet blanket over your plans, but it is important to be aware of the problems that can beset the breeder, and the responsibilities that may have to be faced.

THE BROOD BITCH

Now we assume that your bitch is a good example of the breed, and that she is old enough to mate. As far as I am concerned, that means the bitch should have had two, if not three seasons, and be approximately two years old – she should certainly not be past five years old for her first litter. I work at keeping all my stock in really good trim: fit, healthy, and not carrying excess weight. A bitch should be in this tip-top condition before you embark on mating her. All inoculations must be up to date to enable the pups to acquire as much immunity as possible from their mother during the first few days of life. The bitch must be free from worms, and, most importantly, she should, to your knowledge, be free from hereditary disease and not be a carrier of any disease.

Ch. Warringah's Fair Dinkum: A great example of a roomy, well-constructed brood bitch. She produced eight Champions around the world, from three litters, including three Champion daughters at Warringah.

David Bull.

You should also have your bitch's hips X-rayed, and scored. In the UK the scheme is run by the KC/BVA Hip Dysplasia Scheme. The average score for the breed at present is about 15, but we know that some breeders do not send in the bad hip plates for scoring, so these are not included in our average. I think that a truer score would be about 20 for the breed as a whole. If you were planning to mate a bitch with a score of around 20, you would hopefully use a dog that had a low score of under 10. I have had dogs standing at stud with scores of 0:0, 3:1 and 8:10. By making sure that the 8:10 dog only mated bitches with scores of under ten, I have had only a very small number of his offspring with a higher score than I would like. Of course, I did know his family history – three of his siblings scored under eight, his mother was a 4:4, his father had an HD pass, and generations behind them had good hips.

The hip-scoring scheme is there to help you, the breeder. Once you have the information, you are left to decide whether a planned mating should go ahead. If you see a good dog with a score that you wish was lower, you can weigh up the strength of the hip line behind him, and then decide whether you want to take the risk of using him at stud. It is unfortunate that not all vets are as knowledgeable as they should be when it comes to hip scores. I have heard horror stories of vets getting the score sheets back from the KC/BVA Scheme, and advising their clients to have bitches spayed because the score was too high. In all four instances, the score was under ten.

In the United States the Orthopedic Foundation for Animals operates a rating system. Labradors are not scored, but rated Excellent, Fair or Good. But the OFA will only issue a permanent number for certification if dogs are X-rayed after two years of age.

It is also important that your bitch has a clear certificate for her eyes, and this test can only be carried out by a specialised ophthalmic vet, approved under the KC/BVA scheme. These eye certificates are only valid for one year, and if you are using a young dog and bitch, I would also insist on both sets of parents holding up-to-date clear eye certificates. In Labradors, we are unlucky to have one condition, Generalised Progressive Retinal Atrophy, which does not show up until stock is three years old, or more: in fact, it has been seen for the first time in dogs up to seven years old and older. At present, with so little knowledge available, it is wise to make sure that all four parents of the two dogs you hope to use are clear. You have then done the very best you can.

We have discussed the fact that your prospective brood bitch should be a good example of the breed in terms of conformation, but it is also of utmost importance that she has the correct temperament. A Labrador is known as a gentle, loving dog; biddable, calm, steady and kind with children, with an outgoing disposition. You should not consider using a bitch that does not fall within this criterion. A very excitable or apprehensive bitch will pass on this trait to her pups. We have all heard the excuses "she was frightened as a puppy", "she was attacked by a dog", or "she was scared by a man". This might be true, but if you breed puppies from such a bitch, you could be perpetuating the fault of an unsound temperament. As well as assessing the bitch in question, you should make sure that you know the faults and virtues that appear in the bitch's ancestors. Find out as much as you can about her siblings, her parents, grandparents, and great grandparents, and, hopefully, you will avoid doubling up on any faults when you take the big step of choosing a stud dog.

I suggest that you watch your bitch carefully when she is in season, prior to the one scheduled for mating. As her season progresses, note what days she seems most ready to mate, and take the opportunity to check that she has no strictures. A stricture is a piece of membrane, growing either side of the vagina wall, or as a membrane down the centre of the vagina. It can be detected by scrubbing your hands, applying some Vaseline to an index finger and gently inserting it into the bitch's vagina. If your finger comes up against resistance, it could be a stricture. The vet can remedy this by simply cutting the stricture, but it is better to do this in advance, rather than a day before the bitch is due to be mated, when it could still be rather sore. I once had a maiden bitch presented for mating, and she had been thoroughly checked over by her vet, who, incidentally, was also a friend of mine. When I checked for a stricture, I could only get the first joint of my finger in before it came up against the toughest stricture I had ever felt. I phoned up my friend, the vet, and asked him if he had checked for strictures, because there was no way I could effect a mating with this bitch – only to be told he had never thought of it before! The bitch was taken back and snipped, and we mated her successfully the next day

THE STUD DOG
Choosing a stud dog could be the first big decision you make in the process of starting of a good kennel, or you might go for the easy option of contacting the nearest dog available because you do not want to travel too far. The dog 'down the street' might just be the right one to use on your bitch, and that would be marvellous. However, ninety-nine per cent of the time, you will need your road-map! It really pays to give this important decision a great deal of thought. A large number of beginners opt for the top winning dog of the day, regardless of whether he will be right for their bitch. They reason that if the dog is a Champion, he must inevitably suit their bitch. In fact, only a truly prepotent sire will be able to put something of himself into a variety of bitches. What is worrying is where do they all go in the next generation, when, perhaps, the good dogs around are their half-brothers? I would suggest that the best course of action is to seek advice from your bitch's breeder. The breeder will be in the best position to say which dogs would best suit the bitch; they might name two or three dogs, and then some of the choice is still left to you.

BREEDING PROGRAMMES
LINE BREEDING
I prefer to line breed, as do the majority of successful kennels. It seemed pointless to me to buy in a good line-bred bitch and then go and undo all the years of work by putting her to a dog that did

not match up pedigree-wise. Most breeders would define line breeding as putting grandmother to grandson, grandfather to granddaughter, uncle to niece, aunt to nephew, or cousin to cousin, as well as various other once-removed relatives in the pedigree. With this form of mating, you tend to know what type of puppies to expect in a litter. You know what good and bad points the line carries, and, with careful and judicious choice of mates, you can, hopefully, exclude the bad points and double-up on the good points.

OUTCROSSING
This form of breeding is adopted when you go outside the family and pick a dog that you like because he is a grand type and complements your bitch, having good points where she is weak. However, to be really effective, the stud dog has to be prepotent (i.e. really putting his stamp on the puppies), and unfortunately not too many studs really stamp themselves on a litter. An outcross is also useful when you want to introduce a dash of new blood into a tightly line-bred line, but obviously, this rarely applies to the first-time breeder.

IN-BREEDING
This form of breeding is used very rarely, and it should only be undertaken with a great deal of thought and knowledge of the lines. In-breeding is putting brother to sister, mother to son, etc. It is not something that I have ever tried, and I doubt that I ever will – even with twenty five years experience in the breed.

When you have studied the dogs at shows, and you have narrowed down your field of choice, ask the stud dog owner for a pedigree so you can study it alongside your bitch's pedigree. A stud dog owner is used to these requests, and it does not tie you to any dog at this stage. When you have decided on which dog is best suited to your bitch, the next step is to ask the stud owner if you can use their dog, and give some indication of the month that your bitch will be coming into season. At Warringah, we ask for the bitch's owner to contact us the first day the bitch comes into season. If you leave it later, you might find someone else has phoned before you to book in their bitch, and you might end up having to take second place to them and have to fit in around the times that the stud dog is free. Stud dog owners try to keep some days free for each bitch.

I have seen it stated, in print, that you should keep your dog free for the best part of a week. In an ideal world this would be the best scenario, but most popular stud dogs work hard for a six to eight week period twice a year, and have to fit in at least two bitches a week. This is not true of all breeds, but it is certainly the case with Labradors. A healthy dog is capable of mating at least one bitch a day over a short space of time, although you cannot take too many bitches to one dog in the same week. Therefore, lack of planning can mean that you miss the boat. Remember that approximately eighty per cent of bitches come into season in the same six to eight week period twice a year, the other twenty per cent being sprinkled through the other months. So, the first day that colour shows, phone the stud dog owner and let them know, so that your bitch can be booked in. The stud dog owner might well have asked you to swab the bitch as she comes into season to make sure that she is free from infection. As an owner of stud dogs, I also have my dogs checked at regular intervals to ensure that they are clear too, and not cross-infecting visiting bitches.

THE IN-SEASON BITCH
As previously discussed, you will most likely be mating your bitch when she is about two years old. She will therefore have been in season at least twice if not three times, and by keeping notes

in your diary, you hopefully will have some idea of the days she was ready for mating. A great many bitches are very regular and come into season every six months like clockwork; others have nine or even twelve-month cycles. This is quite normal; my Sussex Spaniel bitch only comes into season every nine months, while my German Shorthaired Pointer bitch only comes into season every twelve months.

However, what is far more worrying is if your bitch only goes three to four months between seasons. I often find that these bitches go on to have false pregnancies, and can end up having a pyometra (inflamed and enlarged reproductive tract), which usually results in the bitch being spayed (removal of the ovaries and uterus). It could be unwise to use this bitch for breeding, as her female offspring might well continue this undesirable trait and introduce the weakness into your line.

Prior to your bitch coming into season, males will find her attractive about two or three weeks before she first shows any colour. The vulva will be a little enlarged, and she will pass water more frequently to scent-mark her territory. Some bitches are so intent on keeping themselves clean that you could well miss the first day or so of the season, when the discharge is rather watery and bright red. It is a good idea to check the bitch each day, pressing a clean tissue to the vulva to see if she has come into season. As the season progresses, the colour will darken and then change yet again, going from bright red to pink, and then to straw-coloured. As the colour changes, the blood-flow will also reduce in quantity.

At Warringah, we always ask brood bitch owners to look for all or some of the following four signs:

1. Flow of blood lessens in amount.
2. Blood changes colour from red, to pink, to straw-coloured.
3. The vulva softens (try prodding it at six to eight days and see how hard it feels then).
   No bitch will stand for a dog until it softens.
4. The tail should swing to one side, when scratched on top at the point where it joins the body.
   The bitch will do this for you one or two days before she is ready for the dog.

Some bitches will display all these signs, others may show only a couple of them – each bitch is different. I have had two bitches myself stay bright red throughout the season, and both have still conceived litters. Although I have never experienced it myself, a bitch can also have a silent season, where no blood loss is seen, and the first indication that the bitch is in season is when she is 'standing' (i.e. ready for the dog and swinging her tail). These bitches can also conceive and bear a litter.

I ask brood bitch owners to telephone on the tenth day of the season – or earlier if the signs are coming together early – in order to give a progress report. We then proceed on a daily basis to make sure we have the right day for the bitch. I have never been an advocate of "We will be with you on the twelfth day". Every bitch is an individual, and she deserves to be mated on the right day *for her*. Having said this, most bitches are mated somewhere between the eleventh and thirteenth days, but never take it for granted that your bitch will be the same each season. One of my foundation bitches was a grand lady called Lawnwoods Hot Pants of Warringah. Hot Pants was aptly named: her first two litters were sixteenth to eighteenth day matings (normal for my line), her third litter was a seventh day mating, and her last litter a twenty-first day mating. All took, all were big litters, and all were conceived on the right day for her at the time.

Do not get complacent and fall into the trap of thinking that a season lasts for exactly twenty-one days – some bitches will be in season for up to four weeks. It is therefore advisable to keep a good eye on your in-season bitch. Everyone has mini disasters; it happens to the best of us. I put a twenty-one day bitch in my puppy run, alongside the big run, for two days. None of the males professed any interest, so on the twenty-third day I put her into the run with the rest of the dogs, and went out to lunch with a friend. When I came back a couple of hours later my son met me at the door with a huge grin on his face. My immediate reaction was "What has happened?" He said he had just got back himself to find all the dogs in the run standing looking at something – that something was the eleven-month-old bitch, twenty-three days in season, and an eleven-month-old dog. This was not a good scenario, especially as the bitch was a Labrador and the dog a German Shorthaired Pointer. I could not take the risk of a litter (our line being such late maters on the whole), so the shot was given and the bitch came back into season.

THE MATING

So now it is the right day for the mating, and I can assure you that it is usually the novices that get the day right, and the so-called 'old-hands' that invariably come a day or two early. It is important that you do arrive at the time arranged between you and the owner of the stud dog. I do not think many people realise how much work and organisation goes into getting everything ready for a visitor at a stud kennel – the rearranged walks, dogs put into kennels so they do not upset the visiting bitch, and meals perhaps given early. In the case of the stud dog to be used, food must be withheld. You cannot feed a stud dog just prior to a mating; he will either bring his meal back up, or have such a full stomach that he will not be interested in the bitch. The kennel owner might even have arranged that an extra person is there to help, so be polite and be on time.

Make sure that you have exercised your bitch prior to arriving at the kennels. She should be wearing a leather collar that is not too loose, and you must have a lead with you. I like to give the bitch a chance to run in the paddock, and allow her time to relax after her journey, so that she feels at home before I introduce the stud dog. Having introduced the pair, I like them to run around and get to know each other. In many cases a bitch will relax and respond to a stud dog after a few minutes play, realising for the first time in her life that she is allowed to flirt and encourage the dog. It can be quite funny to see this realisation dawn on a bitch, and then watch her take advantage, so that soon she has the male running around in circles!

I let this go on for about ten minutes, and if they manage to mate themselves, all well and good. If not, I step in and take charge, as I do not want the dog to tire himself out chasing round the garden after the bitch. I get the owner of the bitch or a helper to hold the bitch firmly by her collar, holding it either side of the neck with the thumbs hooked in for extra support. The bitch should be placed in a good position to compensate for height difference – on either side – and here, I find, the lumps and bumps in the lawn come in useful. I get my dogs used to being handled, and having the bitch held. By holding the bitch's tail to one side and just tipping up the vulva from underneath, it takes no time at all to have the two mated, and we can usually make sure that every bitch that comes for a mating has not had a fruitless journey – providing, of course, that she is spot-on and ready to mate. I am not keen on forced matings. I am sure that a bitch that is forced can will herself not to conceive, or at least reabsorb at a very early stage.

Some bitches need firm handling when it comes to mating – they sometimes identify so much with the human family that they do not realise that they are dogs, and a large, excited stud dog leaping around is the last thing they want! This type of bitch may be spot-on for mating, the rear end is telling you this, and the front end is telling the dog in no uncertain terms to "get lost". When this happens it is best to send the bitch's human family into the kitchen for coffee, and call them out when a tie is already effected. I find a very firm word to the bitch when she realises that the

Ch. Warringah's Fair And Square: a 'gentleman' stud dog.

Anne Roslin Williams.

lifeline of her human family is not around is all that is needed. Once mated she will usually stand as good as gold, and then I call them out to hold her head and collar while the tie is in place.

Just occasionally, you might find that you need to use a muzzle on a bitch. I have known one or two that are perfectly normal bitches, who are great mothers, but they hate being mated. When this has happens I use a pair of tights to improvise as a muzzle. I wrap them a couple of times around the jaw, tie them in a knot underneath, and then take the ends back round the neck and tie them in a bow high on the neck. It is very effective, and restricts the bitch without causing her any pain. However, more often than not the mating will proceed smoothly, and even demure little bitches can turn into raving nymphomaniacs – sex takes over and handles everything. Nature is a marvellous thing!

THE TIE

The tie itself is a phenomenon that is, I believe, exclusive to the dog family. The dog is the only animal that actually has a small bone in the penis, and once the dog has mated the bitch, the bulb at the base of the penis swells inside the vagina of the bitch, and until it subsides we have 'the tie'. This can last for five, ten, fifteen, twenty minutes, or more. When the pair is tied, the dog turns himself around doing a 180 degree turn, so that heads and tails of the two dogs back on to each other. This action, I believe, is to give the dogs a certain amount of freedom to defend themselves should they be attacked, their main weapon, their teeth, being free.

Being a stud dog owner can have its exasperating as well as its funny moments. One of my stud dogs, now gone, appeared to have a low libido, and he needed to be stirred up to mate a bitch. If the visiting bitch was too available, he used to give us this look, which said: "I will mate her, but I am not going all the way," and the so-in-so would do just that. He would mate the bitch, but tie on the outside. I knew what to do when I saw that look on his face. As soon as he started to really mate the bitch, I would push him on with my knees, and hold the two together with my arms round him and the bitch, while a helper pushed a beer crate under the bitch (just the right size to fit under a Labrador bitch). He would then stand quite happily with his front feet either side of her resting on the beer crate for five to ten minutes, while I held on for grim death from behind. Mind you, if the visiting bitch showed a little reluctance, he would get a sparkle in his eye, and say "I like this one", and you knew that you would have a super mating and tie. Apart from this little quirk, he was a gentleman of a dog. If it is convenient, by all means allow the bitch to have a second mating. This is certainly not a bad idea with older stock, and it is most certainly a good idea if your bitch is still standing three days after the first mating. The life of the sperm is approximately three to four days once inside the vagina, so if she is still standing three days later, there will not be too many live sperms around if she is not ovulating till then. With a bitch that stands for the dog for some days, you do not always know exactly when she is shedding eggs. There are tests on offer from the vet that will tell you if the bitch is ovulating or not, and they are an option that you should consider, especially if you will be travelling many miles. To answer that old wives' tale that you may have heard – no, you will not have one lot of puppies smaller than another. It takes approximately ten days before the united egg and sperm nuclei implant in the uterus wall and begin to grow.

Another fallacy to dispel is that you need a tie in order to produce puppies. The first few seconds of the ejaculate is clear seminal fluid, the next thirty seconds to two minutes is the sperm, and for the rest of the tie clear seminal fluid is being pumped in to help the sperms on their long journey to the uterus. If you can hold a dog in place for just a few minutes, you have all that is necessary for conception. Our own stud dog Fair and Square used to tie less than half of his bitches (he had over one hundred and fifty bitches in his lifetime) and he seldom missed – so I have plenty of proof! Ties will vary with each dog – some only last five minutes, some twenty, and others longer. I believe in being comfortable when mating dogs, so once the two are tied, out come my two beer crates (one for me, and one for the owner of the bitch). They make very comfortable stools to sit on while we wait for nature to take its course, and it beats kneeling on wet, muddy grass or concrete any day. When the tie is finished, get your bitch back into the car, on her lead, as quickly as possible She needs to be kept quiet for the next hour or two, and I do not like a bitch to empty herself for the next hour at least.

PAPERWORK

The brood bitch owner should should leave the kennels with a copy of the dog's pedigree, and the litter registration form should also be completed by the stud dog owner. You should also be provided with a photocopy of the dog's KC/BVA Hip Dysplasia Score sheet, and a photocopy of his latest up-to-date eye certificate (these can then be shown, along with your bitch's, to prospective puppy buyers), and last but not least, you should have a receipt for the monies you have just paid. The brood bitch owner pays a fee for the actual mating, but if no pups ensue most stud dog owners will offer a free mating at the next convenient season. Do make sure of these terms before you leave the premises. Because of the amount of stud work I have done over the years, I also issue newcomers to breeding with a pamphlet that I have compiled, taking them through from the first day of the season to when the pups leave home, as well as a copy of my puppy diet sheet to copy and pass on to the new owners of their pups. I find this cuts down on the amount of time it takes to explain everything, and it is also so much easier for the owners of the bitch to refer back to a piece of printed paper than to rely on memory.

As we finish this chapter on the brood bitch, the stud dog and mating, it is sensible to reflect that after the mating your bitch is still in season and you must make sure that no other males can get to her for the remainder of her season. If you are the owner of the stud dog, you also have a part in this litter and should any of the resulting puppies need to be re-homed in the future, you must be ready to accept your part of the responsibilities.

Chapter Thirteen

PREGNANCY AND WHELPING

All being well, we will assume that your bitch is now in whelp, and puppies should be due sixty-three days from the mating. It is not unusual for a bitch to whelp a couple of days early or even a couple of days late; the earliest I know of is a bitch who whelped a whole week early. The pups were all well-formed, if a little small, and all survived.

Following the mating, the bitch should be returned to her normal routine of food and exercise, just making extra sure that no male dog can get at her. Three weeks or so after the mating she will need to be wormed again. All animals are born with dormant worm larvae in the tissues, and when a bitch is in whelp the hormones released during pregnancy stimulate them and they will make their way back to the gut, so it is important to re-worm her at this stage.

SIGNS TO WATCH FOR

Some bitches in the first stages of pregnancy feel very 'precious', and let you know, with a lot of hammy acting, that they are unable to do something that was the norm only a few weeks before. Another sign that a percentage of bitches show is morning sickness; they tend to bring up a yellowish bile at times during the first few weeks. This has happened to only a couple of my bitches. Generally speaking, the bitch becomes very affectionate and usually wants to be around you more, and can become rather demanding of your attention. One of the first signs that you should be able to see on an in-whelp bitch is the enlarging and reddening of the teats, and the hair around them dropping out. This will be seen at about the three to four week stage, and it is a little easier to observe in a maiden bitch. You will also find that the vulva has not quite returned to normal size, but stays a little swollen. By five weeks the bitch will have filled out in the flanks, and by six weeks the majority of bitches will definitely look pregnant. There are those that mislead you both ways. You can be pretty sure that your bitch is not pregnant – and she fools you by producing a litter when she is full term. Others look as though they are in-whelp; they have all the signs, develop milk, and then a day or so before the due date, they seem to deflate like a balloon.

PREGNANCY TESTS

There are various ways to detect if your bitch is pregnant, and then you can avoid changing the diet if she is not in whelp. One method is the laying on of hands at three and a half to four weeks. I have a friend who is brilliant at this, and most vets are pretty good at it too. At this stage in the development, the puppy is the size of a pea, with a very little amniotic fluid around it, which makes it easier to feel. As the pregnancy draws on and the fluid increases, it becomes harder to feel accurately. You may also wish to have your bitch scanned. Ultrasound scanning machines are available in some larger veterinary practices. These are used to diagnose pregnancy in sheep, but it works equally well on dogs, although one or more visits are needed over a couple of weeks. There are some enterprising people in the dog scene who have equipped themselves with this equipment and will actually come to your home, as long as you pay travelling costs.

There is one other pregnancy test, which is relatively new, and all that this involves is a simple blood test. This is done from twenty-eight to thirty-seven days, and is ninety-nine per cent accurate. The protein level in the blood is checked at a laboratory, and so the result will be back in just a couple of days. My own philosophy is that if she is pregnant, I will know sixty-three days after the mating, and if she is not – well, I will hope for better luck next time!

THE IN-WHELP BITCH

From five weeks in whelp the skeletons of the pups are being laid down, and if your bitch is on a mixed diet you might like to add a little bone meal and a multi-vitamin to her daily food. If she is on one of the complete foods this will not be necessary, as she will be getting everything she needs. Whatever type of diet you are feeding, it is essential that the food is of *top quality* throughout the pregnancy, continuing right through to the ceasing of lactation. Do not over-do the calcium; the bitch will only take in so much and excrete the rest, so take advice from your vet.

From six weeks in whelp, I increase the amount of food as additional nourishment is needed on top of your bitch's maintenance diet, and this should be of the best quality. My normal diet for a bitch would be approximately 12oz of biscuit and 14oz (390gm) of raw meat. For the in-whelp bitch I feed the same amount of biscuit, with an additional pack of meat (14oz/390gm), which I now split into two meals. I do nothing extra (in terms of supplements), and this is obviously based on how I feed my own dogs; other people may use different foods and diets for the in-whelp bitch, if the maintenance diet is not of such high quality. Additional nourishment is needed on top of your bitch's maintenance diet, and it should be of the best quality. However, do not over-do the feeding: we want a fit, not fat, bitch when it comes to whelping, to make it easier for her.

Do make sure that you keep your bitch exercised during her pregnancy. I keep to our normal two to three miles for the first seven weeks, but during the last couple of weeks I cut it down as I find the bitch slows down as she gets heavier. There is always the exception to the rule. My brood bitch Hot Pants would not dream of taking things easy, and even at eight to nine weeks in whelp, she would jump over a ditch or a wall rather than walk around. I had to lead walk her during the last two weeks of her pregnancy.

THE LAST WEEK OF PREGNANCY

I like to get the bitch used to the whelping box, and sleeping in it, a week before she is due to whelp. I used to whelp my bitches in the kitchen, but as my veterans have taken over in there, I now whelp my bitches in the study. Both rooms have the advantage of being warm and close to the oven (I will explain the significance of this when it comes to the whelping). The kitchen had the added bonus of being in the hub of family, and so the pups got used to all the comings and goings. The study is a little more comfortable, and I put down one of those clear plastic sheets on the floor (used when decorating), to protect the carpet. My husband, David, designed and built our whelping boxes. For a Labrador bitch, we find that 4ft by 3ft is an ideal size. This gives enough space for the bitch to lie down on her side and stretch out, with space for the puppies, but it is not so big that a pup can wander off and get lost or cold. The box is 14ins high, built of three-quarter inch wood. The edges are covered in aluminium angle to discourage either the bitch or the pups from chewing. The whole box is then given three coats of varnish. The top half of the front can be

Ch. Warringah's Flinders before she was mated.

Anne Roslin Williams.

Ch. Warringah's Flinders, nine weeks in whelp, pictured the day before she had her litter.

removed, and the bottom half folds down flat for when the pups need to get out. I used to use a pig-rail inside but I do not do this any more. I tend to leave my options open, by having holes drilled in the box so I can slip in four broom handles to form a pig rail, should I have a bitch that is a little clumsy with her pups. In the whelping box I use a good thick layer of newspaper and then the fleecy, washable type of bedding, which allows moisture to soak through. I find that this is excellent for whelping, as it keeps the puppies warm and dry, whereas paper tends to get soggy and so the pups can get wet and cold. I also use it when I am rearing puppies, as it has the great bonus of being machine-washable, and so it can be ready to use again in no time.

When I first introduce the bitch to the whelping box, I make sure that only the bottom half of the front of the whelping box is upright, so she only has to step over seven inches into the box. This is easier for her while she is so heavy, and later, when the babies first arrive, it encourages her to be careful stepping back into the box, instead of hopping over a higher barrier and possibly injuring a puppy. During this last week of pregnancy, I take the bitch's temperature daily. The normal temperature of the dog is 101.5 Fahrenheit; in the days before whelping this drops down to 100 degrees, to 99 degrees and finally to 98 degrees Fahrenheit, by which time we know things are starting to happen, and we have only a matter of hours to go.

In these last few days, I make up my 'puppy box', so all is in readiness. This takes the form of a medium-sized strong cardboard box, lined with fleecy bedding material, under which I will place a hot-water bottle. Other items you will need for the whelping include:
Towels for rubbing the puppies to dry them off, and to stimulate breathing.
A small bowl.
Scissors and disinfectant (to cut the cords if necessary).
A tube of lubricating jelly.
A black plastic sack for all the rubbish.
A roll of kitchen paper towel.
Scales for weighing the pups.
A birth chart, and a pen.
Two clean pieces of bedding that fit the whelping box snugly – one to whelp on, the other to put down when all is finished.
A 5ml bottle of Dopram V Drops (a couple of drops under the tongue will often revive a puppy that is failing to breath naturally).
A small tin of Lactol (bitch's milk substitute). If it is not required in the early stages, I use it up when I start to add cereal at weaning time.
A Belcroy Tube Feeder. This is, by far, the best bottle to use for pups should it be necessary to feed them due to lack of milk from the mother, or if supplementary feeding is required.

THE WHELPING
The first stage of labour is usually marked by the bitch going off her food, and her temperature dropping to 98 degrees Fahrenheit, and she will start tearing up the paper in the whelping box, panting like mad and looking a little distressed. I always inform my vet that the first stage has started, just so that the practice knows that a whelping is under way, in case assistance is needed. Labradors are good whelpers, but it is best to have contingency arrangements made before the production line starts.

Over the years I have only had one bitch that ate her dinner normally, and then produced a litter two hours later. Mostly the bitches will either turn their noses up at food as the first stage of labour approaches, or, charmingly, the bitch will eat, and then bring the food back up, usually in the whelping box! At this stage, I make sure the bitch has plenty of paper in her box to tear up and make a nest for her pups. The duration of the first stage of labour can vary widely; it may take only a couple of hours, or it may last up to forty-eight hours. The bitch will need you to be close on hand at this time, in order to reassure her. She will try to convince you that every half an hour or so it is an absolute necessity to go out into the garden to relieve herself, or dig a hole (under a shed, under the house or under a tree). Do not listen to her – or perhaps, accompany her outside every couple of hours if you cannot stand the strain! For some reason, a great many litters seem to be born at night, so if you do take her out, put her on a lead and take a good torch. You do not want her surprising you and dropping the first puppy out in your garden. I note the time of the first proper contraction (you can really see the contraction go down your bitch's body), and I do not leave it for more than one hour of good contractions before contacting the vet, if no pup has emerged. This rule applies throughout the whelping. At the start of whelping, a pup could be stuck across the birth canal, or this could happen towards the end if the bitch is getting too tired to push the pup out by herself. If you need to call the vet, you must be prepared to go to the surgery – it makes little sense to call the vet out to your home, and then to dash to the surgery if more help, like a caesarean, is needed. The surgery has all the equipment on hand, and the time lost could be critical to your bitch and her whelps. If any pups have been born already, take them along in their cardboard box, all snug and warm with the hot-water bottle under the rug, and a towel on top of the box to keep the heat in. The bitch will feel much happier if the pups go along with her. Take a couple of spare towels with you, in case more pups are born at the surgery. Do watch to make sure that your bitch does not deliver the pup that was stuck, en route to the surgery, or on the way back. I once lost a pup because the bitch dropped it just outside the car in my garden, and I did not know until the next morning when I found it in the daylight. I know friends who have lost a whelp down the side of the car (when the back seat is down), so take the torch along with you.

The majority of whelpings are without incident, and night time seems to be the choice of a large number of bitches. Just about anything goes: a couple of pups will come quite close together, and then your bitch may well rest for an hour or even two before starting the contractions again, or the pups may come at nice, regular intervals – it is all normal. I have had entire litters produced in two hours, and others have taken more than twelve hours to deliver.

If the bitch is scrabbling around trying to produce the next puppy, it is a good idea to remove the ones already born to the safety of the puppy box, and then return them, once the newcomer is safely settled. When a puppy has been safely delivered, I give a good brisk rub with the towel and check the sex. I then weight each puppy, and run my finger over the roof of the mouth to check for a cleft palate, before handing the pup back to Mum. I note all these details down on my birth chart; this is not really necessary, but I like to keep details of every litter I have whelped. I take details of time of birth, colour, sex; weight, time since last pup, and type of presentation (i.e. front or rear-end first). It makes interesting reading years later, when you can chart each bitch's litters.

I try to get all the pups suckling right from the start. If your bitch's milk is not already flowing, it will encourage her to let the milk down. Give your bitch the assurance she is looking for: be calm yourself – if you are uptight you will relay your feelings to the bitch, and a nervous bitch is a clumsy one. Some new mums do not realise, at first, that they have to break open the bags and cut the cord. One bitch of mine did not get the idea until halfway through her second litter, and if I had not helped we would have had quite a few dead puppies on our hands. So if this situation arises, I help the whelp out of the bag, and I then cut the cord, though this has seldom been necessary. If I have to cut the cord, I squeeze it tight three inches from the pup, and cut the other side of my fingers, away from the pup's body. I do not tie off the cord, and this has never caused a problem.

With regard to the afterbirth, I usually let my bitches eat what they want. If one is left while she is busy cleaning up a pup, I quickly dispose of it. A bitch will come to no harm if she eats the placentas – they contain a lot of nutrients. This is what a bitch would do in the wild, in order to clear up all traces of the birth so that predators would not detect that the newborn pups were around. The nutrients would also give her energy and keep her going when she would be unable to hunt for some days after the birth.

In all the time I have been in dogs (twenty-five years, and thirty-six litters), I have had only two true breech births (backside and tail presenting, with the back legs being tucked back inside), and these pups can be very difficult to get out. However, it is quite common for bitches to produce up to fifty per cent of their pups with backside and legs presented first. This is not breech, and it does not cause the bitch any problems; the whelp comes out just as easily as head-first presentations. I have been lucky in never having a bitch suffer from inertia. This is the inability to contract and expel the pups, either part-way through the whelping, or right at the beginning. A vet is most definitely needed here. The trend to inertia does tend to run in families, and a bitch who has it is not a good breeding prospect.

As soon as I think labour is over I get someone to take the bitch out in the garden to relieve herself. Obviously, if it has been a long whelping, she will have to be allowed out, accompanied, at some time. I then clean out the whelping box, wiping it down with a mild antiseptic solution. I put clean sheets of paper down under the clean bedding, and then replace the pups in the whelping box and let the mother back inside. I give the bitch a good drink of eggs, milk and glucose, beaten together. This is light and nutritious, and will help give her back some of the energy that she has expended. With any luck, she will then settle down to a good sleep after her hard work. During the whelping, I find that our bitches will only take water, and so I add glucose to this, to give energy. On a few occasions, I have thought all was finished, and have changed the bedding, settled the new mum down – and then a few hours later a final whelp has appeared.

I like my vet to come in during the twenty-four hours following whelping to ensure no pups or afterbirth have been retained, and to give the bitch an inoculation to expel them, if necessary. The vet can also check all the whelps at this stage. It is obviously much better if the vet will come to your home, rather than going to the surgery, which may well upset the bitch at this delicate stage when she is bonding with the puppies, and she needs to feel secure.

I usually sleep downstairs with my bitch for the first night, to make sure she is not clumsy with the pups. Mother and puppies will remain in the study for the next three weeks before moving out to the puppy kennel. The study has the benefits of heat and light, a small TV, comfy chairs, and the kitchen stove is nearby for hot drinks. There is nothing like comfort when there is a long night's work ahead. I always switch the oven on to 200 degrees Fahrenheit, and I leave it on all the time the whelping is in progress. I have managed to revive puppies that appeared to be dead by placing them on to a towel-covered baking tray, and putting them into an *open* oven, for just a few seconds. The hot dry heat sometimes makes the pup take that first vital gasp of air.

When resuscitating a seemingly dead puppy, do not be too gentle; rub the chest area really briskly. If the lungs are full of fluid, hold the pup firmly in a towel with your thumbs over the chest and the rest of your hands supporting the head and body, and, holding your arms above your head, swing downwards quite sharply, more than once, if necessary. This will help to dislodge fluid in the lungs and passages. A couple of drops of Dopram V under the tongue will also help with resuscitation.

CARING FOR THE LACTATING BITCH

I have had bitches that turn round as soon as they have finished whelping and say "Where's my dinner?" Others will take four to five days of coaxing with light, nourishing meals of eggs, chicken, fish and rice, in small quantities, before they get on to a normal diet.

To feed a litter, your bitch will need good food and lots of fresh water. People seem to think that the bitch will need plenty of milk to drink in order to produce milk. This is a strange fallacy. I have found that excessive milk only makes the stools even looser, and they are bad enough anyway after all the hard work of the delivery, plus the afterbirths that have been eaten. I get my nursing bitches on to four meals a day as soon as possible, for it is good food and plenty of water that produces the milk the pups need. A typical diet for a lactating bitch would be:

Breakfast: 8oz biscuit plus milk.
Lunch: meat and biscuits (amounts shown below).
Tea: meat and biscuits.
Supper: canned rice pudding (14-15oz), plus half a can of water.
Fresh water should be available at all times.

If the bitch has a small litter – up to four pups – the two meat meals remain almost as they did before, consisting of two packets of meat (390gm) each, and 16oz of biscuits, split equally between the two meals. If there are up to six pups, the two meat meals will consist of three packets of meat and 1 1/2lb biscuit, and if the litter has eight pups or more, I use four packets of meat and 2lbs of biscuit, divided between lunch and tea. I carry on with the calcium supplement until the bitch stops feeding the pups. When the pups are four weeks old, I start cutting down on the bitch's food. First I cut out supper, then breakfast, and then slowly cut down on lunch and tea, so that by the time the pups are six to seven weeks old, my bitch is back on her maintenance diet. This helps to dry up the bitch's milk as the pups become fully weaned.

As far as exercise is concerned, I allow the bitch to dictate the pace. Some mothers do not want to leave the whelping box for two weeks or more, others will want to go out for a walk the very next day. Your bitch will indicate what she wants. I always wipe her down, after being out, with a mildly disinfectant cloth, strong enough to kill the germs, but not too strong to put the puppies off the milk bar. I also check twice a day to make sure no teats are getting mastitis. You will soon know if she has it: the gland will swell, going from 34A to 36C cup in a very short space of time. If this occurs, the bitch will need antibiotics from the vet, and you must apply hot compresses over the affected teat half a dozen times a day in order to expel the milk. Try to keep the pups off that teat for a day or two, and then it should be back to normal.

After delivering a litter, the bitch will have a discharge from the vulva for a couple of weeks, or perhaps even longer. This will change in colour from dark reddish-brown, to a paler colour as it dries up. The length of time this lasts will be related to the number of whelps, as it is coming from the sites where the placentas were attached to the wall of the uterus. If the discharge should become foul-smelling or contain mucus, you must contact your vet. You should also expect the stools from the bitch to be very dark in colour and loose for a few days to a week after the whelping; this is very normal and it is nothing to worry about. It is merely the combined effect of the strain of the delivery and the placentas consumed, followed by the lavish amounts of food she is now eating.I am never happy about handling a nursing bitch or her puppies too much. I am keen to make sure that the pups get on to the teats, and I retrieve any that wander off from the bitch and get lost; but too much fussing can make a bitch turn against the litter, and she might well turn round and tell you to get on with it, as you seem so keen to look after the litter! I have never had the experience, but I do not think that hand-rearing a litter and bottle-feeding the puppies every two hours is something that I particularly seek!

After five weeks with the pups, I let the bitch sleep separately from them. She is still with them during the day at this point, but staying away for longer periods. By six weeks she is just going in twice a day to drain off any milk she might have. Make sure these times are before her meal, or two to three hours afterwards, otherwise she will regurgitate her food for the pups, which she would do in the wild when she was weaning her litter.

I have never taken a bitch away from her pups abruptly. If she wants to play with them, let her go ahead. The pups learn so much from the bitch, and I have never had the problem of sagging under-carriages, which is what some people fear may happen if the pups are still trying to get milk at eight, nine or ten weeks of age. In fact, there is no need to worry. The pups will soon find there is precious little milk to be had, and they will give it up as a bad job. While the bitch is with her pups, I worm her as often as I worm the pups. After all, she is cleaning up after them all the time, and so she will be re-infesting herself.

After whelping and nursing a litter, your Labrador bitch is not going to be ready to show again until the next time she is in season. She will drop her coat in a spectacular fashion – nearly down to the skin – and her tail is going to look like a piece of string, in no way resembling an otter's tail. So save your money, and do not enter her at any show – it will only be money down the drain.

Chapter Fourteen

REARING A LITTER

We now have a healthy litter in the nest, Mum has settled in well with the puppies, and you feel she is able to cope. As stated in the previous chapter, it is important to keep a very close eye on her for the first couple of days, even to the extent of sleeping near the whelping box for the first night or two, if you feel she might be a little clumsy through tiredness.

WARMTH AND BEDDING

The first three weeks for you, the breeder, are relatively easy; you do not have to do too much for the litter, apart from keeping the box area warm, clean and free from draughts. Pups cannot shiver to compensate for heat-loss for the first two weeks, so you will need to keep the box area at around 70 degrees Fahrenheit during this time, and this should not drop too much for some time afterwards. If you are using a heat lamp, make sure you keep it far enough above the pups to ensure that you do not cook them. The minimum height is three to four feet. If the whelps are cold they will huddle in a heap for warmth; if they are too hot they will spread out around the edges to the box, trying to get away from the heat source. If you get it just right, there will be a loose jumble of pups around the box.

My bitches whelp inside, and the room I use is kept at the right temperature for the pups so I do not need any additional heat at this stage, but when they move outside to the puppy kennel, I use overhead heat. There are other ways of providing heat, such as using a heat-pad, which is put under the bedding. However, knowing the Labrador's penchant for chewing, I have always been a little wary of this method. I am sure others have used them to great advantage – but perhaps I know my dogs too well! The heating-pad has the advantage of heating one part of the box to keep the whelps snug, while having a cooler area for the mother. I use fleecy bedding material in my whelping box; this will need changing (and the newspaper underneath it) every day. I find this type of bedding a great boon, as it keeps the puppies warm and dry. The urine passed goes straight through to the paper underneath, leaving the top layer completely dry. It also gives the puppies a better grip when they are moving around, and, when attached to a teat, their back legs do not keep sliding away. As the pups start to get up on their legs they are able to get a good grip, and if they fall, it is a soft landing.

PROSPECTIVE PURCHASERS

Visitors should be kept to a minimum for the first few weeks: not only do you not want to upset the bitch, you do not want to bring in any infection either. Quite frankly, until the pups are up and actually playing about, they have no individual personality, so it is a pointless for prospective buyers to view them at this stage. I usually encourage people who have booked puppies to come when the pups are between three to four weeks. The prospective purchasers will already have been through some vigorous questioning on my part, before they get on to my puppy list. However, I still leave my options open, because if my gut feeling tells me not to sell when I meet a potential owner, then I will not let the sale go through.

On a couple of occasions I had a little niggle of doubt, but I let the sales go ahead, and later had cause to regret it, as the pups in question had to be re-homed. So now I make it quite clear to any prospective buyers that I do not make up my mind to sell until we meet. If we decide we like each other, and the prospective owner definitely wants a puppy, then I ask for a deposit. This will encourage the purchaser to take the deal seriously, and should the sale fall through, I have enough money to feed the pup and re-advertise (should it be necessary) to find a new home.

NAIL TRIMMING

I keep my pups in the house for the first three weeks. It gives me plenty of opportunities to watch and handle them, as well as getting them used to all the hustle and bustle of the household once they can hear and their eyes are open. The puppies' nails will need attention from four to five days onwards. At this age, when the nails are still relatively soft, ordinary nail scissors will be ideal. If left, the nails become sharp little talons, and as the pups knead the mother to encourage the milk to be let down, they can make the bitch very sore. I cut the nails at least weekly, if not more often, during the first four weeks. Once the pups get out on to a run they tend to wear them down a little themselves, and they may only need trimming every two weeks. As the nails get stronger, I use men's nail-clippers, and eventually I use the guillotine clippers that I use on my older dogs. Cutting the nails regularly will encourage the quick to go back, and you will end up with a better foot shape, with short nails. If the nails are long, the pups splay their toes to accommodate them.

THE DEVELOPING PUPPY

Yellow pups will be born with pink noses and pink pads; the pigmentation takes up to two weeks before it is fully developed. The pigmentation will also present itself around the eye rims at the same time. By the time the whelps reach ten days old, you will find among the smaller pups that the inner corner of the eyes is starting to open. This will open fully during the next few days and it may take a day or two after that before they can focus and see in any great detail. The bigger, fatter whelps always seem to be last in opening their eyes – in fact this applies to most stages of their development. It is the smaller, lighter pups that get up on to their legs first and stagger around the box. This happens at about two weeks, just as the eyes are opening. By three weeks you will see the puppies starting to play together, trying to bite and play with each other, albeit rather clumsily. The character in the litter seems to always be the smallest pup, who is usually the ring leader.

As I said earlier, I am a great chart keeper, and during the first week I weigh the puppies every other day to make sure all are putting on weight. Thereafter, I weigh them weekly until they leave home at nine weeks old. I also note on my charts when I worm the litter, when I cut nails, note when the eyes open, etc. I can then give the new owners a quite detailed report on what has been happening to the pups up until the time they leave home.

THE PUPPY KENNEL

At three weeks of age my puppies are transferred to the outside puppy kennel, which is kept exclusively for puppies and their dam. This coincides with the start of weaning, when the pups need to be able to get out of the box on to newspaper to relieve themselves. The kennel is a well-insulated wooden shed, measuring 5ft by 7ft. The door has been cut in two, to effect a stable door. Both the walls and ceiling are covered in fibre-glass mats, and then covered in plywood to give a smooth surface. The kennel has heat and light, plus a large opening window for light and air. With the door cut in two, we are able to keep the bottom half shut to keep out draughts, while the top is left open to allow fresh air to circulate when the pups are inside.

The whole area of the kennel and run measures 12ft by 10ft, the puppy shed taking up 5ft by 7ft. This gives plenty of space for the pups to run around – but not too much. The whelping box inside measures 4ft by 3ft, leaving an area of 4ft by 5ft for the pups to come out on to when the front of the box is down, to play or relieve themselves. Four feet above the box we have a large hardboard shelf, with a circle cut out to let the lamp and shade fit in; this makes sure that the heat does not dissipate up to the roof and provides a very useful area for storing clean newspapers, bedding etc. If the weather is really cold when a litter first moves out, I hang a blanket over half of the front of the box to help retain the heat.

WORMING

Prior to the start of weaning, you might find that the pups occasionally start to scour, i.e. they produce a foul-smelling, liquid stool, which is very pale in colour. You might reasonably assume that they have caught a tummy bug, but the culprits are frequently worms. I would probably ask my vet for a treatment to settle the stomach, but I also worm, even as early as two weeks of age. By two weeks the worms inside the pups are getting to be quite a size. For this first worming I use a palatable liquid wormer, which slips down easily. I always use a small clean syringe at this stage, it is easy to draw up the correct amount required for the pup (in proportion to individual weights), and you can squeeze it down the throat so easily. In the dim and distant past, trying to get a spoonful of wormer down a puppy's throat was a nightmare, and usually ended up with most of the wormer going over me. I repeat the liquid wormer a week later.

For the following wormings, I use a brand of palatable wormer tablets, which is an effective treatment for both mature and immature roundworms. The tablets have a pleasant meaty taste, and can be given whole to adults, but should be crumbled and mixed into the puppies' food, be it a quarter, a half or a whole tablet, depending on the weight of the pup and the dosage needed. I dose my puppies again at five, seven and nine weeks.

WEANING

If a bitch has a big litter of ten pups or more, I start to wean early, usually when the pups are two weeks old. By this, you will realise that I do not cull, unless I have a sickly or deformed whelp. This is a matter for everyone to decide for themselves. The pups I have reared from big litters have not suffered; in fact, they have ended up the same size at nine weeks as whelps from smaller litters. If I am rearing a normal size litter, I would begin

A four week-old pup at the weekly weighing.

to wean at three weeks, and if it was a small litter of four pups or less, you might find that four weeks is early enough to start.

I have never been able to understand why most people start weaning with milky drinks, as the bitch has so much milk herself at this stage. I have always started with meat meals; I find that the pups love the taste. I use a very good finely ground beef mince with a low fat content (most supermarkets sell this). I start on two meals a day, with a meatball at each the size of a medium-sized marble. I get the pups used to the meat for at least three days before I introduce two meals of cereal, mixed with a good milk powder, especially prepared for puppies (cow's milk is too raw to feed to pups until they are three months plus). I make the powder up to a thick cream consistency, and then I encourage the pups to lap. Usually the first meal or two are hilarious – the puppies wade through it, sit in it, lick it off each other – anything but lap from the bowl! By the time the pups are getting to the end of their first week of solids, they are eating a breakfast and supper of cereal (I use Weetabix) with milk, and a lunch and tea of one meatball each. Over the weeks, I gradually increase the feeds, as detailed below:

THREE WEEKS: **Lunch** and **Snack** A meatball the size of a good marble, working up to walnut-size by the end of the week.

THREE AND A HALF WEEKS: **Breakfast** and **Supper** Two Weetabix mixed sloppy with milk – two to three tablespoons per pup.

FOUR TO FIVE WEEKS: **Breakfast** Half a Weetabix and milk, per pup. **Lunch** and **Tea** meatball (walnut-size), up to 1oz per pup. **Supper** Rice pudding (approx one 15oz can between six to eight pups).

FIVE TO SIX WEEKS **Breakfast** One Weetabix plus milk, per pup. **Lunch** and **Tea** 1-2oz meatball per pup. **Supper** Rice pudding, one can between four to six pups.

SIX TO SEVEN WEEKS **Breakfast** Two Weetabix plus milk, per pup. **Lunch** and **Tea** 3oz meat and 1oz biscuit per pup. **Supper** a quarter of a can of rice pudding per pup.

SEVEN TO EIGHT WEEKS **Breakfast** Two Weetabix plus milk, per pup. **Lunch** and **Tea** 4oz meat and 2oz biscuit per pup. **Supper** a quarter of a can of rice pudding per pup.

EIGHT TO NINE WEEKS **Breakfast** Two to three Weetabix plus milk, per pup. **Lunch** and **Tea** 4-5oz meat plus 2 1/2oz biscuit per pup. **Supper** A third of a can of rice pudding per pup.

I should stress this is the way I go about things – not everyone uses the same type of food or the same amounts. Personally, I do not like to see fat puppies, nor skinny ones for that matter; they should all be just nicely covered.

As you can see, I keep the separate meatball going until the pups are six weeks old. I find that by holding them, continually stroking them, going over them as they eat, and eventually standing them up as they get bigger, while they feed, the puppies get used to showing and baiting, and to being handled. At six weeks old I introduce biscuit to the meat, and change from the butcher's mince to a top-quality dog beef-mince. I do not feed as much meat as some; I like to keep the balance between meat and cereal about equal. As the puppies get older, I make slight adjustments to quantity. A thirteen week-old pup would be given four Weetabix plus milk for breakfast, and lunch and tea would each consist of 6oz meat and 4oz biscuit, making a total of 12oz cereal and 12oz meat a day. This would increase to about about 14oz of meat and between 12 and 16oz of biscuit (depending on the dog), and will stay at that level for most of the dog's life.

SOCIALISATION AND PLAYTIME

I have covered the accommodation, food, worming, and toe nails, but equally important is the 'Tender Loving Care' (known in our house as 'TLC'). Your time will never be wasted sitting and

A cardboard box is ideal for playing and sleeping in – and the puppies also have great fun tearing it to pieces!

playing with the pups, and getting them used to being handled by yourself and by others. This is an absolute necessity for a nice, well rounded-off puppy.

The pups will also need a few toys to play with. There are many goodies that you can buy, but a simple plastic bottle (well washed, and first removing any pieces that can come off) is good fun. A cardboard box does not last too long – but puppies find it the greatest fun for sitting in, on top of or underneath, and then eventually tearing it to little pieces – for the human mother to pick up from all over the run! I do not let puppies stay out too long after their meals, especially if it is a winter litter. It is so easy for a pup to get damp and chilled, and that leads to upset tummies etc. By three weeks, whelps need to walk out of the box on to newspaper to relieve themselves, and by four weeks, I find that if I leave the door of the kennel open after a meal, some of the more adventurous pups will start coming out into the run. By five weeks they all come tumbling out for their meals. I let them have ten minutes play outside in the run, in the garden or in the paddock after every meal, and this increases to thirty minutes by the time the pups are nine weeks old. This gives the puppies the opportunity to learn about grass, sticks, digging holes, and generally having fun. Meanwhile, I get on with tidying up the kennel and run, and when playtime is over, the puppies go back to bed for a good sleep.

ASSESSING THE PUPPIES

While the pups are growing, I look long and hard at them, starting from about five weeks onwards – I am not one of those that can pick pups out at birth. I identify each pup by cutting a small wedge of fur out of the coat (left shoulder, right shoulder, left backside, right backside etc.), and then I stand up each pup and go over the body from nose to tail. I write a critique at five weeks, at seven weeks and at nine weeks (I have to re-do the 'tag' marks as the coat grows back so fast). I find that with this method, I can usually end up with the right pup for me. I sometimes change my mind as they grow, not on structure – that is there for good by six weeks – but the way the head develops etc. I find this an effective way for me; I tend to forget if I just look at a pup and put it back in the nest. Naturally the one I end up with always has the show trim on the tail!

LEAVING HOME

When the pups leave home at nine weeks, I always pack a travelling bag for them, and this contains three to four days of food. The puppy will have to cope with a lot of upheaval, leaving dam and litter mates, and everything that is familiar, so it helps if the food remains the same, and this will hopefully avoid tummy upsets. I give a diet sheet that goes from puppyhood to adulthood, with instructions on worming, inoculation and exercise.

Each pup goes with a pedigree, KC registration, and insurance (all are insured for six weeks after they leave home; this is quite common in the UK, but is rarely the case in the USA). I detail the puppy's worming programme, and any inoculations that have been given. Last, but not least, I give a receipt for the full amount of money paid for the pup. I also stress that the puppy should be returned to me, the breeder, if a problem arises and the owner cannot keep the dog. I do not breed, and then forget my responsibilities. I also tell new owners to telephone if they are worried about anything, at any time.

INOCULATIONS

Every breeder and every vet has their own ideas on inoculation. I very seldom have a puppy inoculated before it leaves me, unless there is a lot of parvovirus around. In this instance the pups will be given a parvovirus shot, as the one I use cuts across any of the mother's immunity that the puppy may still have. I leave all the other inoculations until twelve and fourteen weeks minimum.

This is the programme that works for my dogs. My vet and I found this out the hard way, many years ago, when four pups – two of four months, and two of ten months – suddenly went down with hepatitis. We lost one of the four-month-old pups; the other three nearly died. They went blind, and then regained their sight. The two ten-month-old pups went on to become Sh. Ch. Warringah's Hot Favourite and Sh. Ch. Warringah's Hot Property. Both litters were checked by the drug company, and any pups that were inoculated at ten to twelve weeks of age (like mine) had no immunity. Those inoculated later were well up on immunity.

It was concluded that the immunity given to the pups by their dams (two different ones) was taking some time to diminish, and so the inoculations given between ten and twelve weeks had failed to act. However, I would advise every new owner to take their own vet's advice on when to inoculate – it helps to get off on a good footing with a new dog or a new vet.

I try my best to breed a good, healthy Labrador, but if things do come unstuck, I believe that the breeder must be responsible for attempting to set things right. This can be very expensive, but perhaps if it hurts our pocket, we might be a little more careful the next time we come to breed a litter, and ensure that it will benefit our chosen love, the Labrador.

Chapter Fifteen

TRAINING YOUR LABRADOR

Written by Joy Venturi (Leospring), Field Trial Secretary of Kent, Surrey and Sussex Labrador Club.

The Labrador's original purpose was that of a retrieving gundog, and the breed is acknowledged the world over for its prowess in this field. In fact, there are many forms of work which a Labrador is capable of, but a groundwork of basic Obedience is essential to all disciplines. This entails coming when called, sitting and staying, walking to heel and generally learning to be a polite and sociable animal who will not cause a nuisance to the owner or to anyone else. Even those who only show their dogs should teach these basics. A dog's showing stance will not be ruined by teaching the 'Sit' (some owners believe this is the case) if the dog is taught to stand for food, but to sit for other rewards, such as a retrieve.

Training is made much easier if you are starting with a young puppy, between eight and sixteen weeks. This is a prime socialisation age which enables you to habitualize the puppy, moulding character and behaviour to suit your purpose. After this age, many of the puppy's character and behaviour traits will have been formed. It is by no means impossible to teach an old dog new tricks; but it requires an experienced, patient and thoughtful handler, who also has plenty of time, to reform an older dog that may have acquired bad or undesirable habits, which will need considerable retraining.

Unfortunately, many owners do not realise how actions which they deem to be humorous or harmless in a cute eight-week-old puppy, can become established and cause endless problems later on. For example, if an eight to twelve-week-old puppy is taken for a gentle walk in a new area, with plenty of space, this will give plenty of opportunities to run away. Of course, the puppy is highly unlikely to run off. This is a strange environment, and to a puppy without mother or littermates, you, the owner, are the only familiar thing. Consequently, the puppy, not wishing to get lost, will instantly regard you as pack leader and will eagerly go wherever you go. If the pup should stray, then you, who are bigger and faster, can fetch the puppy back, further compounding your superiority and pack leader status. This behaviour pattern, especially if repeated several times, will be imprinted on the puppy's brain for life, and problems with not coming when called will largely be avoided.

Compare this method with the new owner who has only ever allowed the new puppy to exercise in the garden, usually because the vaccination programme is not complete. The pup, who feels totally confident in these familiar surroundings, will not feel obliged to come when called by the owner, particularly if occupied by an interesting diversion, such as chewing an old flower pot. The owner, thinking the puppy is at least keeping out of mischief, does not enforce the command, i.e. does not go and get the puppy, while repeating the recall command, and then giving plenty of praise. If the command is not enforced, a bad habit has started to imprint itself. After a few similar repeats over the following days, the owner will give the command to come, and the puppy will decide whether or not to respond. No wonder then, at sixteen to twenty weeks of age, vaccination course completed and the puppy is finally allowed into the real world with all its extra temptations, such as other dogs, that troubles are immediately apparent.

At this age the puppy is a lot bigger, and therefore the owner will physically find it harder to go and get a straying dog, who is either very confident, or is terrified by what is happening, and in both cases has the ability to move with a fair degree of speed. The veterinary profession is now more aware of this very important socialisation age, and many practices run puppy parties or other events, as it is recognized that the very slight risk of infection is the lesser evil when compared to the behavioural problems that are created by incorrect socialisation when the puppy is young.

This simple example has far-reaching implications on further training. Yes, things should be kept light-hearted, but the educational purpose of all you do with the puppy should be kept in mind. If the puppy carries out an action which is displeasing to you, then you must step in straightaway, saying "No" in a sharp tone of voice. If you catch the pup in the act of misbehaving, this can be combined with giving the pup a little shake, holding the scruff of the neck, and using a growling noise made in your throat. This is how the puppy's mother would correct, and your action will be fully understood. However, this should only be done at the exact time of the misdemeanour; two seconds afterwards will not do, as the action will not be associated with the punishment.

Likewise, if the puppy does not look worried by your reprimand, than you have just not been firm enough and you are storing up a lack of respect for the future. However, there is an important point to bear in mind if you are hoping your puppy will become a gundog. A reprimand every time the puppy picks up one of your new shoes to chew, will mean that the pup will not retrieve for you. The correct action would be to encourage your puppy to bring the shoe to you, give a lot of praise, and then make sure your shoes are kept out of reach.

All puppies develop at different rates, but by six months of age, all should come when called, respond to the commands sit and stay, down and stay, and walk to heel, ideally on and off the lead. The age at which you start training for more serious work is up to you, but it should be governed by the dog's mental maturity. Many of the top field trialers have their dogs in Novice Stakes by eighteen months of age, and in Opens by the next season. However, other trainers prefer to work at a much slower rate, and I do not start trialing until a dog is over two years of age.

I have also trained several show dogs to compete for their show gundog qualifying certificates at five years, and beyond (the oldest being eight and half years), although all these dogs were ignorant of any aspect of gundog work when I took them on. All of them were basically obedient, which made their further training quite easy. In fact, although training a dog for the gun at this age means several good years work are wasted, it does illustrate the point that older dogs are receptive to new skills, and the extra maturity often makes further training easier, providing they have not fallen into bad habits beforehand.

BASIC OBEDIENCE: THE RULES
START ON DAY ONE

The longer you take to start training, the harder it will become. For a Labrador the odd 'play' retrieves are included here. Try a retrieve with your handkerchief, just once a week, but always make sure that it comes to hand. If you have any problems, stop immediately and retry in a week

An eight-week-old puppy play-retrieves, using a handkerchief.

Venturi.

or two. I also allow my young puppies to retrieve a pheasant wing as a small introduction to later training.

NEVER GIVE A COMMAND WHICH YOU ARE NOT IN A POSITION TO ENFORCE
This also means commands which you are too busy or too tired to enforce. There must never be occasions when the puppy can get away with not obeying a command. Try to stage-manage situations so that the puppy has no real chance of disobeying a command, but is still praised for the correct response. Eventually this becomes habit-forming, and the pup will repeat the correct response in all environments. For example, if you experience difficulty with recalls, practise them in 'alleyway' situations, which limit the possibility of running off sideways and help form a habit of coming straight in to the handler. The alleyways can get progressively wider, before graduating to a large field, where the temptation to run off is greater. This process could take several weeks.

USE SINGLE WORD BASIC COMMANDS (see chart)
Keep your training vocabulary very simple. Write down all the commands you use, with the action they refer to next to them. Each action should have a different word, to avoid confusing your puppy. You may be surprised at the result. It is estimated that the average dog can only learn about twenty-five different word responses, and this soon mounts up if you use two words for every command.

SPEAK CLEARLY AND AUDIBLY
Although dogs have more acute hearing than human beings – perhaps *because* they have – they must have clear sounds by which to recognise the words of command. If we mumble, the sounds become altered. It is not necessary to shout; constant shouting renders the puppy immune, and then the owner has nothing left in reserve for the few, genuine emergencies which arise. On these occasions the puppy, who has always been spoken to with a normal but firm voice, will really take notice should a loud voice become necessary.

GIVE ONE COMMAND, THEN ENSURE THE ACTION IS CARRIED OUT
Never keep repeating a command when a puppy is disobeying that command. Give, for example, the sit command once. If this is not obeyed, press down on the puppy's bottom until you achieve a

sit, and then praise. Even after a command has been taught, there will be times when the pup fails to carry out the required action, but you must always quickly ensure that the command is enforced. Do not keep giving the command, giving second and third chances to get it right, or you will end up with a dog that only obeys after the second or third repetition of any given command.

This rule should also be remembered during advanced training. You may have a dog who is a competent swimmer, but when you give the command to enter water, the dog continually runs the bank. Nothing is achieved by constantly repeating the command and being disobeyed. The trainer must move forward, towards the dog, and ensure the action is carried out, even if this means creating a fresh stimulus by throwing a retrieve article for the dog.

ALWAYS REWARD OBEDIENCE TO A COMMAND
The best reward a Labrador can have is your pleasure. Therefore, show this pleasure with your voice or actions. "Good dog" combined with a good pat. If you have a timid puppy, then proportionally more praise is required to reward an achievement than that required for a rather excitable puppy. Here, one gentle stroke, or a quiet "good dog", may be enough. More praise is generally required when a puppy carries out the action to a command the first few times, compared to when the dog has become proficient at responding to a command. Tidbits can also be used, especially as a reward for coming when called.

KEEP TRAINING SHORT, SWEET AND VARIED
Ten minutes intensive training a day is quite enough. Do not worry if there are some days when you do not have the time, but make sure the pup does not have the licence to disobey any commands which you may find it necessary to give during the rest of the day. Training with dogs, like children, is an on-going activity, and very often the best training sessions are those impromptu moments when you are having to cope with 'domestic' situations. Feeding time is excellent for teaching the 'sit', 'down' and 'stay', with dinner being the reward.

NEVER TRAIN IF YOU ARE IN THE WRONG MOOD
If you attempt to do this, you are much more likely to lose your temper and undo any good work you have already done. Things are also guaranteed to go wrong if you are short of time.

ALWAYS END TRAINING ON A GOOD NOTE
Dogs, like people, have off-days. Sometimes, if things are not going well, it is best to put the dog in the sit, give plenty of praise, and finish the lesson. On another day, training will recommence on a better note. Ending the lesson in this way gives your puppy the opportunity to think things through – the improvement is usually quite surprising.

BE PREPARED TO REPEAT, REPEAT AGAIN, AND PERSEVERE
Owners often do not realise how many times quite simple actions have to be repeated to form a habit in the dog's mind. However, this repetition occurs over many months, or even years. The dog would be very bored if the required number of repeats were carried out in a short space of time. Try to view your dog's training as an exercise in prevention rather than cure. In many cases, your job is to save the dog from its natural instincts, which, if not moulded and channelled correctly, will result in trouble for dog and owner. Always try to anticipate a dog's likely actions in any given set of circumstances, and read ahead. Mistakes will be made, but try to acknowledge them quickly, and avoid making them again in the future.

PROCEDURES FOR BASIC OBEDIENCE

Command	Action if Necessary	Whistle	Comments
Sit	Press down on bottom, pull up on collar/lead.	One long blast.	
Stay	Restrain dog in position, raise faced palm of hand (build up time and distance gradually).		Always replace dog in exact same spot if he moves.
Down	From sit position, pull front leg forward. With hands on shoulders, roll down and sideways.		Psychologically important position, much steadier than sit.
Up	Release command (after praise) for above.		
Heel	Jerk lead and then slacken immediately. (Tap side of leg; dog usually on left side.)		If the dog pulls, walk slower. If dog the lags, walk faster. Use frequent directional changes and circles.
(name) Come sequence: "Come" Praise "Sit" Praise	Choose according to circumstances: a) Walk quietly to dog and, taking control, repeat command, making him come to original call position and praise. b) Run away from dog (he will chase you). c) Ignore him (avoid ineffective shouting).	Several short toots.	Invent your own practice distractions, such as balls or food.

Do not use whistle commands until verbal commands are proficient. If the whistle is disobeyed, resort immediately to verbal command, then act to enforce the command. If you are not in a position to do this, save face, remain quiet. Stage-manage similar situation later.

GUNDOG WORK

This work falls into several different categories, some of which can and do overlap. The largest number of gundogs probably belong either to individuals who wish to shoot over them, or who wish to take their dog picking up or beating on a local shoot. Usually these dogs are also family pets, and from the dog's point of view this kind of life is probably one of the most satisfactory; but it can also hold the most potential for errors in training, as the family may all be contradictory in their approach to the puppy's training. A smaller but fast growing number of dogs belong to owners who wish to enter gundog competitions. The two main types of competition are Field Trials, where the dog is judged under real shooting day conditions and is required to make retrieves of freshly-shot game, and gundog Working Tests, which consist of retrieves in simulated shooting conditions, using canvas dummies or sometimes cold game.

The Labrador is still very popular with gamekeepers, where they are used for a variety of tasks connected with the keeper's job. However, the number of keepers is very much reduced compared with before the Second World War, which means that fewer Labradors belong to full-time keepers; but there are probably more part-time keepers, which helps to maintain the numbers of Labradors in this employ.

The route which our Labrador pup follows to becoming a working gundog will depend upon which category his new owner falls into. The vast majority of owners will train their Labrador themselves, to suit the job that is required. One positive development of today is that more help is available than ever before to assist the potential gundog owner. Most will be in easy reach of a local gundog club which will run training classes; several books have been written, and training videos have been made. First, we should look at the requirements of the ordinary shooting man as a starting point from which all other Labrador work in the gundog field has evolved.

Many of today's guns are shooting men or women first, and dog trainers second. Therefore, if money permits, the dog is usually sent to a professional trainer at anywhere between five and nine months of age. When the dog is returned, providing the trainer's instructions are followed to the letter, and better still, some follow-up lessons with dog and owner are arranged, a good companion shooting dog is achieved.

The work the dog will be trained for is, of course, the original job for which the Labrador was imported to England in the 1800s, i.e. a gentleman's non-slip retriever. This is a dog that will stay quietly with the gun at a drive, remaining steady off the lead, and only retrieving when instructed to do so by the owner. This requires a sensible, but willing temperament. The dog must be a good marker, and although, when necessary, the owner can control by whistle and hand signal, the dog must be able to get on with the job without constant assistance from the handler. The Labrador must hunt cover willingly, take to water when necessary, and retrieve the birds tenderly to hand. This is especially important when it is only possible to pick up game with the aid of a dog, because birds may be wounded, may have run, or fallen into water or dense cover.

TEACHING THE RETRIEVE STEP BY STEP

Command	Action required	Whistle	Hand signal
Retrieving: Sit Stay	Stand slightly in front and to side of dog and throw dummy (to help steadiness).		Raise faced palm of hand.
Back	Send dog. Run outwards to retrieve or throw again if necessary.		
Come	As soon as dog has retrieve (move backwards to help return) clap hands for extra encouragement if necessary.	Several short toots	
Leave	Take dummy (do not grab).		

SUGGESTED COMMANDS FOR ADVANCED RETRIEVING WORK

Command	Action required	Whistle	Hand signal
Sit	Stopping to take further signals.	One long blast.	Raise faced palm of hand.
Back	Going back away from handler.		As above, and moving forward and above head.
Out	Going either left or right.		Arm in direction required.
There	Hunt in that area.		
Get in	Into cover or water.		
Over	Jumping (also ditches and hedges)		
Leave	Release or avoid retrieve.		
No	Don't do that.		

Consistency of the command in relation to the action is more important than the actual word used.

INTRODUCTION TO GUNFIRE

Great care should always be taken with this aspect of your young dog's training. The Labrador is a gundog breed, and there may be many Field Trial Champions in the pedigree, but this does not mean that your dog will automatically be confident with the sound of the gun.

An ideal introduction would be to start when the puppy is still with the dam. Breeders who work their dogs are careful to make feeding time a noisy occasion, with dishes being banged about, doors being slammed etc., while the pups pursue the pleasurable occupation of feeding. As I live in a country area, my own puppies are used to hearing the sound of the rough shooter's gun several fields away, and as their dam is not concerned, neither are they. I held and cuddled my first gundog puppy, aged nine weeks, while a gun was fired about two hundred yards away. The key points to all these situations are that the gun is quite a distance away, and that the puppies are doing something familiar and pleasurable at the same time. This is the situation you must create when introducing an older dog to gunfire. I outline a suitable programme (it requires two people) below:

1. Dog on lead and sitting next to the handler. The handler should be prepared with tidbits and praise.
2. The second person, with ideally a 4.10 or 20 bore shotgun, should stand downwind of the dog and handler, about 200 yards away.
3. Once the gun is fired, the handler must immediately praise the dog or give a tidbit. Most Labradors will either slightly prick their ears to the sound, or be unconcerned. They will quickly become interested in the handler's food and praise.
4. If the above is successful and no worry is exhibited by the dog, the process can be repeated with the gun moving thirty yards nearer.

A selection of retrieve artcles graduating from a puppy dummy (right) to pheasant in a stocking (second left), to fur, and finally to cold game.

Hilly Hoar ARPS.

5. If any worry is shown on the part of the dog, the gun must move further away, and the process should be repeated twice at the further distance. Then a halt should be called for the day. Your dog will probably accept this quite happily. If not, the help of a professional trainer should be sought.

6. If your dog is still happy at step four, the gun can move another thirty yards nearer and the action can be repeated. This last time the dog can also be rewarded with a short retrieve.

7. If this has all been successful, the gun should be unloaded and laid on the ground for the dog to sniff at, while you give praise and encouragement. Many dogs are shy of the weapon, but not of the sound it makes. Once the dog is happy about this, the gun can be lifted and carried, and moved about to get the dog familiar with these actions. Some dogs, even if they have never been hit with a stick, seem to react as if the gun were going to be used to beat them. Therefore much effort and encouragement may be required at this part of the education.

8. Over the next few weeks the gun can gradually come nearer. The lead can be removed from the dog, and the dog instructed to remain in the down or sit position. Eventually the second person can be dispensed with, and the handler can take charge of the gun.

POINTS TO REMEMBER

1. Some dogs do not like the cracking sound of dummy launchers or blank shot, even though they are quite happy with a normal shotgun. Therefore it is better to start with a small 20 bore or 4.10 shotgun, rather than dummy launchers or blanks. I have found starting pistols to be quite acceptable to the majority of dogs. Owners who do not have access to a shotgun could start with this, but remember your dog will have to be introduced to the louder sound of a shotgun, and to the action of the gun being lifted to the shoulder (some of this can be simulated with the aid of a walking-stick) before the dog's education can be completed.

2. Some dogs are thunder-shy, but they are quite happy with the sound of a shotgun.

3. Do not reward your dog with a retrieve every time a shot is fired, or you will make the dog unsteady, associating every shot with running off to get something. One or two early retrieves with shot are, of course, desirable as a reward, but later on just allow your dog to retrieve occasionally.

4. Never take your dog to clay pigeon shoots, even if all the above stages have been successfully completed. The continual barrage of sound going on for hours, with no reward for the dog in the way of retrieving, has turned dogs, which had originally been quite happy with the gun, incurably gunshy. Remember, a dog's hearing is far more sensitive than our own. We are advised to wear ear defenders in this situation, and for a dog the event can become very painful for the ears.

"Quiet" : The bark or whine must be stopped instantly on the first occasion it occurs, or it will become an incurable habit.

Hilly Hoar ARPS.

FIELD TRIALS

It was to preserve the trainability and the gundog characteristics that ensured a high percentage of success, which signalled the beginning of retriever Field Trials, and the rules and format remain largely unchanged. Field trials are walked up, commonly in sugar beet or other root crops, or driven from woodland. Dogs are sent to retrieve in order and are marked by the judges, who have two dogs under them at any one time. Each retrieve is marked, and the judges also make short notes on each dog's work.

ELIMINATING FAULTS: Hard mouth, whining or barking, running in or chasing, out of control, failure to enter water. changing game while retrieving.

MAJOR FAULTS: Failing to find dead or wounded game, unsteadiness at heel, "eye wipe" (when another dog finds game which the first dog could not), disturbing ground, slack and unbusinesslike work, noisy handling, poor control.

After two rounds (dogs get two retrieves in the first round and one or two in the second), the judges take the dogs in any order they require for the number of retrieves they need in order to get a result. Awards can be given for first to fourth, and any number of certificates of merit as decided by the judges. It is not necessary to give all, or any, awards if the judges decide that the standard of dog work is not high enough.

Originally, many competitors were also guns who shot over the dogs they trialed. Today, however, a lesser percentage of trialers shoot over their dogs, but many pick up for the guns on shooting days. Some Field Trialers only keep their dogs for competition purposes, thinking that real gundog work will ruin them. This last situation is not, I feel, to the benefit of Field Trials, or

"Back" : Leospring Mars Marine being sent for a retrieve.

the Labrador breed as a whole. The danger is people could lose sight of the purpose of trials, which is to find good game-finders, and to preserve the bloodlines which the average shooting man will be able to train and control.

GAME-FINDING

It is true that the general standard of handling at trials has improved over the last two decades. Most handlers can control their dogs with whistle and hand signal commands. Steadiness is the norm; it is rare for one or more dogs to run in at a trial. However, marking ability appears to have diminished, and many handlers are afraid to let their dogs get on and hunt without constant interference. It is correct for a dog with natural drive and style to be credited, but this must be coupled with natural game-finding and marking ability. Some modern judges seem to put too much emphasis on speed and handling, and not enough on game-finding ability.

The Kennel Club guide to field trial judges states: "Dogs showing game-finding ability and initiative should be placed above those which have to be handled to their game. Usually the best dog seems to require the least handling. It appears to have an instinctive knowledge of direction and makes a difficult find look simple and easy."

The inability of a few judges to assess good gundog work without resorting to trick retrieves, can lead to situations where the best game-finding dogs may be lost from a trial for picking the wrong bird. This is because they have been asked to pick one specific dead bird among several others, often while runners are left unattended, to be collected by the ordinary picker-uppers on the shoot at a later stage. This does not give Field Trialing a good name; it does not find natural game-finders, and it does not set the right example to new people coming into the sport. It also contradicts Kennel Club regulations (and humane considerations) which state that: "Wounded game should be gathered and despatched at the earliest opportunity. And wounded game should normally be tried for before dead game."

BREED REQUIREMENTS
Fortunately, the majority of working Labrador breeders and Field Trial judges are well aware of the type of working dog that needs to be preserved. A visit to most local Labrador breed club Field Trials will give the opportunity to see some examples of excellent dog work, and quiet, effective handling. The Labrador's popularity as a gundog will only continue if the breed fulfils the requirements of the average working gundog owner. This must continue to be borne in mind by all those judging trials, and by those breeding and competing with working Labradors.

Firstly, there is a requirement that the dog has the type of temperament which enables the ordinary handler to be able to control and work it. Secondly, there is evidence (judging by the telephone calls I receive each week from potential purchasers) that working Labrador owners are becoming more concerned that the Labrador should look like a Labrador, and not a black Whippet. This has been a criticism of some of the Field Trial lines of today.

At a recent Labrador Club Annual General meeting a letter was read from the Duke of Wellington (Stratfieldsaye) deploring the split between the working and the show Labrador. Both sides can be blamed for this split, as both type and working ability should be considered together. Sadly, since 1946, when the last Dual Champion was whelped, an increasing proportion of breeders, on both sides, have not kept this ideal in mind.

However, it appears that more recently this trend seems to have been reversed a little. Many of the present Field Trial dogs have improved in type, and more show people are, again, taking an interest in the working aspects of the breed. Fortunately, there have always been a few Field Trial kennels that have insisted on maintaining true Labrador type within their breeding programmes.

GETTING INVOLVED IN FIELD TRIALS
Field Trials are still the main shop window for the working Labrador. However, it is an expensive sport, and serious Field Trialers need to join numerous clubs throughout the country, to be sure to get a run in the very over-subscribed trials. The bank balance is likely to go in the red on January 1st each year with the cost of all the subscriptions!

Many trials are only open to twelve dogs, with at least fifty and usually many more entries. Luck is necessary to get drawn, and then luck plays its part on which retrieves you get on the day, as no two are the same. Most breeders are happy only to gain the satisfaction of breeding and/or owning a Field Trial winner, or the ultimate, a Field Trial Champion. Although a top winning dog may earn quite an income in stud fees, the prize money will hardly cover the entry fee. It will certainly not cover the petrol and hotel bill. Most professional trainers hope that Field Trial success will bring in enquiries to take on the training of other dogs, and that the publicity involved in qualifying to run in the Retriever Championship will improve their reputation.

THE RETRIEVER CHAMPIONSHIP
To qualify for the Championships, which are run each year by the International Gundog League, a

dog must gain either an 'A' qualification by winning a two-day Open stake, or three 'Bs', which are obtained either by coming second in a two-day stake, or first in a one-day Open stake. Thus, winning a two-day stake not only gives the dog the first leg to becoming a Field Trial Champion, but also the extra kudos of going to the Championships.

As a result of this, most clubs which are able to run Open stakes eventually aim to organise a two-day stakes, thereby sending a representative to the Championships. Whether this rush for two-day stakes does anything to produce a better gundog is open to debate. Twice the number of dogs are run (twenty-four), and so the dogs very rarely retrieve any more birds over the two days than they would have done in a one-day stake. The norm is three birds on the first day, often with an early finish, and two or three birds on the second day, for the dogs kept in.

BECOMING A FIELD TRIAL CHAMPION
To make up a Field Trial Champion a dog must win over three days i.e. one Open two-day stake and an Open one-day stake, or three one-day Open stakes. Obviously, two two-day stakes would also count. One stake must be open to all types of retriever. A dog must also qualify to gain preference in draw in order to run in open stakes. This is done by winning a first, second, or third in lower stakes, within the two preceding seasons of the open stake in question. It is certainly more difficult for the modern-day trialer to make a dog into a Field Trial Champion, because of the larger number of competitors and tougher qualifying entry requirements. However, trialers are still very keen, and once bitten by the trialing bug, it is a hard sport to give up. It has become an enjoyable, although at times a frustrating way of life for many owners.

GETTING STARTED IN FIELD TRIALS
First read the paragraphs on Picking Up and Working Tests. Make sure you fully understand what is written and carry it out. Then, if you are still interested in Field Trialing your dog, contact the Field Trial Secretary of a local club and ask to attend a trial, either to spectate, or to help on the day. In this way you will find out exactly what is required from the dogs and handlers. A word of warning: non-competing dogs are not allowed at Field Trials, so on this occasion, you will have to leave your own dog at home.

PICKING UP
Fortunately, most field trialers do pick up with their dogs. They, along with many other gundog owners, work on shoots throughout the season, performing an essential job on any modern shoot. It is impossible for someone who is shooting, even with the help of a really good Labrador, to mark down all birds, particularly the wounded birds which often fly a long way behind the line of the guns, before landing. These birds are the main concern of the good picker-up. It has always been desirable that these wounded birds are picked up quickly to prevent suffering and a lingering death. In these days of anti-field sports campaigners, it is even more essential that shoots ensure that competent handlers and dogs are available for this job. The good picker-up will therefore need to stand up to one or two hundred yards behind the guns, depending on the type of cover and the terrain, and be prepared to send his or her dog as soon as the bird is down, to ensure maximum success.

Once the drive is finished, the handler can move forward with the dogs and clear the ground in front where other dead birds have been marked down. Although picking up is a good grounding in game-finding ability for any dog which is to be field trialed, it must be acknowledged that the work required does have some differences. However, in my opinion, these differences can be

Picking up is usually carried out well behind the gun-line.

Jan West

Sometimes the opportunity arises to stand in the gun-line, which is good training for Field Trials. Note the young dog in training still has a lead on – but the check-chain would be removed for work.

Jan West

Field Trial winner Treherne Wideawake returns at speed with a bird.

Jan West

reconciled, providing you are not expecting to take only one dog. I always take three dogs with me. One or two experienced dogs – often, at least one of these is currently being field trialed – and a youngster which I am bringing on, although I will be more selective about this dog's work.

I would certainly not let a youngster retrieve during the drive, but insist that the dog stays steady and quiet in the down position, while the older dogs do the work. I am really looking for younger dogs to become almost bored, and certainly resigned, to doing nothing during drives. I find that during their second season, the dogs very quickly get interested again, once they realise they will sometimes be sent for a retrieve. If the early steadiness habit (in their eyes, sitting and doing nothing much) has not been well and truly ingrained, you will never have a truly steady dog.

During the drive, one of the older dogs is sent whenever a runner comes down. As the dogs are not sent in any order or routine, I find that they are easy to keep steady, because the element of surprise never allows them to think that it is automatically their turn. The dog I choose to send will depend upon where the bird has fallen, whether or not the dogs have marked it, and whether there happens to be a particular training aspect that I am concentrating on with either of the dogs.

For example, if one dog has not had much experience retrieving over fences or ditches and a bird goes over a fence or ditch, then the inexperienced dog will get that retrieve. Dead birds are usually left until the drive is finished. It is then sometimes possible for an inexperienced dog to be sent for one or two birds, especially if they have been dropped into light cover. This will require hunting out, but will give a high guarantee of success. This helps to build confidence in the younger dog.

Although I never send my young dogs during the drive in their first season, I always give them plenty of opportunity to hunt for and find birds when the drive is over. Eventually, because the dogs have built up confidence in retrieving game, the first retrieve of a wounded bird usually "just happens". The event often occurs before I get round to stage-managing this part of the dog's education, and it always seems to pass off successfully, with the dog just taking it in his stride, and regarding the whole thing as a normal development.

Once the dog is confident in picking wounded birds, I add a further lesson. Whenever an older dog brings back a wounded bird during the drive, I dispatch the bird and then throw it down, about five yards in front of the young dog, while the bird's nervous system is still causing it to flap. I insist that the young dog still stays in the down position, and makes no moves to grab the bird. This action helps consolidate the steadiness lesson, without making the dog afraid of flapping birds.

SOME WORDS OF WARNING
Although it is pretty safe to send dogs for runners behind the line, always make sure, with the keeper, that the drive is not a back-to-back, or you may be sending your dog into the next drive. With runners that fall in front of you towards the guns, make sure that the dog you send has marked it well. If other birds are shot, and the dog is not sure of the mark, in the heat of the moment the dog may run in and retrieve one of these birds, lose the runner and cause you embarrassment. When in doubt avoid sending a dog, but make a note of the bird's whereabouts, so if it is not retrieved by the guns' dogs or a beater, it can be retrieved at the end of the drive.

GETTING STARTED IN PICKING UP
If you are the new owner of only one dog, you may be forgiven for wondering how you are ever to get started. If you wish to pick up without rushing and ruining your dog, my advice is to first speak to the breeder, as, if he or she is local, they may invite you to take the dog along and stand with them. This will give your dog a chance to watch and behave, while the breeder's dogs do their

THE DELIVERY

Standing or sitting when delivering a bird are both equally acceptable.

Jan West

LEFT: Three birds are brought back at the same time.

Jan West

Good temperament is essential when a number of dogs are crowded into a small vehicle. FT winners (pictured left to right): Leospring Mars Marine, Treherne Wideawake, Mardi Gras Down at Leospring and Treherne Gamefall at Leospring.

Jan West

work. The breeder will probably be helpful, as they will be interested to find out how the dog they bred is coming on. Alternatively, try to find another gundog enthusiast who will take you along with them. You must of course have the keeper's permission.

GUNDOG WORKING TESTS

These tests now have to be run under Kennel Club license. This recent ruling was despite disagreement by most clubs and individuals involved in working gundogs and Field Trials. This disagreement arose, not because the benefits of working tests to dogs and owners were not acknowledged, but because there was a general concern that their recognition by the Kennel Club would confer too much importance on these events, rather than placing them in their true light.

Their real purpose is as a measure of the level of training reached by a dog and handler. They are viewed as a means to an end, rather than an end in itself. Working Tests test steadiness, retrieving, handling and marking ability, but they cannot test whether a dog is hard in the mouth, or controllable and quiet under real shooting conditions. The Kennel Club, however, rules virtually all dog events, and there are harsh penalties for dogs, owners and judges who become involved in un-licensed events. However, this said, Working Tests are now a very competitive sport; they are enjoyed by hundreds of people and their dogs throughout the year. Some events even raise considerable sums of money for charity, and others give more prize money than Field Trials. Most are modest events run by local dog training clubs. They cater for each stage of development from puppy tests through to novice, intermediate, and open tests. Some clubs also run novice dog/ novice handler tests, or test instruction days.

Many competitors also Field Trial and Pick Up with their dogs, but this is not a necessity. Those who do not work their dogs on game, either through lack of opportunity or lack of interest, can still have great fun competing in Working Tests while at the same time allowing their Labrador to use its natural instincts, and become better trained. It is true that many of today's trialers have graduated by starting out in Working Tests, and this is probably responsible for the higher standard

Langshott Honeybee: a strongly built bitch with Working Test and show awards. Owned by Mr B. Yeowart.

of handling at trials. Test critics will claim they also highlight the worst aspects, where dogs are handled on to their retrieves, instead of being allowed to use their own game sense and nose.

However, despite this criticism, it is far more sensible to test your dog out in competition at a Working Test, and later perhaps at a Field Trial training day (a useful service offered by some clubs to their members), and Picking Up, before entering a Field Trial proper. This is especially true if you are new to gundog competitions. It is quite wrong to insult a Field Trial host by turning up with a dog which is not ready to trial because it possesses eliminating faults. This dog would be depriving another more experienced, dog of a run. If the above route is followed by novice handlers who would like to run their dogs in trials they are less likely to get on the wrong side of Field Trial organisers and officials by running sub-standard dogs.

GETTING STARTED IN WORKING TESTS
Make sure your dog has basic Obedience training, and then join a local Gundog Club. Find out all you can on the subject of gundogs – reading books, and talking to experts – and then enjoy yourself. All the above events are run on private ground by the generous permission of the host. It

behoves all owners to behave in a responsible manner and not push their dogs into events too quickly. If dogs and owners are not properly educated, embarrassing situations may arise, which may mean the individual, and the club, may not get a future invitation.

COMPETITIVE GUNDOG WORK IN AMERICA
FIELD TRIALS

Today these events are highly competitive. They are usually run over several days, taking place all the year round and over the majority of the country. The standard of training required is very high, being highly demanding of both dog and handler. Consequently the majority of dogs are handled by professional handlers, which tends to make it somewhat costly for participators. However, there can be no doubt that the spectacle of a dog completing triple, two-hundred yard marks, in a dead straight line and avoiding all distractions, is very impressive.

The aim to achieve completely equal tests for each dog is founded, no doubt, on the will to avoid the element of luck, which plays a great part in English Field Trials (and also in early American Trials). However, when this means that bad falls have to be rethrown, and cripples cannot be picked up because each dog cannot be given the same opportunity, the judging of a dog on its ability to perform in a way required by the hunter or shooting man, is lost. In Helen Warwick's book *The New Complete Labrador Retriever*, published by Howell Book House, Dave Elliot compares the trial dogs of yesteryear with those of today: "I have no hesitation in saying that the former were better game finders.....They had to find the cripples as well as the dead." In his opinion, because this aspect is no longer trained for, today's dogs lack self-reliance.

Joan Hayes, a respected English breeder and Field Trial handler of the Staindrop Labradors, fulfilled a lifelong ambition in 1986 when she visited the United States. Her father, the late Edgar Winter, had founded the Staindrop kennels in 1929. He visited the United States in 1948, and many of the early Field Champions carried his prefix, including Field Champions Staindrop Kam, Murton, Spanker, Striker and Ringleader. Ringleader was one of the few yellows to be made up.

Joan had the opportunity to see Labradors working and she comments: "I was impressed by the excellent memories of dogs, who are usually required to mark three or four thrown birds. Although some dogs marked the bird throwers, rather than the actual fall of the bird, especially on the tests where flyers were used. In America game is very limited, and on an ordinary shooting day one may be licensed to shoot five doves, or quail etc. depending on where one is. Therefore, our American friends have devised a Field Trial system which is nearer to, but in some ways more difficult than our Cold Game Working Tests. In a nutshell, the difference is that in some tests live birds are thrown, then shot. These are called 'flyers'; the others are dead and are thrown by hand.

"It was somewhat difficult to adjust to the degree of licence allowed in whining, or occasional barking, coupled with unsteadiness on the line". These dogs, are however, eliminated later on in the series and full run-ins or breaks are eliminated whenever they occur.

"Interestingly, at this trial the helpers that fired the guns and threw the birds included music students from a local College." This, I feel would be a rarity in England and is another of the differences between the sports either side of the Atlantic.

At this particular trial, a Limited All-aged Stake (the equivalent of an English Open Stake) run by the East Texas Retriever Club, there were forty-six Starters. There is, therefore, considerable pressure on judges, and, in return, on the dogs and handlers, for the tests to become tougher and tougher in order to separate dogs by ability, and then to find the winners. The dogs have become better and better, and as a result, it is an opinion held by some, that part of the work required has deviated further and further from actual hunting situations. However, despite this high standard, we must give full credit for the number of dual Champions which have been made up, including some in quite recent times. These include Dual & AFC Ch. Hiwood Shadow, who was born in 1979 and had achieved his various titles by 1984.

THE AKC HUNTING RETRIEVING TESTS

These tests are a relatively new innovation in America. They were devised by concerned individuals who recognised the need to develop a system which would evaluate the natural hunting and game-finding ability of their dogs. It was hoped that this would help to fill the void left in the gap between pure show and trial dogs, and much has been done to encourage a wide body of Labrador owners to train and work their dogs to a set standard.

Overseen by the American Kennel Club, the aim of the Tests, which are on three levels, is to judge dogs against the criteria required by the average hunter (shooting man) – not against the performance of other dogs competing in the test. They are based as closely as is possible on real hunting situations, for both dog and handler. The tests do not consist of artificial or trick problems, but include: walk-ups, working from blinds, boats, or other situations occurring during wildfowling; marking ability, handling, nose, steadiness, style, courage and manners, are assessed, as well as tracking wounded game.

All tests are conducted within a 'real hunting range', and most call for the handler to carry an empty shotgun, which he must shoulder or carry in a safe manner. Bird throwers must not be in view unless at the point of origin (i.e. in line with the dog.) Intentional hard mouth, in the opinion of the two judges shall be grounds for failing the test. Sloppy retrieving is marked down, and at all levels dogs must retrieve to hand. It is only at the Junior level that the dog may be gently restrained and brought to line on a lead in the walk up. The levels are based on ability, not age, and are divided as follows:

JUNIOR HUNTER: The judges want to see evidence of basic hunting instincts. The test includes simple tests and aims to encourage and guide. Hyperactivity, barking and excessive disobedience, lack of interest and lethargy to be marked down.

SENIOR HUNTER: This requires a hunting dog that will do a respectable job in the field. The judges assess natural ability and handler control. The dog must be steady but will not have quite the degree of experience required by a dog in the higher level. (There is a bigger jump from Junior to Senior, than from Senior to Master.)

MASTER HUNTER: This last level requires the dog to be steady (as the Senior dogs) once the judges have given the ready signal. A controlled break will mark the dog down to a nought. All birds must be delivered to hand. The dogs should handle to whistle, voice, and hand signals. But on marked retrieves the dog will be marked down if their use is required. Tests will be over more difficult terrain and will include blinds and/or marks, which will be no further than 100 yards. Distractions can also be used, and the dog must be steady to shot, falling birds, and fur. (Chasing is an eliminating fault.) Trailing tests and retrieves simulating cripples will be judged on natural ability and use of nose. Dogs must be steady – even if some distance from the handler – while other dogs are worked.

WORKING CERTIFICATE

Dogs must complete one land retrieve, and a back-to-back water retrieve. The dog does not have to retrieve to hand, but will be allowed to drop the bird within a discretionary distance of the judge in the radius of the handler. The dog must show a soft mouth. i.e. not maul the bird. The idea is that no training is given, but that the dog shows natural ability to retrieve over land, to enter water,

Killingworth Sadie MH, WR (Ch. Kuros Spartacus – Dolofon Black Lass). The Master Hunter qualification is the most difficult title to win of the three hunting tests in the USA.

and possesses a soft mouth. The tests are run on a points system. On each retrieve the dog is given marks from 1-10 on four points, Marking, Style, Presentation/Courage, and Trainability. The dog might have four retrieves, and must score more than 5 for each element, across the board. The overall average of the four sections added together must be seven or more to pass the complete test. If a dog is failed on any one of the four sections by both the judges he is immediately put out of the test.

For a Junior Hunter title a dog must pass on four occasions to qualify for the Junior Hunter Certificate. The dog may continue to run in Junior tests until qualifying once in Senior Hunter Tests (remember it is a very big step from Junior to Senior. Senior dogs must pass the section on four occasions to receive the title of Senior Hunter. (If the dog has not already been awarded the JH, this increases to five.) A Master Hunter dog must pass on five occasions, if already holding the Senior Hunter title. (If not, the dog must pass on six occasions.) The titles JH, SH and MH titles may all be added to the dog's pedigree. Each year the top Master Hunters are invited to an invitational event to demonstrate what top dogs can achieve. They must have passed a Master Hunter test three times in that calendar year to be asked to the event, which is held in the autumn.

With the introduction of these tests, it can be seen that strenuous efforts have been made to preserve the instincts of the working Labrador and other gundogs. There is now a range of events which will fulfil the requirements of all Labrador enthusiasts, as well as preserving the best qualities of the breed we all love.

Chapter Sixteen

LEADING FIELD TRIAL KENNELS

Whether you Field Trial, Hunt, work or show your Labrador, the same great founding kennel prefixes appear behind all today's successful dogs and kennels. Labrador students the world over are united in their respect and gratitude for those men and women who are synonymous with such names as Banchory, Glenhead, Hiwood, Munden, Shavington, Staindrop, Whitmore and Zelstone. It is from these common roots that the Labrador appears in its many facets today. The export of British bloodlines to Labrador enthusiasts continues, complementing the lines developed by the original importing pioneers, who quickly popularised the 'English' Labrador, proving its worth in work, looks and character.

The following kennels are among the most prominent in Britain today, and are much appreciated by American Field Trial followers who have imported stock from them. They will also be of equal interest to the new Hunter Trial enthusiasts, whose aims embrace many of those currently pursued on the English scene.

ABBOTSLEIGH

This kennel was established in 1945 by Trish Hales, who bred her Labradors mainly for picking up. It was her daughter Sarah, now Sarah Coomber, who started to compete in tests and trials with the dogs. The first to be made up was FT Ch. Abbotsleigh Lynx, by Abbotsleigh Ivan (FT Ch. Holdgate Willie – Abbotsleigh Gala) out of Susan of Brackenbank. Although not a flashy dog, he was an excellent game-finder. Susan was also mated to their next Field Trial Champion, Abbotsleigh Kossack, to produce FT Ch. Abbotsleigh Nimrod.

FT winner Leospring Mars Marine. Jan West.

Kossack was by FT Ch. Spudtamsons Berry of Mirstan out of a FT Ch. Holdgate Willie daughter, Manymills Wistful. This line of breeding produced good-looking stylish Labradors.

A Nimrod son, Pluto of Abbotsleigh, gained awards in the Championship show ring as well as in open Field Trials. Along with the Lynx descendants, they have had a large impact on the working lines in the south of England. Many first-time gundog trainers have found success in dogs from this line, which seem to show inherent traits for trainability, marking and game-finding ability. FT Ch. Abbotsleigh Joshua was also made up by Jill Gill. He, in turn, sired Mr D. Raven's FT Ch. Bravenhyde Holly and Mrs McCullen's FT Ch. Kilderkin Renoir.

BARNAVARA

Dione Ryan blames her husband for the fact that she has owned or bred four Field Trial Champion Labradors, and one Field Trial Champion Pointer, as he had no interest in her passion for horses, and was therefore reluctant to finance it. She decided to increase the chances of a successful marriage by taking an interest in *his* sport of shooting. Being of a naturally competitive nature, and also rather embarrassed by the behaviour of the shooting dogs her husband took out, Dione took the matter into her own hands, and the snowball effect led on to trials.

A bitch, Sapperton Dawn, was to have the greatest effect on the kennels. Sired by Roveacre Tilt out of Kievton Whisper, she went back to FT Ch. Galleywood Shot and FT Ch. Zelstone Moss through her dam's sire, FT Ch. Sendhurst Zelstone Tinker, and to Bench, a yellow son of Dual Ch. Knaith Banjo, on both the sire and dam sides. 'Dawn' was intelligent, and an excellent game-finder, and when mated to Stonerpoint Nathaniel (FT Ch. Palgrave Edward – Bedingham Hall Jey), she produced FT Ch. Barnavara Mayfly.

Mayfly possessed her mother's intelligence and game-finding ability, as well as the factor which seems to be the 'je ne sais quoi' of top field trial dogs. Many dogs possess the factors which enable them to work brilliantly *for themselves*, but if a dog uses these factors to work one hundred

The fruits of a successful Field Trial kennel. FT Ch. Alltmoor Dee (left) and FT Ch. Barnavara Minnow (right).

per cent for the handler – then you have a dog *par excellence*. Mayfly was mated to FT Ch. Swift of Swinbrook, by FT Ch. Swinbrook Tan – Holdgate Swallow (a Willie – Boffin daughter – see Holdgate, listed below) to produce FT Ch. Barnavara Minnow. Minnow, in turn, was mated to FT Ch. Kenswick Hamish (Dambrias Black Tern – FT Ch. Stonerpoint Be Hopeful of Kenswick). These dogs went back on the Zelstone, Scotney and Hedenham Park lines to FT Ch. Gallywood Shot and FT Ch. Glengarg Ben. This mating produced FT Ch. Barnavara Black Zulu.

All these Barnavara FT Champions have BVA/HD passes, Breeders Letters, or low hip scores recorded. Dione also made up FT Ch. Alltmoor Dee, by FT Ch. Stratfield Saye Dipper – Halkmoor Debbie (out of a Willie daughter by FT Ch. Westead Shot of Drakeshead).

DRAKESHEAD

This kennel, owned by the remarkable husband and wife team, John and Sandra Halstead, may well be regarded as the most successful Field Trial kennel of recent years, if not of all time. When John and Sandra met, John was a shooting man who worked his Labradors, and Sandra was a keen show-goer who finally got her way in showing some of John's dogs, achieving several Best of Breed wins. Sandra is a Championship show judge in her own right, and both she and John are "A" Panel Field Trial judges.

The Drakeshead kennel review in the *Midland Counties Labrador Year Book,* 1974, shows five Field Trial winners, and a proud achievement of two seconds, and a certificate of merit in Open Stakes. By 1979 FT Ch. Westead Shot of Drakeshead (no descendant of the show dogs) had been made up, been retired and spent two years hunting up like a Spaniel. Rumours started to circulate that the dog was retired for being too hot, so John, who was busy with FT Ch. Drakeshead Tinker and FT Ch. Drakeshead Anna, persuaded Sandra to campaign the dog. Shot went on to win another Open Stake and then took the 1979 Retriever Championship.

Shot's sister, FT Ch. Westead Tan of Drakeshead, was also campaigned to her title. Both these dogs, and Tinker, were by FT Ch. Swinbrook Tan out of FT Ch. Sendhurst Sweep daughters. Anna was Tan's daughter by FT Ch. Holdgate Willie. The kennel has gone on to make up fourteen Field Trial Champions, with four of these being home-bred, as well as breeding or handling Field Trial Champions for other owners.

FT Ch. Glencoin Drummer of Drakeshead was a Shot grandson out of Glencoin Daffodil. Daffodil, owned and bred by Mrs Nairn-

John Halstead pictured with FT Ch. Glencoin Drummer of Drakeshead.

Hayward, was a superb producer, being mother of three FT Ch. sons. They were the brothers FT Ch. Glencoin Drummer of Drakeshead and FT Ch. Glencoin Digger of Saddleworth, who was owned by Mr and Mrs Mayall; then, when Daffodil was put to FT Ch. Breeze of Drakeshead, the offspring included FT Ch. Glencoin Dean of Drakeshead. Drummer was a good-looking yellow dog who was used widely at stud. He sired FT Ch. Raughlin Pete of Drakeshead from a mating with FT Ch. Raughlin Rose. This dog won the 1992 Retriever Championship – the first yellow ever to do so.

In 1981 a black dog was born by Tinker out of Carrington Fay, a bitch who only had Field Trial Champions in later generations of her pedigree. The litter was bred by Mr W. G. Bickley, and the black dog, FT Ch. Breeze of Drakeshead, made up before he was three years old. He went on to make history by becoming the only dog to win the Championship on three occasions, 1985, 1986 and 1987. John describes his remarkable skills, saying: "He was a dog with uncanny marking and game-finding ability. You always went to a trial hoping that the scenting conditions were poor, because then he was at his best. Many dogs will run well when scenting is good, then it is more difficult for a single dog to shine."

Obviously the scenting conditions at the Championships, which are always held in December, were just what Breeze required. It is very unlikely that Breeze's record will ever be broken. FT Ch. Drakeshead Luke and FT Ch. Drakeshead Lace were both by FT Ch. Earshampark Sabre out of Anna. John regards Drakeshead Dipper (Tinker's dam) as one of the best producing bitches. A Field Trial winner herself, she was grandmother to Drummer and Breeze. She was also the mother of FT Ch. Drakeshead Thorn, who, when mated to FT Ch. Spudtamsons Berry of Mirstan, produced FT Ch. Brenjon Dirk of Drakeshead. Dirk was the sire of the influential stud dog FT Ch. Haretor Mark of Drakeshead. The other Haretor Field Trial Champion made up by the Halsteads was FT Ch. Haretor Shadow of Drakeshead (see under Haretor). John and Sandra feel strongly that Field Trial dogs should combine normal picking up and hunting with trialing, and dogs are never saved or rested just for trials, not even the Championship.

GUNSTOCK

This kennel is owned by Terry and Gaynor Bailey, who both shoot. Gaynor started trialing in 1967 as the result of a £1 bet that she could not win a first, second or third award in a field trial with a yellow. Of course, anyone who knows Gaynor will realise she just had to take up the challenge, and she won the bet with a dog called Rancho Grande, who got third – and Gaynor got the trialing bug!

Terry and Gaynor were married two years later and he started to run a dog called Gunstock Black Sambo. This dog was excellent on runners and on the whistle. He won six trial awards but finances did not permit serious campaigning. His daughter, Gunstock Flannog Barberry, had more opportunity and won a novice stake as well as winning seven seconds, five of which were in two-day Opens. She was mated to a dog they had made up, FT Ch. Gunstock Teal. Teal was by the famous sire FT Ch. Swinbrook Tan out of FT Ch. Angeltowns Black Sapphire. The Baileys believe Teal to be the first Field Trial Champion who also had a hip pass and eye certificate. The breeding of sound dogs is very important to them, and Teal seems to have stamped good hip scores on his descendants.

Terry says: "Up until the time he died at thirteen and half years old, he was still rock steady and the perfect shooting dog." Teal probably set a record by winning the Scottish Gundog Society two-day Open Stake three years in succession from 1977 to 1979, on the same ground.

From the mating of Teal and Barberry, a two day Open Stake winner, Gunstock Matador, was

Gaynor Bailey and the Gunstock Labradors: (left to right) FTAW G. Black Sambo, FTW G. Hutch, FTW G. Fendrake, FT Ch. G. Teal, FT Ch. G. Lisleholme Black Bun and FTW G. Flannog Barberry.

produced. He had twelve other awards and was top Retriever at the CLA Game Fair in 1983. FT Ch. Gunstock Lisleholme Black Bun was also made up by this kennel. Reputed to be an excellent marker and still steady at twelve years of age, she is most interesting because she was entirely show-bred, sired by Poolstead Pirate out of Lisleholme Dusky Aphrodite (descended from Kinley and Reanacre breeding). Working ability, soundness and looks are the hallmarks of this kennel, and both Gaynor and Terry are "A" panel Field Trial judges.

HARETOR
The owner of this kennel was the skilful gundog breeder, June Crowden. Although she did not compete in trials herself, she was, before she emigrated, a regular spectator at trials. As well as breeding three Field Trial Champions, she was regarded as one of the pioneers in trying to improve and maintain the hip and eye status of the working Labrador.

Haretor Abel of Bellever (FT Ch. Stratfieldsaye Dipper – Sladbrook Twiggy of Haretor, a Swinbrook Tan grand-daughter) won five Open Stakes, and was runner-up in the 1983 Retriever Championship. Owned by Rupert Hill, who picks up and shoots over all his dogs (also

Haretor Abel of Bellever: Runner-up in the 1983 Retriever Championship.

well-known for his Field Trial English Springer Spaniels), Abel was used as a beating dog for two seasons before he was taught to handle. Obviously an exceptional, as well as being a goodlooking Labrador, he was also the sire of John and Sandra Halstead's FT Ch. Haretor Shadow of Drakeshead. June also bred FT Ch. Haretor Mark of Drakeshead, who is one of the top working sires of today, if not *the* top.

HOLDGATE

Gabriella Benson's kennel started in 1955 with an eight-week-old puppy chosen by her father-in-law to wean her from the more dangerous pastime of horse riding. With the aid of a book and with help from Col. Kingsforth Lethbridge (the breeder), Gabriella and Stella (who was to become FT Ch. Creedpark Stella) won their First Trial. She went on to win her next two Open Stakes as well as the IGL two-day Open.

Gabriella says: "She was a truly unique bitch, because I knew absolutely nothing about trialing. We taught each other, and our rapport became almost telepathic. The professionals called her a 'natural', and said I would never have another like her; and although I have had some very good ones over the years, I don't think I have ever been quite so 'at one' with another dog."

Nevertheless, the Holdgate kennel made up another eight Field Trial Champions: Holdgate Boffin, Holdgate Vesta, Holdgate Willie, Cefnperfa Gypsy of Holdgate, Greenwood Timothy of Holdgate, Myddlecourt Willow of Holdgate, Holdgate Winter and Holdgate Bebe.

Stella was mated to FT Ch. Galleywood Shot, who had won the Retriever Championship. A bitch from this litter, called Bramble (who won two stakes) was mated to FT Ch. Hiwood Dipper, and this produced FT Ch. Holdgate Vesta. She was mated to Jerico Rocket and produced Holdgate Steven. Rocket was chosen to improve the looks of Vesta, who was rather small and light-boned. Steven gained seven seconds in trials, proving his consistency, but he was a rather small dog who never showed himself off. However, when he was mated to Wing of Ruckley, a bitch from Glenbruar Smiler out of Berrystead Zelstone Bramble, a dog resulted which epitomised the true Holdgate type and temperament. This was FT Ch. Holdgate Willie. Willie was a Retriever Championship winner, as well as winning a first at Crufts, the only time he was ever shown.

Gabriella says: "If a perfect dog existed, it was Willie. He was a natural game-finder, easy to teach and willing to please." Willie ran in the Championship four times in all, winning the first time and being placed each subsequent time, ending with a fourth when he was five years old. Willie appears behind many of the pedigrees of today's trialing dogs, and in practically all of the dual purpose pedigrees. He and his son, Holdgate Dibble (a superb game-finder and gundog, but with an ultra light mouth which put him down at trials), seemed to do the most in fixing a gene which improved the looks and conformation of working Labradors. Willie is also directly behind the most recent Holdgate Field Trial Champions, Greenwood Timothy of Holdgate, Myddlecourt Willow of Holdgate and Holdgate Winter.

The Holdgate kennel has consistently produced good-looking dogs, with special emphasis placed on good noses and *natural* game-finding ability. Even though their mistress has been dogged with a thrice-fractured spine, numerous broken bones and remodelling of joints, the Holdgate dogs have always been first and foremost working gundogs, besides their success as trial dogs. As a result of their owner's disabilities, the Holdgate kennel has concentrated on dog line breeding, as opposed to bitch line breeding, since rearing litters is now out of the question. This does not seem to have reduced the kennel's success.

Gabriella, a successful and experienced trainer, as well as being a long-standing and respected "A" panel judge, says: "I could write a book on what I have learnt from other people about dog

ABOVE: FT. Ch. Holdgate Winter (1984).

LEFT: Gabriella Benson, pictured with FT Ch. Creedpark Stella in 1958.

training. No two dogs are ever the same, and with each new one comes new problems to solve, and new challenges to face." When asked about her feelings on today's dogs, she commnents: "It is such a pity that judges at Field Trials will almost invariably put a 'robot' whistle dog above a natural game-finder, and the handler with most control is placed above those who expect their dogs to do their work unaided."

LETTERMORE

This is another kennel which has achieved great success in breeding typical-looking, working Labradors and which has been greatly influenced in its breeding programme by FT Ch. Holdgate Willie. Val and Pat O'Brien's FT Ch. Quail of Lettermore was sired by Willie, homebred from Pat's first bitch, who ran in Field Trials. Quail was used continually for picking up, and what is even more notable was that she was the only picking up dog which Val owned at the time. Quail was made up when she was eight years old, and she won the Essex Open Stake, with eight eye-wipes over two days.

Another of their bitches, Lettermore May, won the IGL Open Stake and knocked on the door with many other awards, but found that the title just eluded her. However, when mated to FT Ch. Carnochway Daniel (FT Ch. Leacross Rinkals – Killyleagh Wanda), she produced FT Ch. Lettermore Trout – a good-looking dog with the required natural nose, marking ability and sensible temperament – as well as four other Field Trial winners in the same litter.

PALGRAVE

The late Eric Baldwin's prefix is equally well-known in Labradors, Golden Retrievers and Spaniels. Even after his death, Eric's line of working black Labradors exerts a strong influence on the Field Trial lines of today. He bred Nigel Rowson's 1984 Championship winner, FT Ch. Palgrave Nettle (FT Ch. Shot of Palgrave – FT Ch. Palgrave Holly). This has produced several Field Trial Champions including Mr D. Openshaw's FT Ch. Palgrave Quin and Stan Harvey's FT Ch. Palgrave Quest. Shot was also runner-up in the 1977 Championships. The sire of the pre-potent FT Ch. Swinbrook Tan was FT Ch. Palgrave Edward (FT Ch. Sendhurst Sweep – Palgrave Glenfarg Tessa).

POCKLEA

David Garbutt is the owner of this kennel. He won the Championship in 1991 with Pocklea Remus (FT Ch. Haretor Mark of Drakeshead – Drakeshead Gypsy), as well as being second in 1989. He also bred and handled David Benson's FT Ch. Pocklea Tide of Middlegate (FT Ch. Breeze of Drakeshead – Gypsy) to win the Championship in 1988. This win was all the more remarkable because Tide had not seen her breeder since leaving home as a six-week-old puppy.

She had been trained and handled by David Benson, who qualified her at the North West Field Trials Association two-day stake. However, the Championship was shortly before Christmas, and David had just taken on a new meat trade business, so he did not have the time to run her. David Garbutt had Tide for only six days before running her. This ultra-short partnership says a lot for both the dog and the handling and training abilities of the two Davids. Tide went on to win three more Open Stakes with David Benson, qualifying twice more for the Championship. David Garbutt had also won the Championship in 1981 with FT Ch. Pocklington Glen. He also made up FT Ch. Pocklington Tessa, and another bitch, FT Ch. Sandringham Magpie, who when put to FT Ch. Swinbrook Mosquito produced FT Ch. Pocklington Ben.

SANDRINGHAM

The Labrador world is indeed privileged to have such a patron as Her Majesty the Queen. The Royal Family have long owned Labradors, with King George V also breeding under the Wolferton affix. Although always worked, several Labradors were also shown. Her Majesty became Patron of the Labrador Retriever Club in 1946. After her accession to the throne, the Queen built up the Sandringham kennel with the emphasis on the working side.

FT Ch. Sandringham Ranger was made up, as well as several other Field Trial winners being campaigned. Her Majesty's handler since 1964 was Bill Meldrum. A remarkable bitch, Sherry of Biteabout, who was an Open Stake winner, also proved to have a strong influence on further breeding. When mated to FT Ch. Creedy Park Digger she produced FT Ch. Sandringham Sydney. Sydney won four Open Stakes, as well as an Award of Honour at the Championship. He also sired FT Ch. Sandringham Salt (out of Sandringham Mustard). FT Ch. Sandringham Slipper was also made up, going from a Novice Stake winner to Champion in just ten days. Slipper also came fourth in the 1969 Championship and second in the 1970 Championship at Sandringham. Occasionally puppies are sold to working homes and campaigned to success, and this includes FT Ch. Sandringham Magpie and FT Ch. Sandringham Moccasin. The Royal Labradors are good representatives of the Standard and are regularly used by members of the Royal Family, both to be shot over and for picking up. Her Majesty is a proficient handler and has judged several trials. Princess Anne and the Queen have both hosted several trials and tests, and both take an informed interest in the dog work.

STRATFIELDSAYE

Owned by His Grace the Duke of Wellington, the dogs are handled by the experienced and calm Arnold White Robinson. Arnold's apprenticeship began in the early thirties, covering all breeds, especially Pointers. His experience in working Labradors goes back to some of the classic kennels of the past – Cornbury, Galleywood, Hiwood and Ruro, to name a few. Having worked for Mr H. Henderson (Beinnmhor), Arnold eventually started working at Stratfieldsaye in 1969.

FT Ch. Stratfieldsaye Beinnmhor Lomond, a son of the FT Ch. bitch, Cornbury Ruro Teal, was one of the dogs to move with him. This dog was made up in 1972, and then went on to win the Retriever Championship in the same year. Lomond was mated to Ciddyhayfield Tansy, a bitch from Stratfieldsaye lines, to produce FT Ch. Stratfieldsaye Dipper, who won the Championship in 1980. FT Ch. Stratfieldsaye Calcot Crossbow, made up in 1974, was virtually all show-bred. His sire was Calcot Blaise (Ch. Sandylands Tandy – Calcot Braeduke Lance), and his dam was Persian Pride (Scwarlodge Drummer – Laret Sunset). The Duke has always aimed for working Labradors which adhere to the Breed Standard, and the occasional infusion of show blood has helped to maintain this objective. The dogs are all used regularly for picking up.

SWINBROOK

No catalogue of working Labrador kennels would be complete without mentioning this kennel, owned by the late Duncan Mackinnon. The prefix is now in the ownership of his handler, Phillip White. Phillip made up seven Field Trial Champions for the kennel, with two, FT Ch. Swinbrook Tan and FT Ch. Swinbrook Beatle, being bred there. It is Swinbrook Tan who has stamped his mark on the working lines of today's dogs. He was by FT Ch. Palgrave Edward out of a remarkable bitch, FT Ch. Beinnmhor Tide. Bred by Mr Henderson and owned by Mr Mackinnon, Phillip handled her to her title, and to win the Retriever Championship in 1969 and 1970.

An examination of the pedigrees of practically all the modern Field Trial Champions will show one or more lines to Tan. In the words of one well-known trialer: "He *must* have been sound. Had he not been, the working Labradors of today would have been a disaster." FT Ch. Swinbrook Mosquito (second in the 1975 Championship), FT Ch. Swinbrook Fern (litter sister to Tan), and FT Ch. Swinbrook Swift also contributed to the Swinbrook legend.

All the dogs were firstly hard-working, picking up dogs and trials had to fit around this job. Recently, FT Ch. Swinbrook Twig (FT Ch. Drakeshead Actor of Shotgate – Palgrave Kay) was second in the 1987 Retriever Championships, handled by Ian Openshaw.

TIBEA

This kennel was built up by the late Robin Watson. Robin was an "A" panel judge, and an excellent sportsman, as well as breeding a top Field Trial line, along with his wife, Marlene. Many working Labradors in the west and south of England are descendants of FT Ch. Oday Alice of Tibea, who has similar breeding to FT Ch. Swinbrook Tan, i.e. FT Ch. Palgrave Edward – FT Ch. Beinnmhor Tern. When Alice was mated to FT Ch. Hedenham Park Dash of Philray, she produced FT Ch. Tibea Topaz. This bitch was considered their most prominent, as her progeny were very consistent at trials. One of these, FT Ch. Tibea Tosh, is behind many current Field Trial Champions. Another, Tibea Tea, won five seconds in Open Stakes.

The Tibea dogs were not large, and Marlene believes this may account for their low hip scores. All the dogs were, and still are, regularly used for picking up. Robin Watson Junior has started to campaign the dogs once again, but although Marlene works them in the field, she is reluctant to actively campaign the dogs, for fear of lowering the high Tibea standards. She says: "Robin only ever campaigned the best dogs, and among his achievements was winning fourteen Novice Stakes, with fourteen different dogs. His principal aims within the breeding programme were for good temperament, and, although he appreciated a good-looking dog, this had to come first."

Marlene is a dog trainer and handler in her own right, and acted as judge's steward for her late husband at many trials. She certainly has a good eye for a working dog, and with her breeding programme and her son's interest in Field Trialing, the Tibea dogs may well come to the fore once again.

THE DUAL PURPOSE KENNELS
The road followed by those interested in both showing and Field Trialing is certainly a very challenging one. There has not been a Dual Champion since Mrs Wormald's Knaith Banjo, born in 1946, but a few kennels can claim achievements in both areas. The influence of the Holdgate kennel, particularly FT Ch. Holdgate Willie, has already been mentioned. He is grandfather to Susan Scales' Manymills Drake, a two-day Open Stake winner and a winning show dog. Drake sired Ch. Abbeystead Herons Court, born in 1985, out of Charway Seashell. Herons Court, owned by Mrs L. Minchella, won several Field Trial awards.

Drake also sired the Field Trial winners, Treheme Fairly Game at Leospring and Treherne Game Fall at Leospring, who both won awards at Championship shows. Leospring Mars Marine (sired by Pluto of Abbotsleigh), was another two-day Open Stake winning dog with Championship show awards, and all three of these dogs were out of Buttsash Polly Flinders of Leospring. This bitch was a daughter of Bridget Docking's Ch. Squire of Ballyduff, who was a winner of Field Trial awards, and the fourth in a line of Ballyduff black dog Champions, who were also good workers.

Ch. Timspring Sirius was a son of Eng. Am. Ch. Ballyduff Seaman, the first in this line of Champions. Sirius was owned by Joan Macan, who owned several dogs who were successful at trials, and he was sire to Secret Song of Lawnwood, owned by Marjorie Satterthwaite. Song sired FT Ch. Styleside Hawk, owned by Mr J. Leeson, as well as Ch. Elowood Soul Singer, owned by Jean Reader, who also had Field Trial awards. He, in turn, sired Eileen Ayling's Meadowmill Tap on Wood, who won a novice dog/novice handler stake and a Reserve CC. Soul Singer was also grandfather to another Reserve CC winner with Field Trial awards, and this was Westonholme Dark Warlock, owned by Ann Clements.

The dual purpose route, although difficult, will, hopefully, always have its followers. There are still a few kennels who insist upon their working dogs being good representatives of the Standard, and there are also still some show judges who work their dogs and therefore bear this aspect in mind when judging. The dream of another Dual Champion may prove to be permanently elusive. However, its pursuit can only be a good thing for the breed, helping to maintain the true Labrador type, which the forefathers of the breed sought to preserve.

Written by Joy Venturi ("Leospring"), Field Trial Secretary of Kent, Surrey & Sussex Labrador Retriever Club.

Chapter Seventeen

HEALTH CARE

I am not medically trained, but having owned Labradors for twenty-five years, I have learnt a little about the health and well-being of the Labrador. I will therefore touch briefly on some of the major hereditary problems and ailments that can affect the Labrador. I hope that readers are as lucky as me in finding a vet whom you have the utmost confidence in and can converse with.

I spent some six months investigating the various vets in my area, chose one, and have had eighteen years faithful service to date. I prefer the smaller practices: mine has only two vets, whom I know very well. Consequently, they also know my dogs very well, and we have a marvellous working relationship. Common sense and a little first aid might be all you need at times, but always go to your vet if in any doubt whatsoever.

FIRST AID
It is sensible to keep a small first aid kit handy. It should include:
Thermometer.
Bottle of Arnica solution.
Bandages (cotton and crepe).
Roll of plaster.
Scissors.
Lint.
Antiseptic cream.
Packet of cooking soda.
Liquid paraffin.
Potassium permanganate.
Plastic syringe for medicines, (obtainable from your vet – makes getting liquid medicines into your dogs so much easier than from a spoon).
TCP or Savlon Disinfectant (or failing that, use salt).
TAKING YOUR DOG'S TEMPERATURE
One of the first things you should do if you feel your dog is unwell is to take the temperature. This should be done before you telephone for the vet, and the reading will be invaluable in determining if you should bring in the dog to the surgery at once. A dog's normal temperature is 101.5 degrees Fahrenheit (38.5 degrees Centigrade). With puppies of up to six months of age, you can expect it to be slightly higher – 102-102.5 Fahrenheit (39 Centigrade). A temperature that is either higher or lower than these norms, will indicate that something is amiss.

Use a thermometer with a rounded end, and shake it down, to ensure the mercury has fallen.

Then insert the thermometer into the dog's rectum. Keep one hand pressed against the stifle, so that your dog cannot bend the knee and sit down, and with the other hand, keep hold of the thermometer. Leave the thermometer inserted for one minute to get a correct reading.

ARNICA SOLUTION

This is a ticture for sprains and bruises. It helps the healing process and also reduces bruising and swelling. If I have dog with a cut pad, I make up the solution to the recommended strength, and keep it in a small plastic box. Then after cleaning, I can soak the dog's foot in the solution, three or four times a day, until the cut is healed.

COOKING SODA

This may seem like an unlikely item to include in a first aid kit, but there is a good reason for it. Labradors are notorious scavengers, and to date, I have had two experiences of a dog getting hold of a dangerous substance. If you pop a couple of half-inch long nuggets of cooking soda down the dog's throat, it instantly makes the dog vomit, thus bringing up whatever has just been eaten. This can be done immediately at home, before dashing off to have the dog seen by a veterinary surgeon.

LIQUID PARAFFIN

This comes in handy if your dog has managed to get into the biscuit bag and has gorged on food. It is also useful if your dog has eaten a bone and is straining to pass a stool. A good couple of tablespoons of liquid paraffin will coat the inside of the intestine, which will help the stool to be passed more easily. If this does not work, you will need to take your dog to the vet.

POTASSIUM PERMANGANATE

This comes in crystal form, and can be bought very cheaply from a pharmacist. It has a two-fold use. When diluted in water it will make an antiseptic solution, or in its dry state, it can be pressed on to a small cut or wound (such as a bleeding toenail, if you have cut too close to the quick) and it will instantly stem the blood flow. This is also used when removing dewclaws at three to four days old, although it is quite normal to keep the front dewclaws on Labradors. We find that they are a help rather than a hindrance in the field, and very seldom tear when the dogs are adults.

COMMON AILMENTS AND DISEASES

ANAL GLANDS

The two small glands situated either side of the anus can become full and uncomfortable. A classic sign is when a dog drags its rear end along the ground. I have always found these glands very easy to empty myself. Your vet will, of course, perform this simple operation for you, or will show you how to do it.

I put a large wad of cotton-wool (cotton) over the rectum, and squeeze firmly from either side. It should discharge a rather foul-smelling fluid on to the cotton wool, and this should be swiftly disposed of. If frightened, a dog can evacuate these glands itself. As I said, I took a long time to choose my vet, and the first time I visited him, my young bitch shot the contents of her anal glands right down his clean, white coat. His comment was "I won't forget you in a hurry!" We are still good friends, eighteen years on.

ARTHRITIS

This is a rather common complaint in elderly Labradors; just like humans, as they get older they tend to seize up a little. Arthritis is the inflammation of a joint, resulting in pain, which may affect the way the dog moves. Your vet will be able to prescribe drugs that will alleviate the pain to some degree, but there is no known cure.

BROKEN TAIL

A funny-sounding ailment, but that is exactly the way to describe it. The tail hangs forlornly down, a few inches from the base. It can be painful for the dog, but recovery only takes a few days. It is usually seen after the dog has been out in the cold and wet, or has taken a swim in very cold water. If you ensure that the tail is thoroughly dried, especially under the tail near the base, and ensure that your dog sleeps in a warm draught-free room, the problem will cure itself.

CANKER OF THE EAR

Some dogs seem to go through their entire life without any trouble with their ears, and others seem to have more than their fair share of problems. The usual sign is shaking of the head, or one ear held lower than the other. On closer inspection, you will see that the ear canal will be reddened and hot. I invariably seem to have at least one dog with ear problems, so I always keep a spirit-based ear-cleaner and ear-drops in stock, which will alleviate the problem. These can be obtained from your vet. When treating a dog, hold up the ear by its tip, apply some ear cleaning fluid, and then massage the ear at the base (from the outside) for at least thirty seconds to a minute. Then gently wipe out any excess with a tissue. Do not be rough, and at no time dig down into the ear. Once the ear is clean, put in the recommended number of ear-drops, and massage again, to work it well down into the ear canal. Repeat this on the other ear, and continue with the treatment daily until the problem has cleared. A regular weekly check helps to keep on top of any ear problems.

CLEFT PALATE

This occurs fairly infrequently in the Labrador, but every new-born whelp should be checked over. This is done by running your finger down the centre of the mouth, and you will be able to tell if the puppy has cleft palate. If this is the case, the kindest thing you can do is to ask the vet put the pup down. A puppy with a cleft palate cannot suckle properly, and milk will continually be coming back down the nose. This means that the puppy cannot take in sufficient nourishment, and will soon start to fade and eventually die. In mild cases, surgical correction is effective.

CONTAGIOUS DISEASES

Your dog should have a course of inoculations in puppyhood, as the maternal antibodies lose their strength. This should be followed up by yearly boosters to give your dog cover from the scourges of Distemper, Hepatitis, Leptospirosis and Parvovirus. These are all killers, and we should all take advantage of the vaccines that are available. It does not mean that your dog will not contract the above diseases; but the attack will, most likely, be very mild, or hardly noticeable at all, if your dog is inoculated.

DEPRAVED APPETITE

The eating of faeces (stools) is always considered to be a horrible habit, but one that can be prevalent in many kennels, especially as the chain is seen to be kept going, with mothers cleaning up after their pups. The best way to get on top of the situation is to make sure that the area the dogs are kennelled in, and their run, is kept clean. If you catch a dog trying to eat the stools of another dog, pick up immediately, and show your distaste, making your voice sound hard.

If you have only one or two dogs, you can try various remedies that do meet with some success. You can leave stools around on purpose, but liberally sprinkled with pepper, or even mustard. The dogs will very quickly get the message. I have not tried it myself but I have heard that charcoal biscuits, fed with the meat, make the stools quite unpalatable.

Do check that your dog is being fed a well-balanced diet, and that you are supplying all the nutrients that are required. It used to be thought that dogs were trying to supplement something that was missing from their diet, but dogs who eat stools can be just as healthy as those that do not get into this habit.

DEAFNESS

I have found that some of my 'oldies' do develop a certain amount of deafness – again, just like us humans. It is nothing to worry about, but accept that you might have to go thundering off over the lawn to tap an oldie on the rear, because you want the dog to come in. When walking away from you, there is little chance of the dog hearing, or of seeing your hand signals.

DIARRHOEA

Most dogs will get diarrhoea at some time or another during their lifetime. Usually it can be put down to something the dog has eaten, but it is also a symptom of some illnesses. First, take your dog's temperature, and if this is normal, the best way to tackle the problem is to withhold food for at least twelve, if not twenty-four hours. Make sure the dog has access to plenty of fluids, preferably with a packet of rehydrant added, to replace salts and sugars that the dog is losing in the very liquid stools.

Often, this is all that is needed to clear up the problem. Your dog should then be weaned back to normal rations, making sure that no milk is fed for another week or two. If the problem persists after two days, consult your vet. If the stool contains more than a streaking of blood, go to your vet immediately, as this could be the start of haemorrhagic enteritis.

ECLAMPSIA

Eclampsia or 'Milk Fever', needs *immediate* veterinary help. This condition can happen any time from the last week of pregnancy until after weaning. It usually happens when the bitch is in her peak lactation period, when the pups are two to three weeks old. The levels of calcium in the bitch's bloodstream decrease to such an extent that she can go into a coma. The first signs are restlessness and rapid breathing in the bitch, followed by shaking, muscular tremors, and loss of co-ordination so she staggers around and eventually collapses.

The remedy is an intravenous injection of calcium, administered by the vet, which brings about a rapid result. If left unattended, the bitch will die. My only experience of this condition occurred when the pups were nearly six weeks old, and were just about weaned off the mother. She had been given calcium supplement in her diet during the pregnancy and lactation, and, in fact, was still on it. The vet came out, and the bitch failed to respond to two inoculations of calcium. He left me caring for the bitch, as there was nothing more he could do, and eventually at 2am, four hours after the first calcium shot, she started to respond, and was able to return to the pups in the morning.

ECTOPARASITES

Ectoparasites are the four main outside invaders which attack the dog's skin; namely, fleas, lice, mites and ticks. All can be treated, and even the very cleanest of dogs can pick them up from time to time. Vigorous scratching and hair loss are the symptoms that you will notice. You might even find a flea – and if you see one flea, there will be many more lurking around. It is usually easier to see the droppings of the fleas, which are like tiny dark grains of sand. It is important to use the medication given by your vet correctly, following the instructions carefully, and ensuring that the parasites are eliminated from bedding, kennel walls and the area the dog lives in. Lice do not move around at the same rate as fleas. They are even smaller, and they get into crevices, and the folds of skin, especially around the ears. The minute mite is a basic cause of mange, and can often only be diagnosed by doing skin scrapes and examining them under a microscope. Mites are also found in dogs' ears, often passed on to the dog by a cat living in the same house.

Ticks are picked up by dogs when exercised over fields, especially where sheep have been on the same ground, or in woodland areas where deer are found. They can be removed by a insecticidal shampoo. They should not be pulled off the dog, as they tend to leave the mouth-part embedded in the skin, which will continue to irritate. A drop of ether, or lighter fuel, may encourage the tick to let go – but if the tick is anywhere near the dog's eyes, this is not possible.

GASTRIC TORSION (BLOAT)

This is not a common occurrence in Labradors, by any means, but it does crop up very, very rarely. If it happens, it is a real emergency, and you must get your dog to the vet quickly, trying to keep the dog as quiet as possible. The signs are the dog appearing anxious and failing to settle; the stomach is hard and taut, and will start to swell. This is due to a twisting (torsion) of the stomach, cutting off the escape of gas from fermenting food. Immediate surgery is necessary, which can be very successful, but the shock the dog goes into afterwards can be the killer. It is, unfortunately, something that can occur again in the same animal. Some breeds are more prone to it than others; it usually occurs more frequently in the very deep-chested breeds.

HAEMATOMA (BLOOD BLISTER)

I have had a couple of Labradors, who have suffered from this, this over the years. It is usually seen on the ear flap, caused by the dog shaking the head and damaging the ear. This causes small blood vessels to break, and a blood clot forms. This can become quite swollen and painful.

The condition is alleviated by simple surgery, using buttons, or sutures in a circle around the opening from which the blood has been drained. This exerts pressure, and prevents the clot from accumulating a second time. Haematomas can appear at the site of any injury or blow, but in a Labrador they seem to happen most often on the ear.

KENNEL COUGH (Infectious Canine Tracheobronchitis)

This is a bane to breeders and kennel owners – not in itself life threatening, but a problem that every owner of a number of dogs dreads. There are several agents associated with this condition – mainly viral, but only one bacterium, Bordetella bronchiseptica. The viral particles are extremely small, and can travel through the air from animal to animal. Fortunately, they do not survive for long outside the host animal, and infection is picked up by direct contact. The bacterial agent tends to be a secondary invader, and causes the ocular and nasal discharge which is so often associated with KC. Older dogs may become immune to several of the strains, but the youngsters will always pick them up, if they have not been in contact with them before. There are vaccines available which help to protect dogs against this disease. Nasal drops will help protect dogs against Bordetella *only*, while the injectable vaccines will help to protect dogs against some of the viral elements. They need to be administered every six months, and once the drops are given to a dog, it is quite a headache trying to administer on successive occasions, as the dogs hate it.

A dog with KC usually develops swollen glands in the throat, and a hard, rasping cough. This is most commonly heard first thing in the morning, and after any exertion at all. The condition will last some weeks, and the dog needs to be isolated from other dogs for six weeks. *This means that you do not go out to the shows because you don't want to waste your entry fee.* I take about six dogs to a Championship Show at a time, and I go to most of the shows, and if my dogs are infected, the subsequent loss to my pocket in lost entries is enormous, not to mention the round-the-clock barrier nursing I will have to take on to keep the infection at bay from my other dogs, and perhaps a litter of pups.

Kennel cough in a puppy can have after-effects; they can develop pneumonia complications. One of my dogs, Ch. W. Fore Square had very bad scarring to his lungs after contacting KC at twelve weeks of age, and he suffered on cold, damp days in winter for the rest of his life.

Kennel Cough does not seem to affect the dog's appetite, but, to help ease the symptoms, a good cough linctus or honey will help. This can be easily administered with a clean, empty syringe. Antibiotic treatment is usually effective, but so are homoeopathic remedies, and I have found the homoeopathic tablets are fast-acting. I administer them crushed in a teaspoon with a little honey, and they go down very easily.

LARYNGEAL PARALYSIS

Laryngeal Paralysis is a disease of the older dog, and more than fifty per cent of all cases presented to the University Veterinary Hospitals in the UK are Labradors. Once diagnosed, the necessary delicate operation should be performed by a specialist. The symptoms are very loud, distressed breathing, coughing, (often mistaken for a heart cough), a muted bark, and the inability to take very much exercise. The larynx actually collapses slowly over the wind pipe, cutting down the air intake into the lungs. The operation entails pinning back the larynx, either side of the windpipe, so that the dog can breathe easily again. An eleven-year-old Labrador of mine was operated on, and recovered to such an extent that she was going out on three-mile hikes less than five weeks after the operation. After the operation, we had to make sure that she did not have any flaky food that could be inhaled into her lungs, and an after-effect of the operation was that she had a muted bark. This was a bonus point in 'Slipper's' case, as she had been a very noisy old bird up till then! She lived the remaining eighteen months of her life in less pain, and with dignity and vigour. Most of the dogs that have this operation range between ten to thirteen years of age. All take the stress of the operation well, and have an improved life afterwards. If you think your old Labrador could possibly have this disease, please discuss it with your vet.

MASTITIS

Mastitis is the inflammation of one or more of the mammary glands. It can happen at any time, but mainly during the lactation period. A wise precaution is to run your hands over the teats at least twice a day, while the bitch is feeding her puppies, to ensure that they have not become inflamed. You will know if your bitch has mastitis; the teat becomes hot, very hard and inflamed, and is most painful. The bitch may also show signs of fever. Antibiotic treatment from the vet is required, but you will be able to help the healing process by applying hot towel compresses, and expressing the discoloured contaminated milk. This should be done at least five or six times a day.

Once the situation begins to improve, try to get the pups back on to the teat in question (they will avoid it by themselves in the early stages); this will help to prevent the condition recurring. In severe cases, the mammary gland may become completely destroyed and replaced by scar tissue, which is non-productive, leading to a 'blind' teat in later pregnancies. Some bitches produce so much milk that the pups cannot use it all. If a bitch is nursing a small litter, cutting down on the food intake can help. When weaning the pups, reduce the bitch's food slowly, as they need less of her milk, and this will ensure that the situation does not arise at this time.

PYOMETRA

This is a condition that can affect bitches of any age after their first season, but the incidence increases in middle-aged and elderly bitches. It is an inflammation of the uterus, and it should be treated promptly or you could lose your bitch. I have found that bitches that have had litters, or are prone to false pregnancies and frequent seasons (i.e. less than the normal six months) seem to be more at risk. To make sure that I never put my bitches through a pyrometra, I always have my bitches spayed (uterus removed), once they have had the litters I have planned for them.

The symptoms of Pyometra are loss of appetite, raised temperature, excess drinking, a swollen abdomen, and vomiting. There is often an evil-smelling discharge or pus from the vulva. At least this is easy to see, and your vet might well try antibiotics to clear up the situation before resorting to surgery. When the uterus remains closed, the discharge and pus remain in the abdomen. This is a more serious condition, and usually the uterus has to be removed. The bitch will make an excellent recovery, and it often seems to give older bitches a new lease of life. Careful management of the diet afterwards will insure that your bitch does not become obese. Think of all those guide dogs walking the streets – all have been spayed or castrated, and none are fat!

STRICTURE

This is a piece of membrane growing either side of the vagina wall, or as a membrane down the centre of the vagina. A few bitches have them, and so it is best to check a bitch, prior to her first mating. If she has a stricture, the vet can quickly dispose of it, so that the mating can go on unhindered.

UMBILICAL HERNIA

This is a small hernia at the site where the umbilical cord was attached. It can be hereditary, or caused by the bitch being too enthusiastic when severing the cord at birth. It is rarely serious, and the hernia tends to get smaller or disappear in time. If this does not happen, your dog may require surgical correction.

WARTS AND LUMPS

The elderly Labrador seems to be prone to getting lumps and bumps, and nearly all of them will cause no harm at all. However, you should always check with your vet to make sure a growth is benign, especially if it seems to be growing at a fast rate.

WET ECZEMA

This is something that seems to affect a lot of Labradors. It is usually from a site that is causing irritation, usually around the neck area. Labradors love to find something to roll in – a little fox dirt behind each ear is, I think, the Labrador equivalent to Chanel No 5 – and unless you make sure all is removed, it will very quickly turn into a site for wet eczema. Fleas, lice, mites etc. will also cause irritation, and the scratching will produce the same results.

The first indication is a small, wet patch of hair, which will come away in your hands quite readily. This can start from the size of small coin, and will grow rapidly go up to the size of an orange. My method is drastic, but it works. I remove all the hair from the site, and scrub it three to four times a day with a solution made from one teaspoon of salt, dissolved in a small basin of warm water. I dry the area thoroughly, and then apply a cream with a cortisone base, which will lessen the desire to scratch. I do this for two to three days, removing the yellow crusty cover that forms, until new skin is regrowing. The hair seems to grow back quite rapidly. If you fail to remove all the hair from the site in the first instance, the eczema seems to go on growing.

WORMS

The outward signs that your dog has worms are: poor condition, a staring coat, and in a puppy especially, a bloated stomach. Different worms can infest the dog; puppies are mostly prone to roundworms (toxacara canis), as are adult dogs. The commonest tapeworms (Dipylidium caninum), are easily picked up, as their hosts are fleas and lice. These days hookworm (Ucinaria stenocephala) and whipworm (Trichuris vulpis) are only occasionally seen. Consult your vet as to the best way to eradicate them, as different worms are susceptible to different treatments. A regular worming regime is advised to keep the more common worms at bay.

HEARTWORM

Heartworm (Dirofilaria immitis) is not seen in the UK (the climate is not warm enough), but is widespread in the United States and Australasia. The disease is carried by mosquitoes which have bitten infected animals. Clinical signs of the disease include tiredness, coughing and shortness of breath; major organs may be damaged before detection. Your dog can be put on a preventative programme, which includes regular dosing. Your vet will advise.

HEREDITARY CONDITIONS

EPILEPSY

This is a condition that occurs in many breeds. It is not widespread, and it is thought that it could be inherited, so dogs displaying the condition should not be bred from. A dog experiencing a fit will froth at the mouth, clamping the jaws; the whole body stiffens and the legs are extended. After a few minutes, the dog will relax and start to move his limbs as if running. It is possible, at this stage, that the dog may lose control of the bladder and bowels. The duration of the fit varies, but in many cases it will be as much as a few minutes. The dog will be dazed and unsteady as conciousness returns, and should be kept in a dark, warm room to recover.

Veterinary attention should be sought. If a dog is fitting a lot, this can be controlled with drugs. The fitting dog usually follows a pattern of regular intervals. It is thought that many fits occur that owners are not aware of, as they take place in the night when you are not with the dog.

EYES

In Labradors, we do have hereditary eye diseases to contend with. It is not an easy problem, and it is one that has been added to in the last few years with the addition of GENERALISED PROGRESSIVE RETINAL ATROPHY to our list of CENTRALISED PROGRESSIVE RETINAL ATROPHY, RETINAL DYSPLASIA, CATARACTS and ENTROPION. Listing them all together sounds horrific, but a lot of work has been done, and is still being carried out at many research centres around the world, to help us overcome our difficulties.

We are all hoping that in the future, with a breakthrough in the research into DNA, a simple blood test will tell us who is a carrier. With this information, we will be able to use a really superb dog that is a carrier, as well as clear dogs, at stud, because with a simple blood test, we can determine which members of a litter are clear and which members are carriers. The carrier puppies' registration can be endorsed 'not to be bred from'. In this way, we will eventually hope to eradicate some of these diseases. For the present, a sensible attitude to the problem, with yearly eye examinations of your breeding stock, is essential. When buying puppies, you should ensure that both the parents have current clear certificates for eye abnormalities, and, if possible, the grandparents should also be certified clear.

HEREDITARY CATARACTS

These are usually found in two types in Labradors:

POSTERIOR POLAR CATARACTS: These can be present in one eye only. They appear as a small pin-prick, rarely seem to get any bigger, and do not cause the dog to go blind. We call these by the common name of Polar cataracts.

CORTICAL OPACITY: This type of cataract is found in both eyes, and can be seen as early as one year, or much later in life, from six to seven years of age. They can lead to total blindness. The mode of inheritance is an incomplete dominant gene, so they can be carried down one side of the family, or on both sides if you are unlucky. Because of the incomplete mode of inheritance, the occasional affected puppy can be produced from clear parents.

ENTROPION

This can be detected from an early age. It is caused by part of the eyelid rotating inwards, and the lashes irritating the cornea. If not treated, this condition will result in ulceration and impaired sight. The signs you see are a continually watering eye, and this can be seen on puppies in the nest. The condition can be remedied by surgery.

However, you would not then breed from the infected animal, as the condition is inherited. It is not carried by a simple recessive gene, and so it is quite hard to pin down. Even if you avoid lines that you think are carriers, it may well pop up a generation or two later. This should not be confused with the rather droopy bottom eyelid that is sometimes seen in puppies; I would personally prefer to see the puppy grow into its head, before any decisions are made regarding this.

RETINAL DYSPLASIA

This is a folding or detachment of the retina at the back of the eye. It is possible to diagnose it as early as eight weeks of age. The inheritance mode is in a recessive fashion, and because it can be detected early, it is reasonably simple to eliminate from breeding programmes.

Small retinal tears can be seen in older dogs. These do not seem to lead to detachment of the retina, and do not seem to affect the sight of the eye. Both types are relatively rare in the Labrador.

CENTRALISED PROGRESSIVE RETINAL ATROPHY

This condition has been with us for many years. It was first detected as 'night blindness', usually noticed when a dog was about five years of age and had difficulty in seeing in a failing light. It is thought to be inherited in a dominant fashion in Labradors, and because of years of checking stock, it is now found vary rarely in eye examinations today. Interestingly, it is never seen in the Labradors in Sweden, and this poses a problem in the training of young vets, because of the lack of cases to demonstrate on.

CPRA will lead to eventual blindness in those diagnosed at a young age. However, when seen in the older dog for the first time, it seems to progress at a slower rate, and often will not impair the eyesight to the same extent. The dog is likely to retain some sight for the remainder of his life.

GENERALISED PROGRESSIVE RETINAL ATROPHY

Again, this condition has been with us many years, but it was not brought out to the light of day until the last year or two. Unfortunately, I discovered that one of my top stud dogs, Ch. W. Fair and Square, was a carrier at over nine years old. I believe in being honest and up-front, and so I went public. Little is still known about the condition, but it is thought to be inherited in a recessive fashion. Therefore, if an animal is diagnosed as having GPRA, it means that both parents are carriers. The condition develops at quite a late age, the earliest signs being seen at three to five years old, eventually leading to complete blindness. Again this is first seen as 'night blindness', as with CPRA.

Because of its relatively late onset and its mode of inheritance, the elimination of GPRA in the Labrador is going to be a problem. This will often mean that an individual may have produced progeny before any signs of GPRA have developed. When this situation arises, the only way forward is for the owners of progeny already produced to be notified. Eye tests are done on an annual basis, and until genetic fingerprinting is available, the use of regular eye tests for all breeding stock – and a sensible attitude to the published results – is the best way forward.

HIP DYSPLASIA (HD)

This condition can be seen in most breeds. It is a multifactorial condition of the hip joint, which is a typical ball-and-socket joint. Any deformity in the head of the femur, or the socket, can impair its efficient function. In a puppy, it is usually evident by four to five months. The signs are: loss of musculature on the thighs, signs of pain on getting up, and, when running, the pup may use the hind legs as one unit, tending to bunny-hop.

It is impossible to cure a puppy, but by making sure the dog is not too heavy, and by building up the muscle (swimming is a wonderful way to do it), the Labrador will most likely be able to lead a reasonable life. Arthritis may well develop in later life in these joints, and veterinary help will be needed at that stage. There are surgical procedures that can be performed, but as these are changing all the time, I would suggest you consult your own vet as to the best method of treatment. People enquiring about puppies invariably say: "Oh Labradors have Hip Dysplasia, don't they? I have been told to ask if the parents are free." This always annoys me, and if they are paying for the call, I launch into a lecture about how we Labrador breeders have been addressing the problem for the past twenty years or more – and that is why they have heard about it.

I am a great believer in using the accredited hip-testing scheme. It is a tool to help us in deciding which dogs or bitches to breed together. When being X-rayed a dog is either sedated or given an anaesthetic, and laid on its back. The hind legs are extended fully and then rotated inwards, to allow the clearest picture possible to be taken of the joint. It is most important that both hips are correctly aligned, and that the X-ray is crisp and clear, to enable the panel of experts to grade or score them accurately. In the UK we X-ray from twelve months of age; in the United States a permanent grading is made after the dog is two years of age. As hips are likely to take on some wear and tear as the dog grows older, the age at which the dog is X-rayed is a point to bear in mind, in order to get the best possible evaluation. Over the years, more and more Labrador breeders have had their dogs' hips X-rayed; those that do not are now very much in the minority.

I do not think that the overall score has dropped over the years – in fact, it has gone up a little. Now that we see most X-rays being sent up for scoring, this is giving us a truer picture. We cannot get a complete one, because we still get people who will not send up bad X-rays – but is better than in the past, when *no* bad X-rays were sent up for scoring, and therefore could not be included in evaluating the overall score. We do not see the number of very high scores these days; the overall picture is much healthier, with good, medium, and low scores coming through.

In some other countries there are restrictions on the dogs that can be used for breeding, with only the very highest grades being used. I am glad that in the United States and in the UK, we do not have these controls, and we are still allowed to use which dogs we choose. If you were using a really excellent Labrador, with less good hips, you would, hopefully, be mating it to a dog that had really good hips, and a good hip line behind it. We have to be careful with HD, it can cause pain, but we must not put so much emphasis on one defect that we lose the overall picture, balance and character that makes up the Labrador. With a sensible attitude we will retain the good qualities of our breed, as we work towards reducing faults.

OCD (Osteochondrosis dissecans – Osteochondritis dissecans).
This affects many breeds of dogs. It occurs in the shoulder, elbow, hock and stifle joints, usually in the bigger, faster growing breeds. In Labradors, it is mainly seen in the elbow, and is likely to affect young puppies from four to eight months of age upwards. It is noticed that the puppy goes lame usually on one or both front legs. This could, of course, be caused by simple injury, so the first course of action is to restrict exercise for a couple of weeks and see if the dog improves. However, if the dog is still intermittently lame, you should ask if OCD is the problem. My vet, Colin Clark, who has a far greater understanding of the subject, outlines the condition:

"This is part of an extremely complex group of conditions, which affects one or more joints of the growing dog. The suffix '-itis' generally implies an inflammatory process, associated with that particular organ or structure: e.g. Osteitis: inflammation of the bone; Chondritis: inflammation of the cartilage; Osteochondritis: inflammation of bone and cartilage.

"Since OCD is, strictly speaking, *not* an inflammatory reaction, it is more accurate to use the term Osteochondrosis when referring to a single lesion, and Osteochondroses when referring to the multiple lesions which are now recognised in the dog.

"The basic problem associated with the osteochondroses occurs when the cartilaginous precursor of the skeleton becomes bony (ossified) in a disorganised manner, or fails to ossify at all. At some stage during the development of the pup, the normal procedure of joint formation is disrupted. The cause of this disruption is unknown (idiopathic), but there are several factors known to influence the development of osteochondrosis.

"OCD (Osteochondrosis dissecans) is a specific kind of osteochondrosis, which is used to describe a condition in one or more joints, where the articular cartilage undergoes necrosis (death) due to insufficient nutrition, and forms fine cracks or fissures. These fissures may join together to form a flap, which may remain attached to the underlying bone, or break off and float freely within the joint. Should this flap become ossified, it can be seen on X-ray.

"Since there is more than one type of cartilage associated with the development of each joint, it follows that there are several classifications of osteochondrosis; and since there are several joints in the body (one or more of which can be affected at the same time), it is, therefore, not so surprising that the condition causes some confusion, both outside and inside the veterinary profession, and is difficult to diagnose.

"Some of the factors associated with OCD (and other osteochondroses) are trauma, breed of dog (larger breeds being more susceptible than smaller breeds), endocrine imbalance, genetic factors within a breed, and over-feeding.

"Osteochondrosis is a disease of the young dog, although lesions, once present, will often persist throughout life, and will invariably lead to osteoarthritis in later life. Clinical signs of stiffness/lameness start from between four and eight months, with a higher incidence in the male, which tends to be heavier than the female. Because the early evidence of the condition may be very subtle, it may be difficult to diagnose, even with the use of X-rays, and often repeat examinations with strenuous investigation is required before a final diagnosis is reached.

"Until more is understood about the cause (aetiology) of this condition, there is little that can be done to prevent it. Attention to breeding programmes, sensible feeding and exercise programmes, and general commonsense will help, as will free and open discussion between all people associated with the welfare of dogs."

I have had some cases of OCD over the years (most breeders, if they are honest with themselves, will have had some also). In all cases, the dogs have been operated on and placed in good homes once they have recovered from the operation, and all are still going well. I have not bred from any of these affected dogs; I have also avoided using their siblings, and I have tried not to use the parents. I was once told that the dogs I presented at the Veterinary University should have been smaller, and that I should restrict the feeding. In a perfect world, this would be fine, but in my line I am dealing with good up-to-size Labradors in the parents, and I know the pups will have obtained full height at seven to eight months of age. This is just my particular kennel, so I cannot change the size they are when they are presented, but I have made sure that my dogs carry a lot less weight during their puppyhood, and I think it has been a positive step in my management of the problem.